IMAGES
of America

COLUMBUS

ON THE COVER: The 1947 Stephen D. Lee High School Homecoming Parade is pictured on Main Street. The floats showcased the school's various clubs and organizations, such as the Student Government Association. Following the parade, Adelaide Howard was crowned homecoming queen. (Courtesy of the Southern Historical Collection, Wilson Library, the University of North Carolina at Chapel Hill.)

IMAGES
of America

COLUMBUS

Mona K. Vance on behalf of the
Columbus-Lowndes Public Library

ARCADIA
PUBLISHING

ISBN 978-0-7385-8806-3

Published by Arcadia Publishing
Charleston, South Carolina

Printed in the United States of America

Library of Congress Control Number: 2011927525

For all general information, please contact Arcadia Publishing:
Telephone 843-853-2070
Fax 843-853-0044
E-mail sales@arcadiapublishing.com
For customer service and orders:
Toll-Free 1-888-313-2665

Visit us on the Internet at www.arcadiapublishing.com

This book is dedicated to my mother, Katharine S. Vance, who has been a constant source of love, encouragement, and guidance.

Contents

ACKNOWLEDGMENTS

The Columbus-Lowndes Public Library, founded in 1934, has a strong commitment to the preservation of local history. When the current library building in Columbus was built in the 1970s, space was provided for Lowndes County history and genealogy materials. In 1992, the library completed a major renovation, tripling the size of and providing climate controlled stacks for its Local History Department, made up of the Billups-Garth Archives and the Margaret L. Buckley Genealogy Room. This expansion was funded by the Snowdoun Association (now the Billups-Garth Foundation). Currently, the Local History Department is one of the largest archival repositories in a public library in the state of Mississippi.

It is the mission of the Local History Department to collect, preserve, and make accessible the history and culture of Lowndes County. The collections are diverse, capturing the various people, businesses, activities, events, buildings, and organizations that make up the history of Columbus and Lowndes County.

Every image included in this volume can be found at the Columbus-Lowndes Public Library.

I would like to thank the following individuals for their guidance and assistance is researching and editing this book: Gary Lancaster, Sam and Carolyn B. Kaye, Rufus Ward, Mike Lowery, and Tom Mayfield. I would also like to thank Alice Shands, director of the Columbus-Lowndes Public Library, for giving me the direction and encouragement to accomplish this volume on behalf of the library.

I would also like to thank J. Carlos Rosales of CS Digital Productions in Columbus for use of the images by photographer Carl Brown. In addition, many thanks to Dr. Berkley Hudson, associate professor with the Missouri School of Journalism, for granting use of the O.N. Pruitt photographs through the Southern Historical Collection at the University of North Carolina at Chapel Hill.

Most of all, thanks go to my friends and family, for your support, encouragement, and patience during this process.

Finally, thanks go to all of the people who have donated materials and collections to the Columbus-Lowndes Public Library over the years. It is each and every one of you who deserves recognition for your commitment to preserving the history and culture of Columbus and Lowndes County. For, without you, the memory and traditions of Columbus would be lost.

Unless otherwise noted, all images are courtesy of the Local History Department at the Columbus-Lowndes Public Library.

INTRODUCTION

Columbus, Mississippi, is situated largely on the east bank of the Tombigbee River. In December 1540, the Spanish explorer Hernando de Soto crossed the Tombigbee near present-day Columbus while leading one of the first European expeditions into what is now the United States. Native Americans of the Choctaw and Chickasaw tribes predominately inhabited the area prior to European settlement. In 1810, John Pitchlynn moved to Plymouth Bluff and worked as a US interpreter and assistant agent for the Choctaw Nation. During the Creek War phase of the War of 1812, his residence was fortified and was known as Fort Smith. It was a supply depot and meeting place for US officers and allied Choctaw Indian chiefs. A year prior to Mississippi gaining statehood in 1817, the future site of Columbus was ceded to the United States government by the Choctaw Treaty. It was Silas McBee who suggested the new name of Columbus for the town that had developed in 1819 where Andrew Jackson's Military Road crossed the Tombigbee. Prior to being named Columbus, the settlement was referred to as Possum's Town by Native Americans, a nickname referring to an early storekeeper, Spirus Roach, and his long pointed nose.

An official survey of the state line between Mississippi and Alabama was not completed until late 1820, which caused many people to initially consider Columbus as part of Marion County, Alabama. Once the survey was concluded, Columbus was incorporated as a Mississippi town and was included in the creation of Monroe County, Mississippi, in February 1821. That same year, the state's first public school, known as Franklin Academy, opened in Columbus. In 1830, the Treaty of Dancing Rabbit Creek was signed, resulting in the opening of millions of acres of the Choctaw Nation to European-American settlements. Many families moved from places like Tennessee, North Carolina, Alabama, Virginia, and Georgia looking for new opportunities and fertile farmland. It was a result of the increase in population that, in 1830, Lowndes County was formed and Columbus became the county seat. The county was named Lowndes after William Jones Lowndes (1782–1822), a lawyer, planter, and congressman from South Carolina.

The rich soil that greeted settlers yielded crops such as cotton, corn, and tobacco. Cotton, however, was the major money crop, and by 1860, Lowndes County was producing over 50,000 bales of cotton and over a million bushels of corn annually. It was during these prosperous years prior to the Civil War that many of the ornate Columbus homes were built that still exist today.

During the Civil War, Columbus served as a hospital center, an arsenal, a major food producing center, and, briefly, as the state capital. After the Battle of Shiloh in April 1862, many of the homes, churches, schools, and businesses were converted into hospitals for the treatment of the wounded and sick soldiers. The Brierfield Arsenal in Columbus, which was operated by the Confederate government, produced cannons, ammunition, wagons, swords, belts, canteens, and many other items needed for an army in the field. Local businesses and individuals were also contracted to manufacture uniforms, tents, pontoon boats, ambulances, shoes, and much more. In 1864 and early 1865, after the state capital of Jackson was burned by Union troops, the government of Mississippi moved to Columbus in order to continue operations. Also, several attempts were made to invade Columbus by the Union army, but they were all stopped by forces under the command of Gen. Nathan Bedford Forrest.

Memorial Day, originally known as Decoration Day, has its origins in Columbus. On April 25, 1866, four Columbus ladies decorated the graves of both the Union and Confederate soldiers in Friendship Cemetery. Francis Miles Finch memorialized this act in his poem *The Blue and the Gray*.

Columbus was a pioneer in education, not only with the establishment of Franklin Academy, but also with the creation in 1884 of the first public college for women in the country, the Industrial Institute and College (now Mississippi University for Women). The school was unique in its combination of industrial, liberal arts, and normal (or teacher) training. The school can trace its beginnings, however, to the Columbus Female Institute, a private school founded in 1847. Columbus is also home to the Mississippi School for Mathematics and Science, the state's only public, residential, coeducational high school for academically talented juniors and seniors.

Vital to the success and growth of Columbus has been the Tombigbee River. The city's proximity to the waterway allowed for both the transportation of goods and the travel of people to and from Columbus. It continues to be an integral part of this area's business, industry, and recreation.

The turn of the century saw the growth of industrial businesses in brick, clothing, building stone, gravel, cheese, dairy, and butter. The principal industries in Columbus included railroad shops, lumber mills, a large brick plant, greenhouses, a marble works, cotton oil mills, creameries, a cotton compress, and garment plant.

Beginning in 1940, Columbus began an annual event known as the Columbus Pilgrimage. During the Pilgrimage, celebrated every spring, visitors receive tours of city homes and gardens complete with tour guides dressed in period costumes.

In 1941, the Air Corps Advanced Flying School (now the Columbus Air Force Base) opened as a twin-engine flying school just north of Columbus. The base continues to train US Air Force pilots and its operation now includes a population of over 3,200 people.

The city of Columbus has been the birthplace or hometown of many national figures, such as writer and playwright Thomas Lanier "Tennessee" Williams, boxer Henry Armstrong (born Henry Jackson Jr.), Walt Disney Oscar-winning animator Joshua Meador, and sports announcer Walter Lanier "Red" Barber. Lenore L. Prather, the first female chief justice of the Mississippi Supreme Court, is also from Columbus, and Pulitzer prizewinner Eudora Welty found inspiration here while a student at Mississippi University for Women. Other figures either born or raised throughout Lowndes County include negro-league and major-league baseball players Samuel Harding Hairston and Samuel Jethroe, blues artist Big Joe Williams, former NBA basketball player Clarence Weatherspoon Sr., and retired NFL football player Jerry Lee Rice.

Today, around 25,000 people call the city of Columbus their home.

The images in this volume offer only a glimpse into the many people, businesses, organizations, and events that have shaped the city of Columbus.

One

EDUCATION

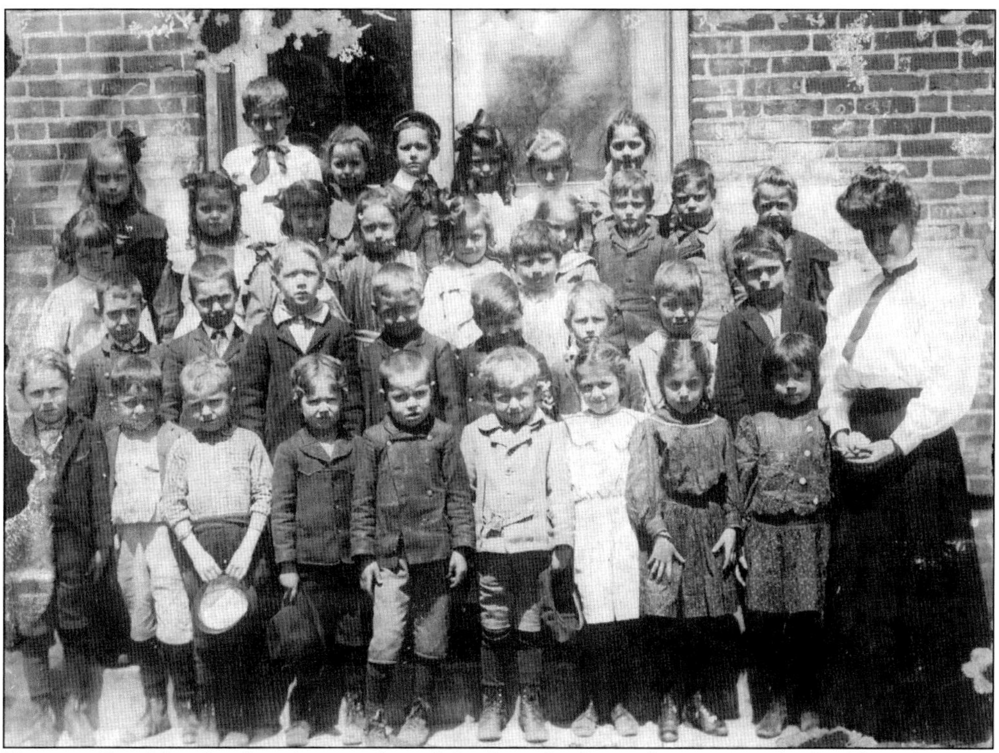

Here are Franklin Academy's second- and third-grade classes from 1904. The building shown is what was known as the "Kitchen." Their teacher, Sadie Hudson, is shown on the right.

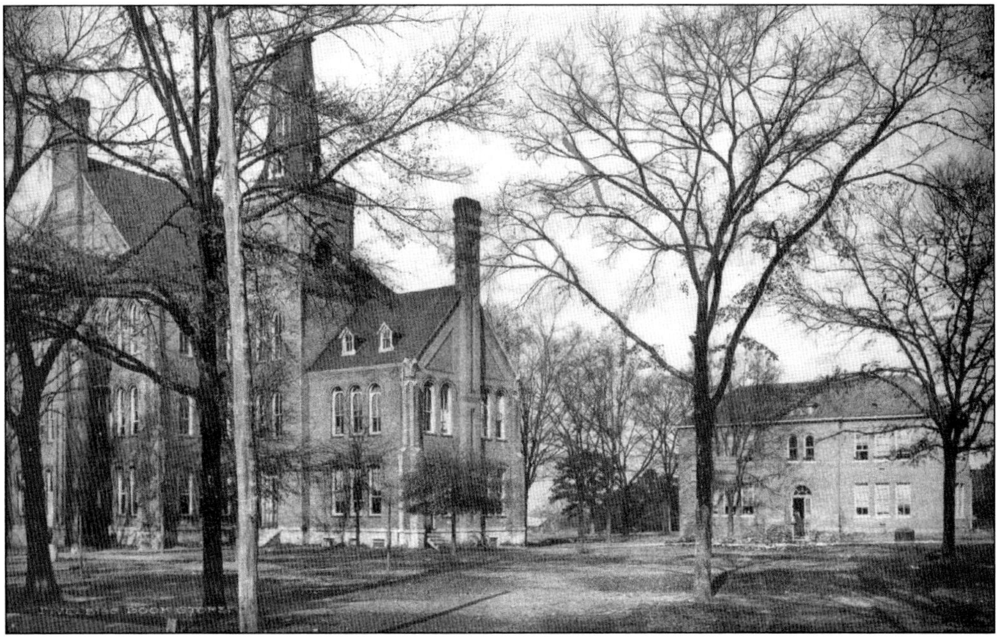

Franklin Academy, chartered in 1821, is the oldest public school in Mississippi. This image shows the 1886 school building (left) and the 1904 Annex (right). The main school building contained 14 rooms along with a chapel, while the Annex contained an additional five classrooms. The 1886 building was replaced by the current brick structure in 1939.

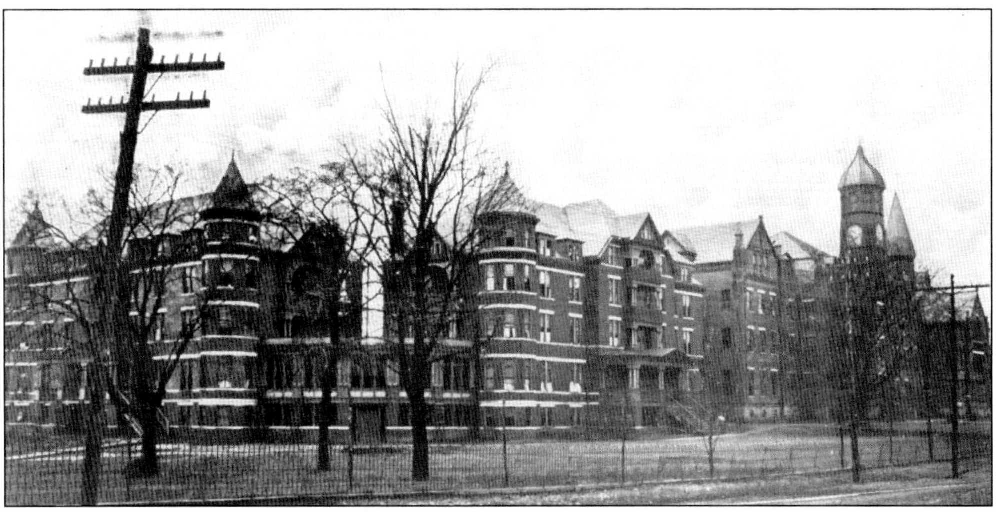

On March 12, 1884, Mississippi chartered the first public college for women in the country, the Mississippi Industrial Institute and College for the Education of White Girls of the State of Mississippi in the Arts and Sciences, or Industrial Institute and College (II&C). II&C, a combination of classical, normal (or teaching), and industrial training, was hailed around the world as revolutionary. The school changed its name to Mississippi University for Women in 1974 and became coeducational in 1982.

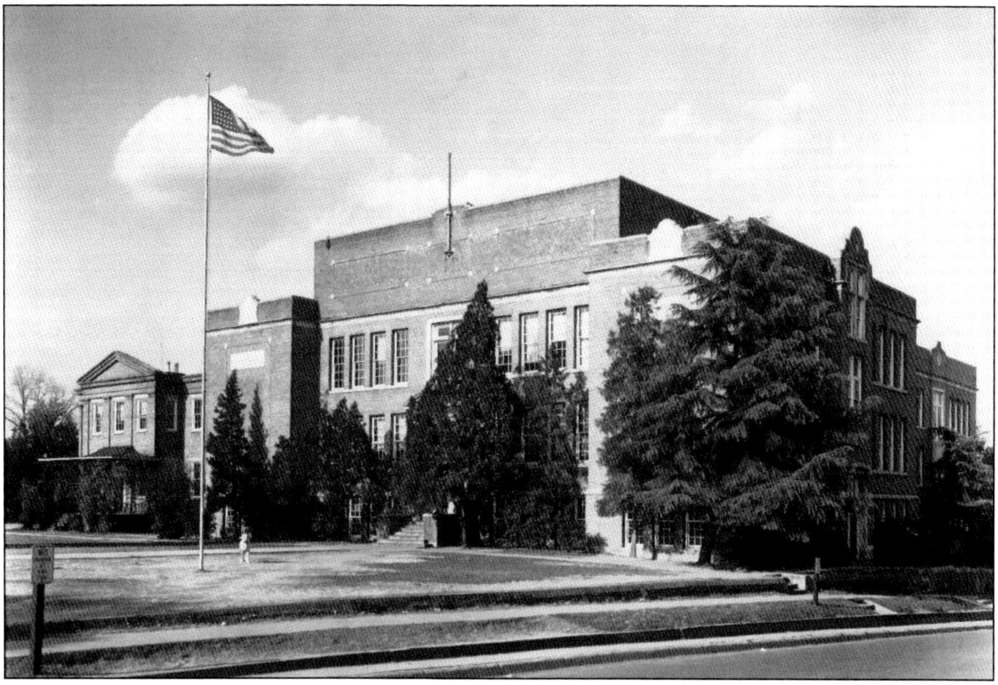

This image captures Stephen D. Lee High School around 1920 on the corner of Seventh Street and Third Avenue North, the current location of the Columbus-Lowndes Public Library Chebie G. Bateman Building. The school was constructed in 1918, and the addition to the rear was built in 1925. In 1953, a new senior high school was built on Military Road (below) and later used as a middle school. The 1918 building above was being used as a junior high when it burned in 1959.

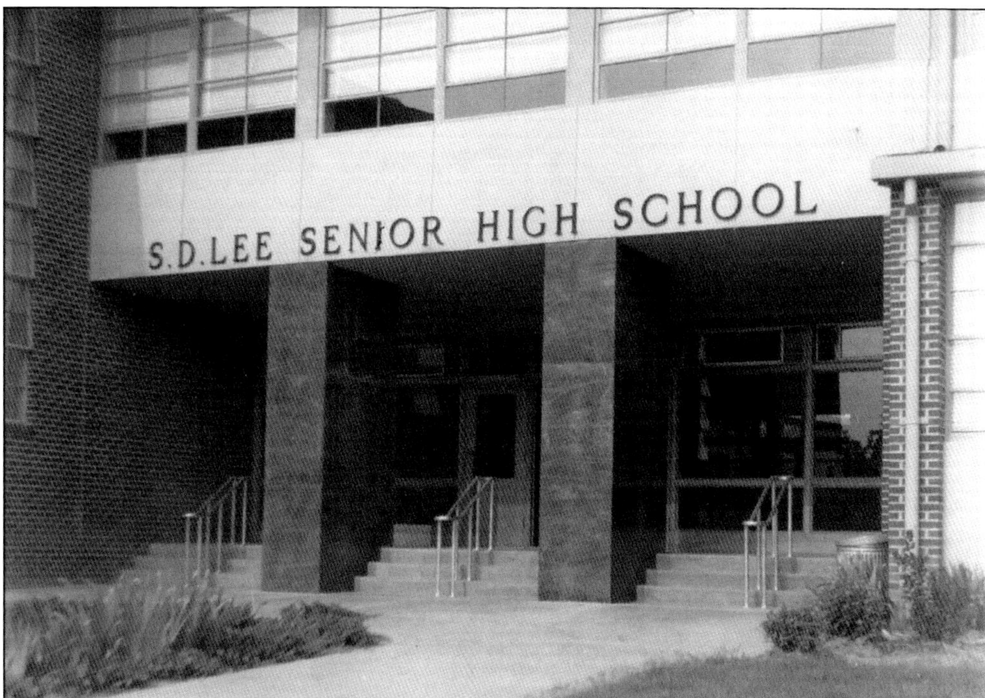

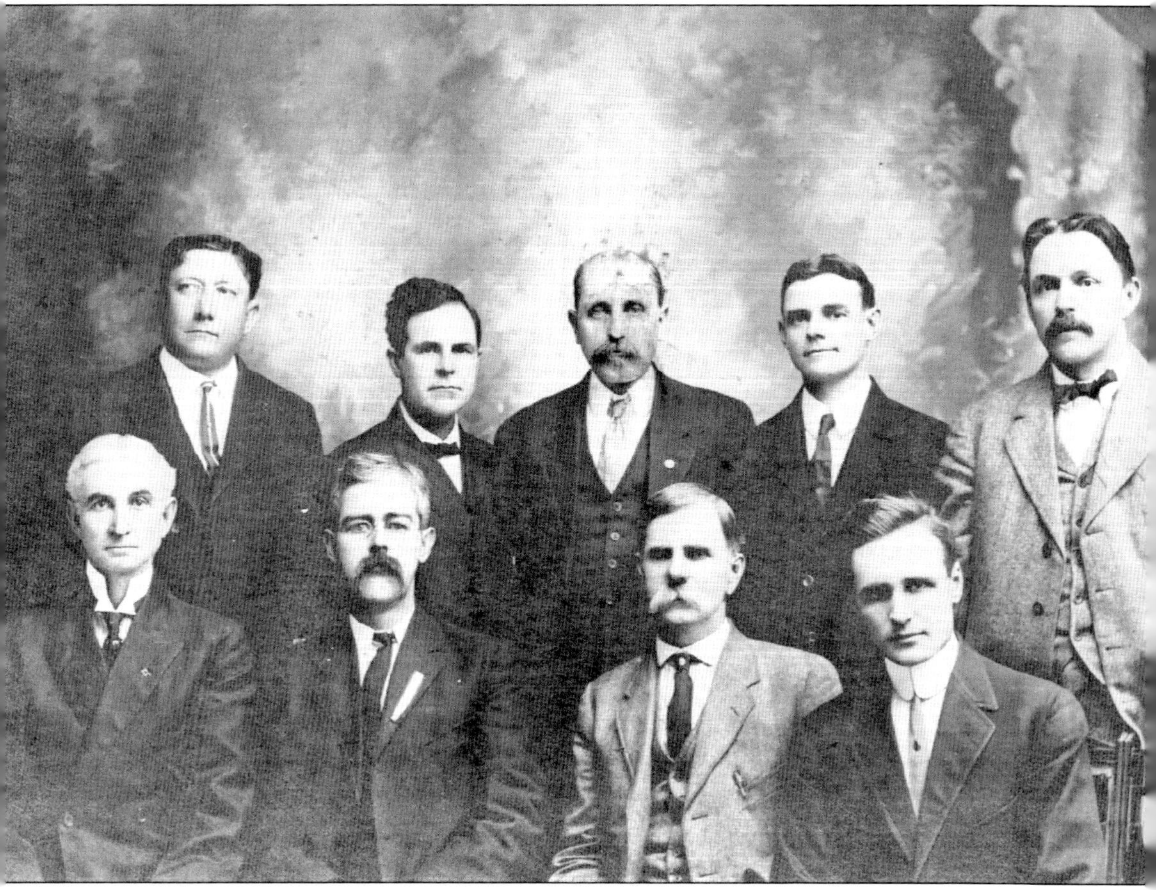

Joseph "Joe" Anderson Cook, standing second from left, was a pioneer of education in Mississippi. He was born in 1862 in Artesia and in 1902 was elected superintendent of Columbus city schools. Beginning in 1907 he served as president of the Mississippi Teachers Association before becoming the first president of the Mississippi Normal College (now the University of Southern Mississippi) in Hattiesburg in 1911. Cook was elected state senator for Lowndes County and served two terms before his death in 1940. In 1962, Joe Cook Junior High School (now Joe Cook Fine Arts Magnet School) was named in his honor. Others pictured here include, from left to right, (seated) Dr. R.S. Curry, William H. Carter, A.C. Goree, and Birney Imes Sr; (standing) E.C. Chapman, Joe Cook, George McCown, W.E. Kennedy, and John Stinson.

This sketch shows the University of Columbus, erected in 1844. The building, located at present-day 715 Second Avenue North, was initially used by the Methodist church. Eventually, it was used as a school that also housed a concert hall and stage. Beginning in 1907, the building was used as the Jewish synagogue for the Temple B'nai Israel.

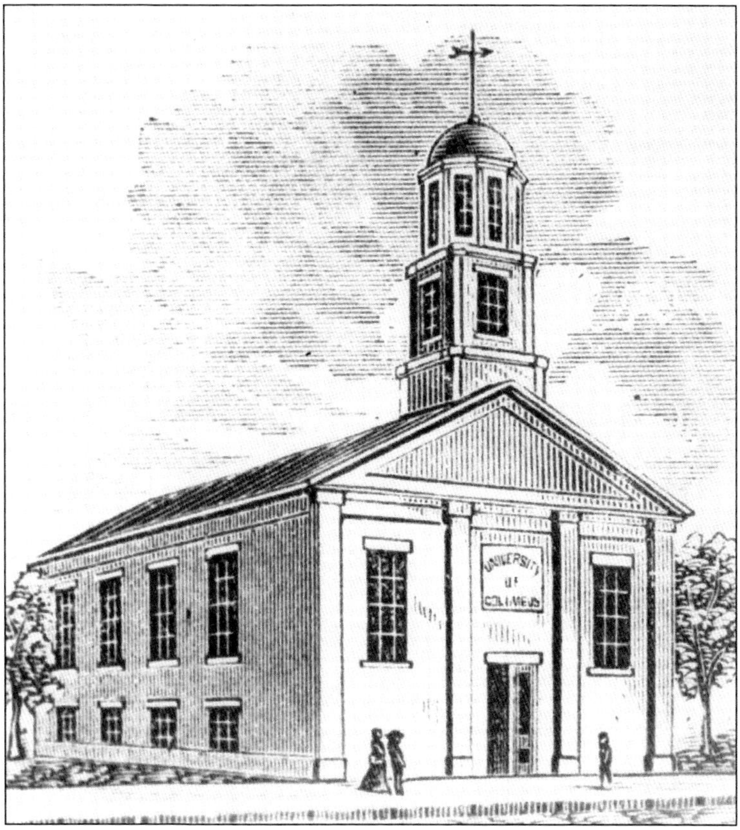

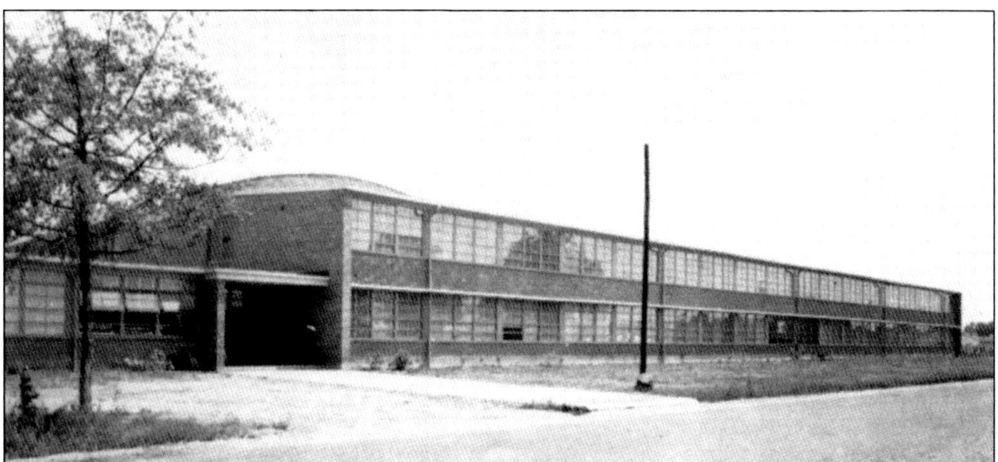

Robert E. Hunt High School, named for longtime educator Dr. Robert E. Hunt (1898–1978), was built in 1954 as an African American school. It was consolidated with Stephen D. Lee High School in 1970.

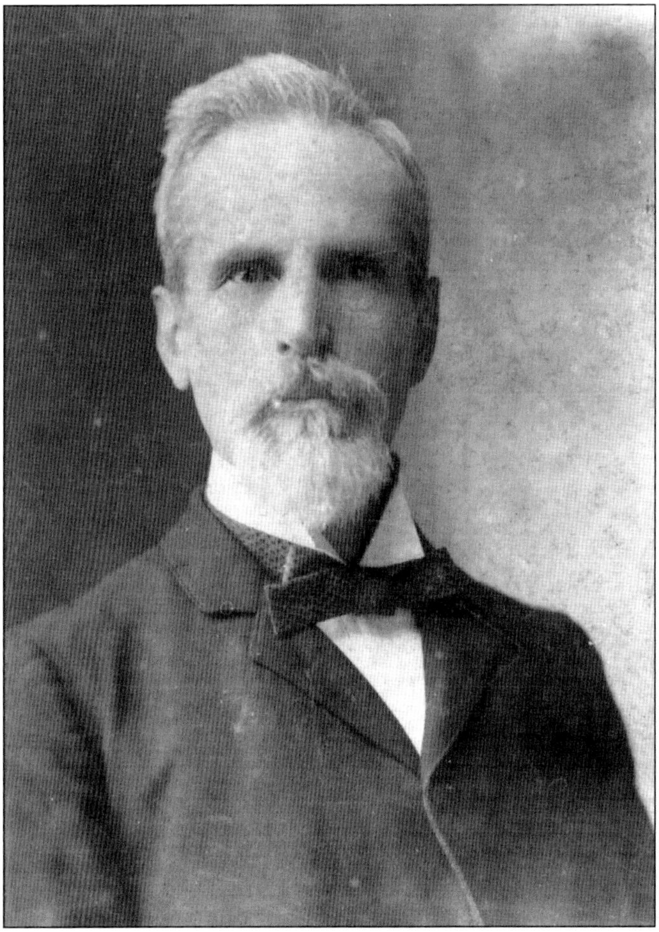

James McCaden Barrow was born in Petersburg, Virginia, in 1841. As a Confederate soldier during the Civil War, he was held prisoner at Point Lookout prison in Maryland. After coming to Mississippi, he first operated a private school in Artesia. Later, he became superintendent of Franklin Academy and served 33 years as superintendent of Columbus city schools. He died on November 26, 1904. In 1907, the two-story brick school below was completed and named in his honor. It served students from the first to sixth grades and included a cafeteria in the basement. Long-term educator Mary Stokes once served as principle. It underwent a major renovation in 1965 but was closed in 1976. The following year, Mississippi University for Women, near which the school is located, purchased the property and still maintains it.

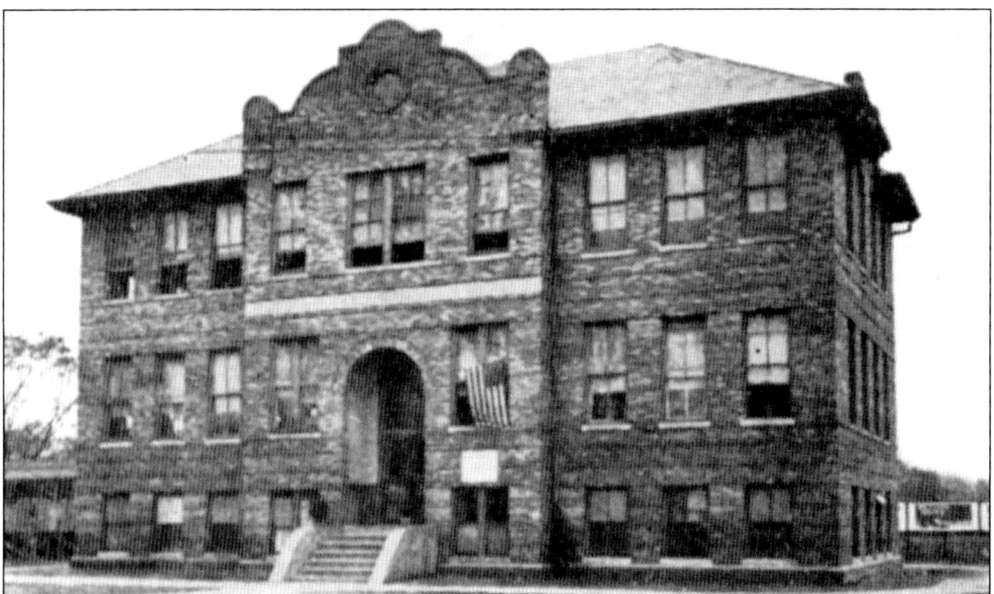

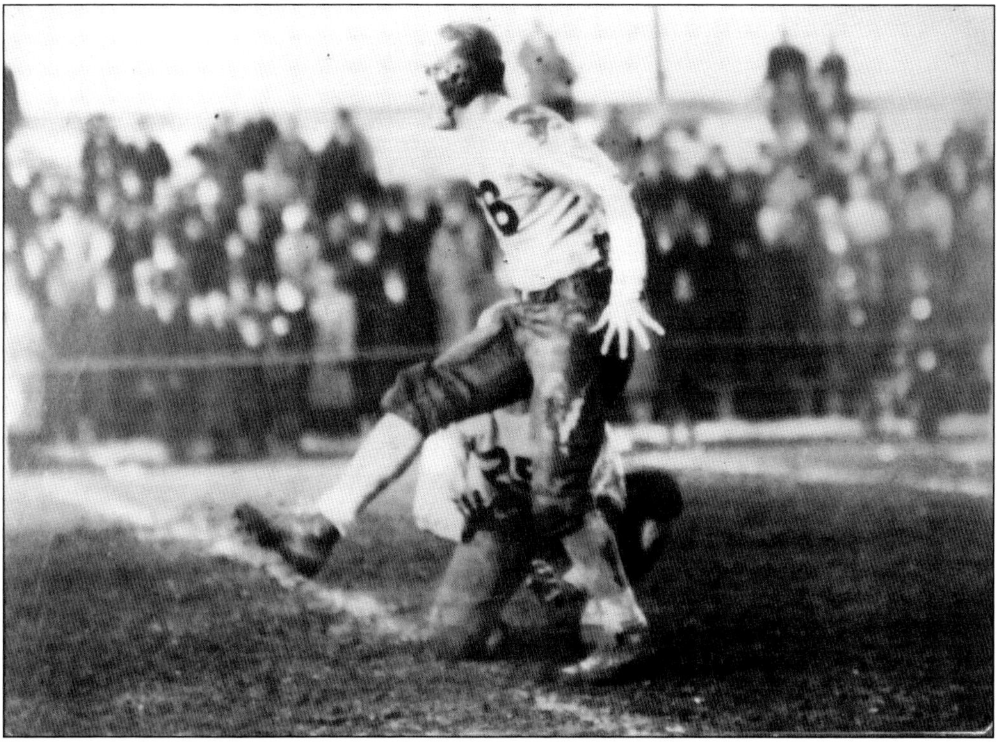

This photograph captures the winning kick of the 1936 championship game between the Stephen D. Lee High School Generals and the Austin High Maroons of Chicago. Team captain Leslie Dodson scored the game-winning extra point, bringing the final score to 7 to 6, and made the Lee High Generals national champions.

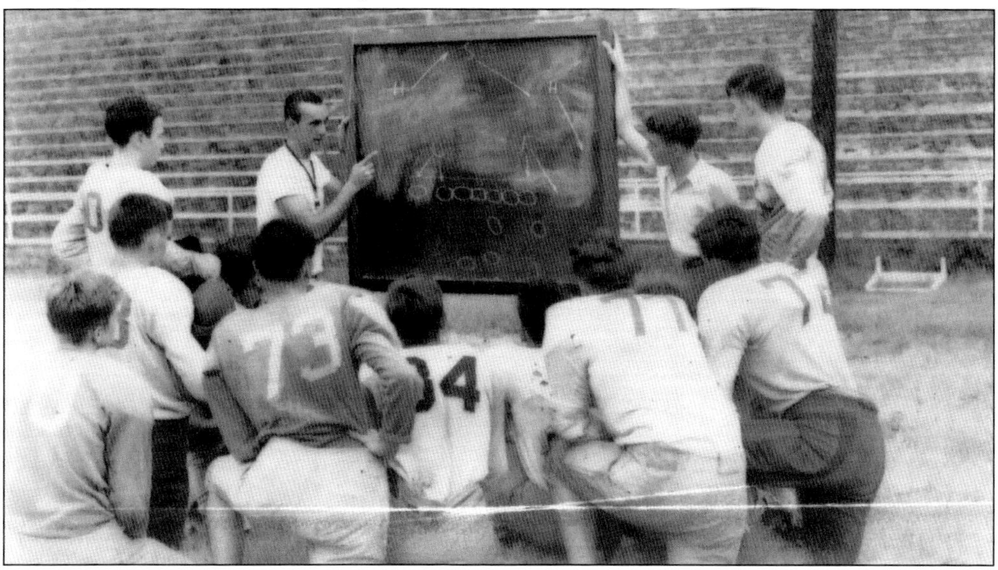

Former Stephen D. Lee High School coach W.F. "Sonny" Bruce is seen holding practice inside the Magnolia Bowl with the football team around 1944. Bruce went on to serve as superintendent of the Vicksburg, Mississippi, City School System. (Courtesy of the Southern Historical Collection, Wilson Library, the University of North Carolina at Chapel Hill.)

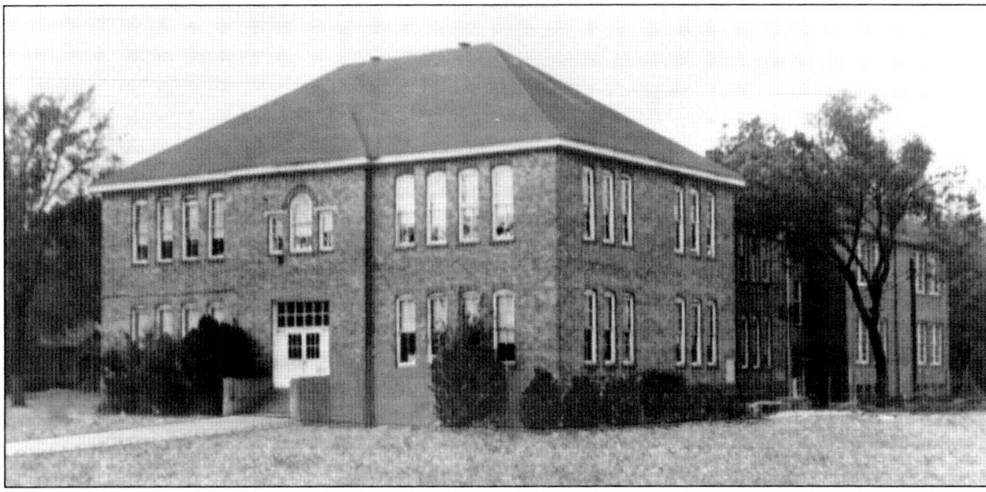

Union Academy was established following the Civil War. The institution began as an African American school that was run through the American Missionary Association until 1877, when it became a branch of the all-white Franklin Academy. Professor William Isaac Mitchell served as the school's first African American principal from 1878 to 1916. The brick structure seen above opened in March 1903 and was large enough for 1,000 children. In the early 1900s, the school added a high school curriculum but was converted into an elementary school in 1954. This building, located on Tenth Avenue North, was replaced by a new school building in the early 1960s. The image below shows the 1948 Union Academy graduating class. Professor and principal William Isaac Mitchell is in the second row from the bottom on the far left.

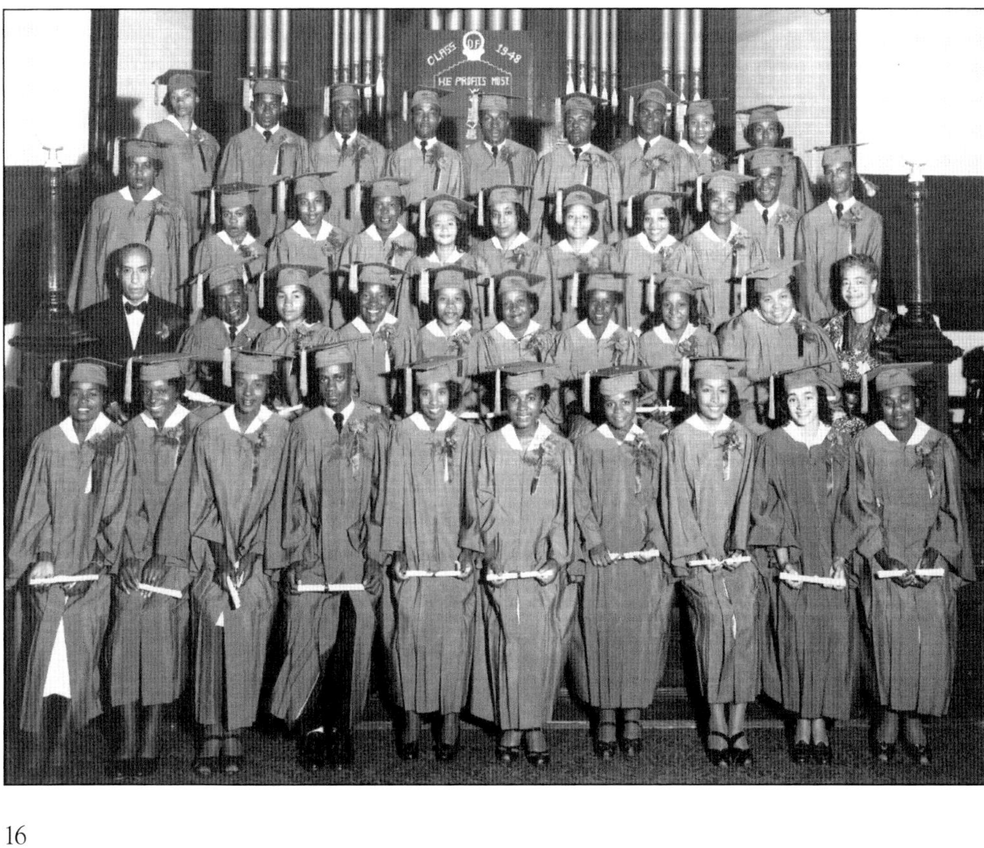

Two

Business and Industry

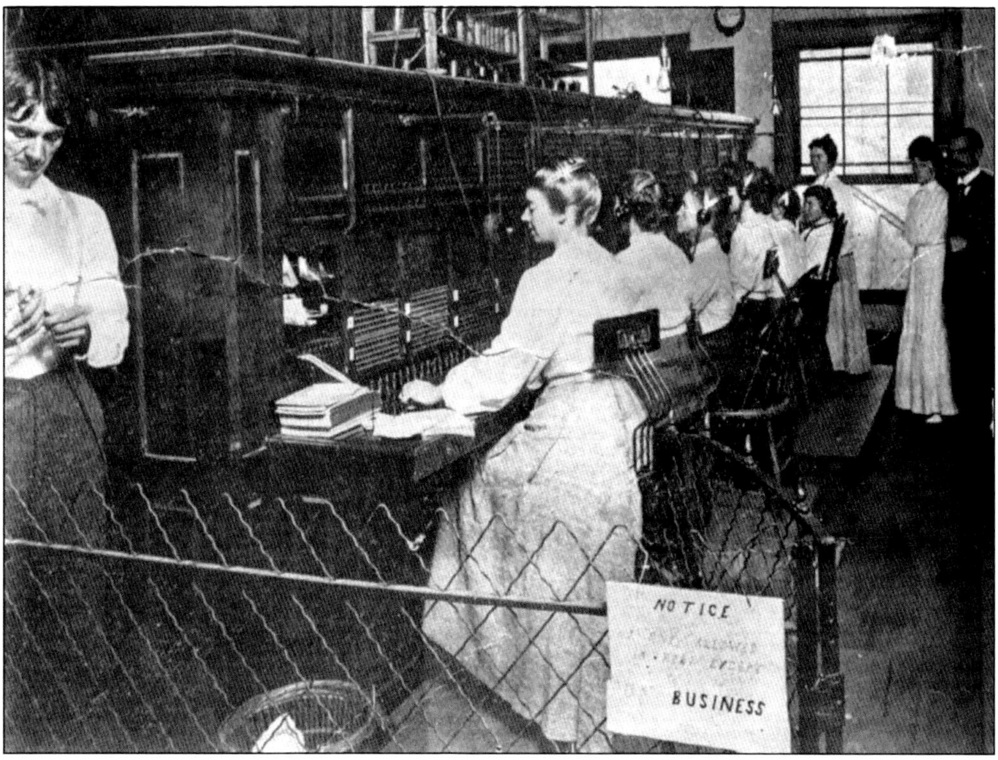

In 1905, the Cumberland and Telephone and Telegraph Company opened operations in Columbus. The local exchange conducted business at 509 ½ Main Street and employed around 20 employees. Managed by J.M. Thornberg, the business handled both telephone calls and commercial telegrams. The machine used to handle telephone calls was a multiple switchboard containing a double-metallic wire system. The women shown here were known as "hello girls."

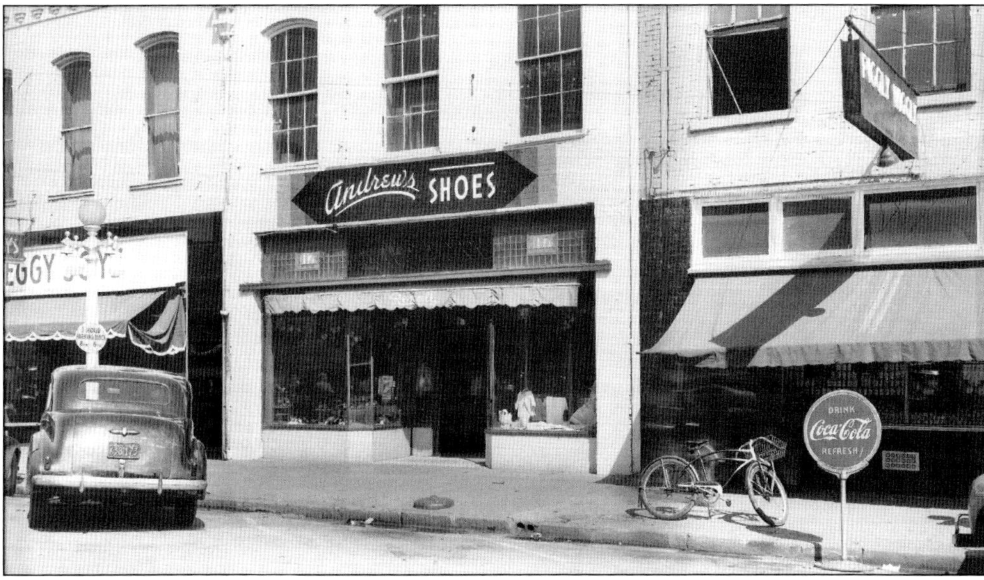

Here is the Fenton Andrews Shoe Store sometime between 1942 and 1947. Located at 117 Fifth Street South, it was owned by T.J. Moody and Fenton Andrews. To the left of the shoe store was Peggy Joys Ladies Shop and to the right was the Piggly-Wiggly grocery store. Below is the interior of Andrews Shoe Store.

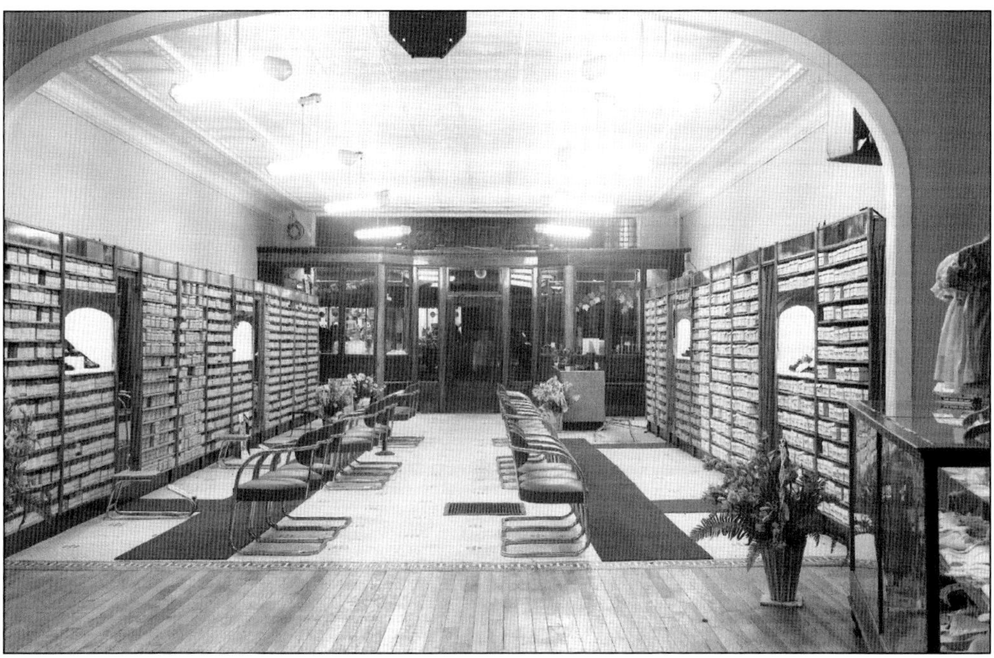

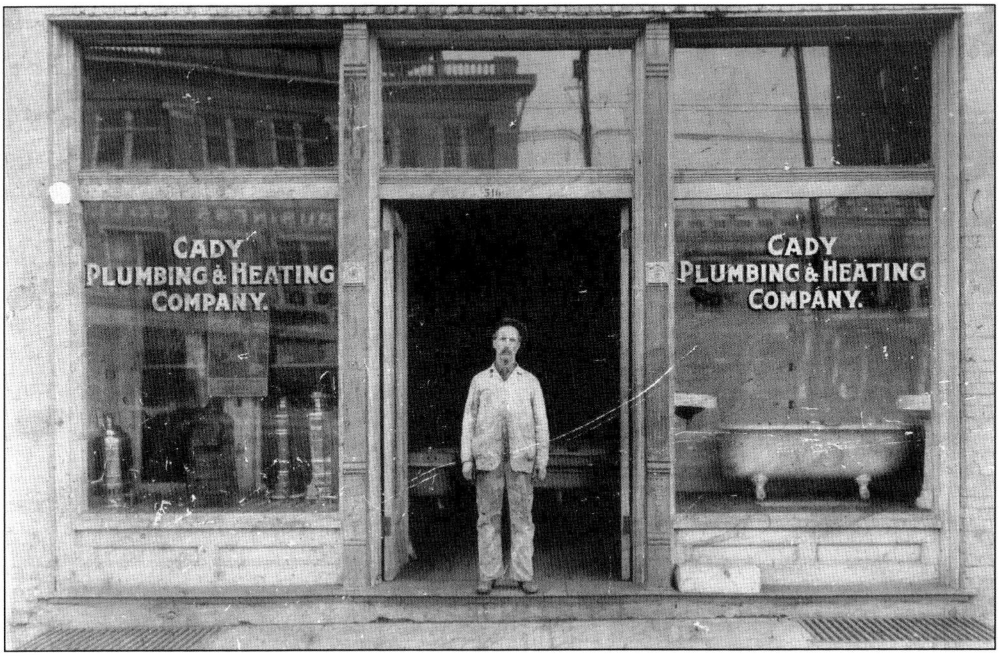

Here is the Cady Plumbing and Heating Company around 1906. Operated by Thomas J. Cady, the store offered products for sanitary plumbing as well as steam and hot water heating. Located at 516 Main Street, it is the current site of offices for the *Commercial Dispatch* newspaper.

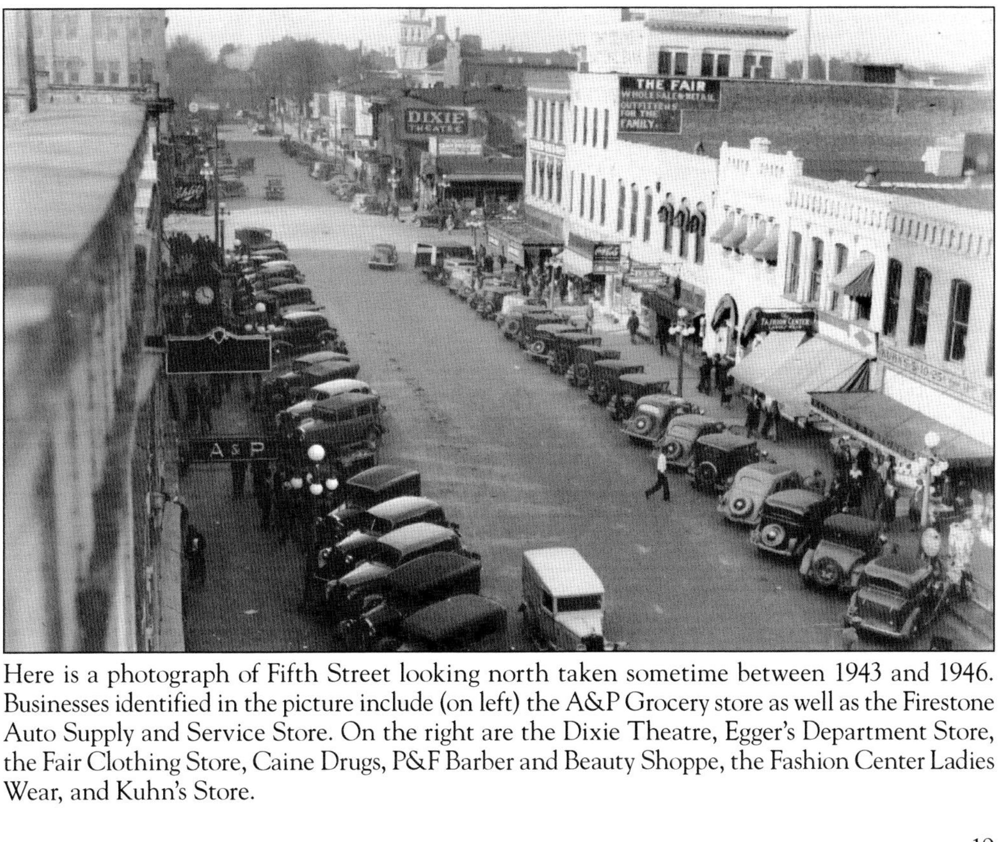

Here is a photograph of Fifth Street looking north taken sometime between 1943 and 1946. Businesses identified in the picture include (on left) the A&P Grocery store as well as the Firestone Auto Supply and Service Store. On the right are the Dixie Theatre, Egger's Department Store, the Fair Clothing Store, Caine Drugs, P&F Barber and Beauty Shoppe, the Fashion Center Ladies Wear, and Kuhn's Store.

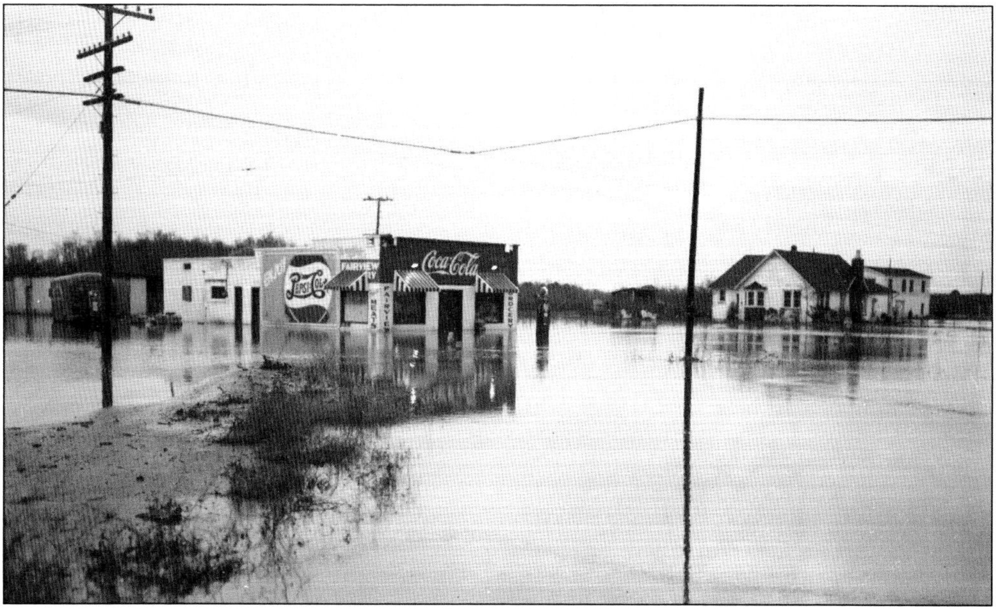

This image shows waters receding from Fairview Grocery and Meats after the 1949 flood. The grocery store was located at the northeast corner of Highway 69 and Highway 82. The Tombigbee River crested on January 6 at around 40 feet. Three Columbus residents, Jewell Hooper, David Livingston, and Robert Haskett, clung to trees above the rising Luxapallila River for over 30 minutes after their boat overturned. They were rescued by city water works employees.

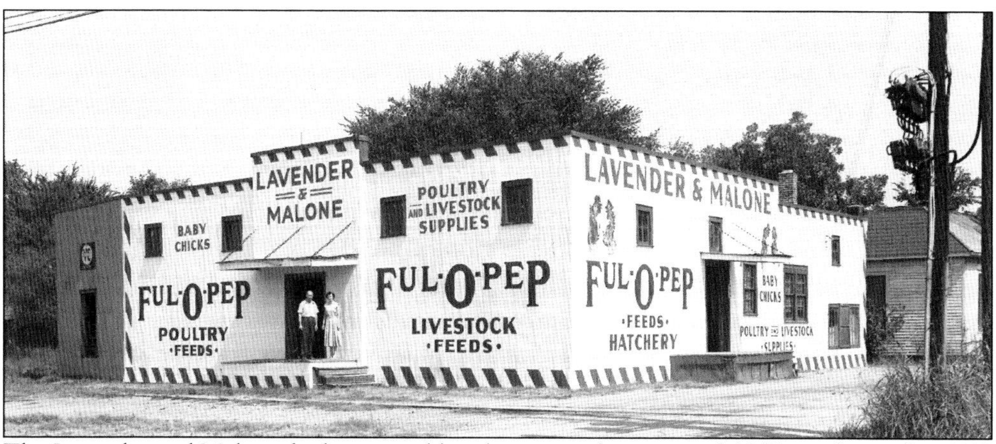

The Lavender and Malone feed store and hatchery, seen here around 1947, was located at 1419 Main Street and supplied feed, baby chicks, and livestock supplies. The store sat in front of what is now the Mississippi Valley Gas Company.

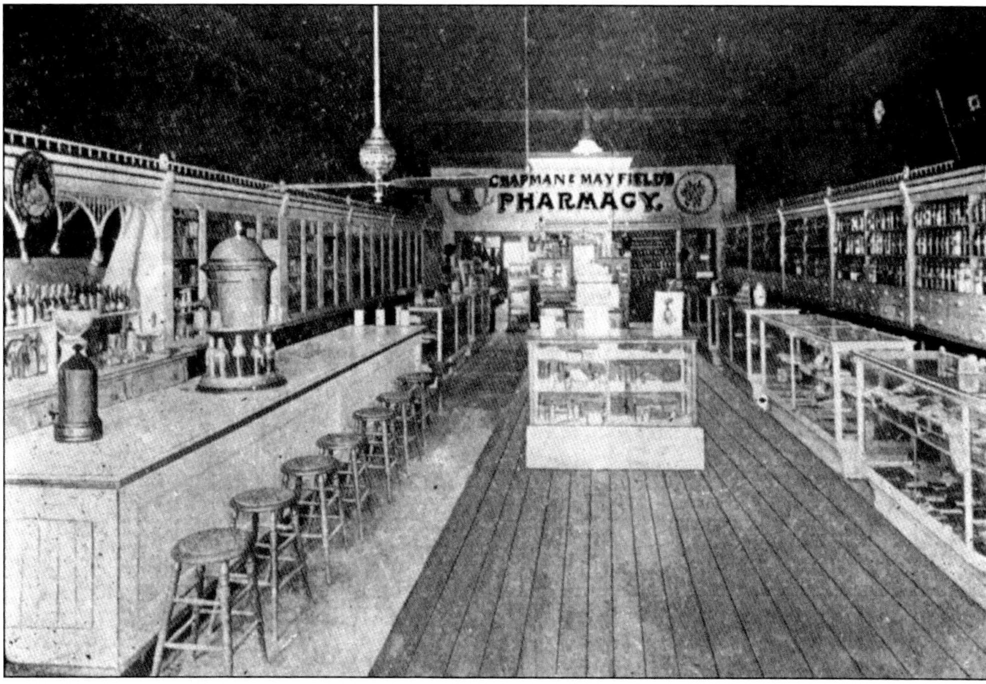

The Chapman and Mayfield Pharmacy, seen here around 1905, was owned by druggists E.C. Chapman and L.E. Mayfield and was located at 117 Fifth Street South. The pharmacy sold a variety of goods including "drugs, proprietary remedies, fancy and toilet articles" and promoted the idea that "the BEST is at Chapman & Mayfield's."

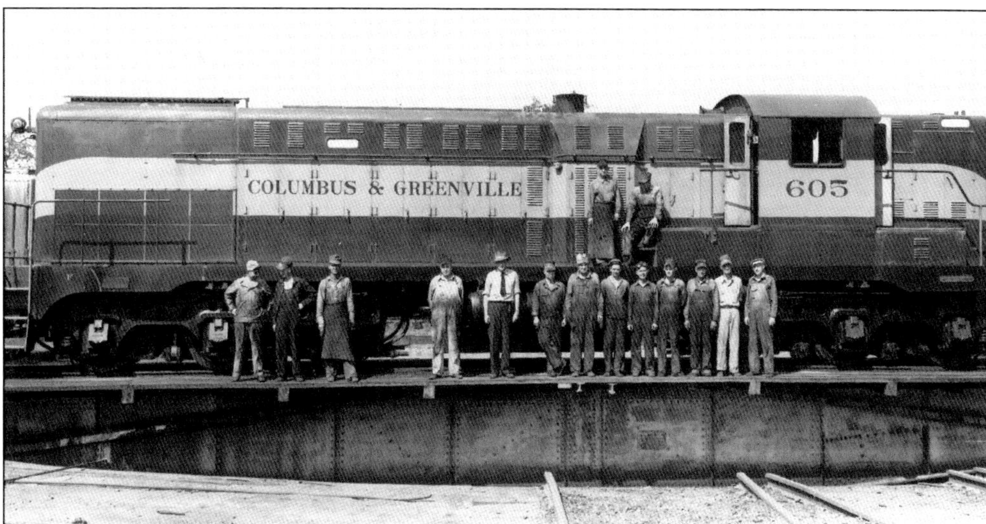

The Columbus & Greenville Railway Company (C&G) was one of several railroad companies that operated in Lowndes County over the years. Originally called the Southern Railway Company, it was renamed the C&G in 1920 and operated as both a freight and passenger train. The above image shows workers standing on the turntable, which allowed locomotives to turn around and return in the opposite direction, near the roundhouse or engine maintenance facility, which still exists today.

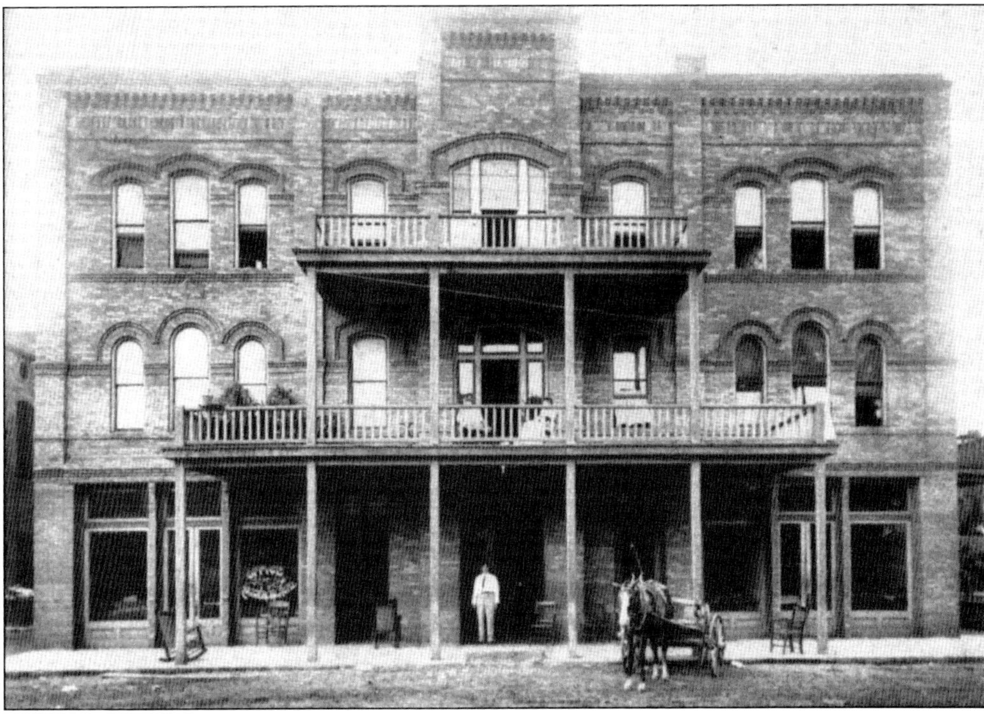

The Commercial Hotel (above), a three-story building, was built in 1898 by Thomas J. Gunter. The hotel was located on College Street between Market Street and Fourth Street South. In 1940, Gus and Jim Talantis remodeled the structure and gave it a new name, the Alexandra Hotel (below). In 1969, the hotel was torn down to make way for a parking lot.

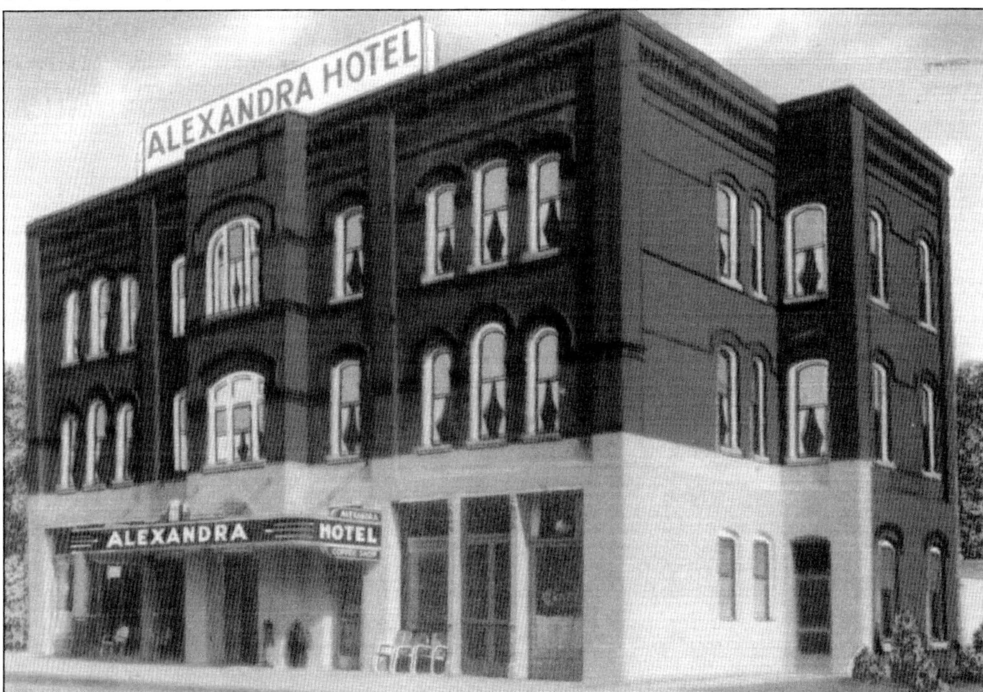

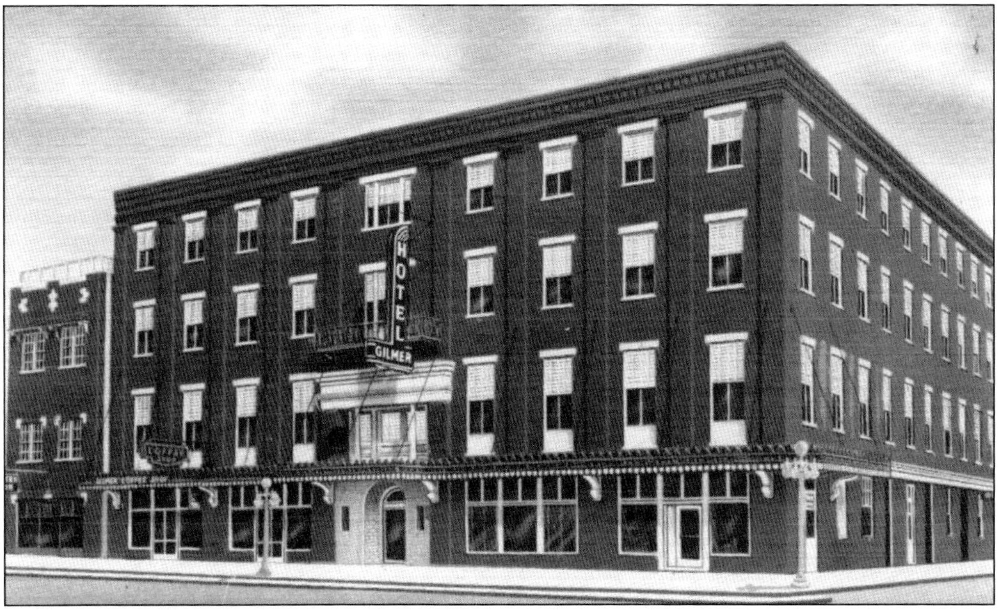

Construction of the Gilmer Hotel, named for Col. John Gilmer, began in 1860 on the corner of Main Street and Fourth Street North. The first floor had a post office, drugstore, barbershop, and a drummer's sample room. The hotel was known for lavish parties and balls, which were housed on the second floor. During the Civil War, the unfinished hotel was used as a hospital for those wounded in the Battle of Shiloh. Later, celebrities such as Clark Gable, Bob Hope, Jack Dempsey, Doris Day, and Will Rogers were all once guests of the hotel. The lobby, seen below around 1908, witnessed evolving decorative interiors over the years. Torn down in 1963, the site is now the location of the Gilmer Inn Motel.

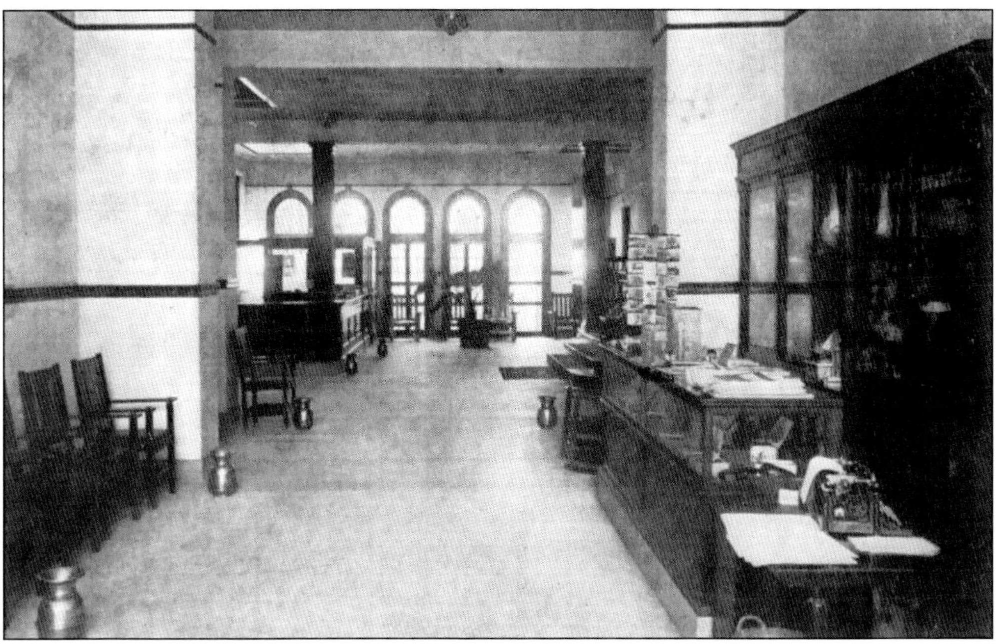

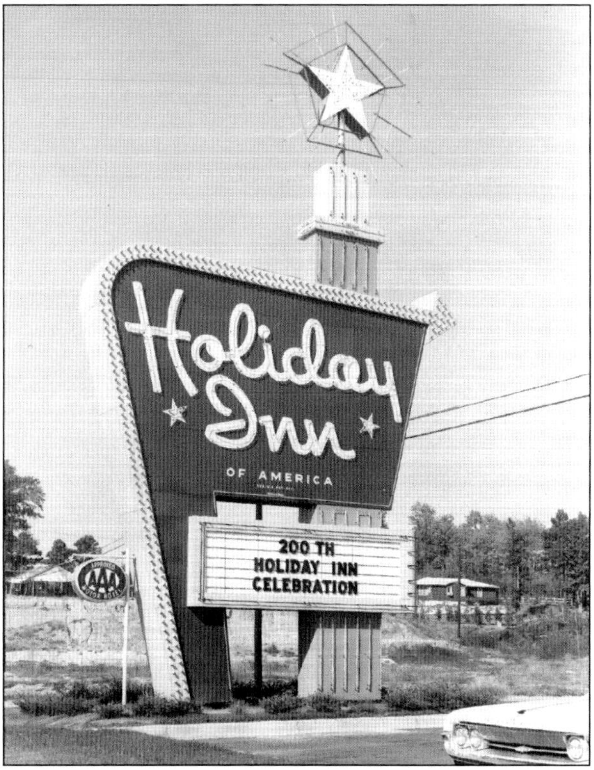

The Holiday Inn, built in 1960, was operated by Leo Spatz and was located on Highway 45 North across the street from the Magnolia Bowl. It originally contained 62 rentals, a banquet room dubbed the "Magnolia Room" (below), and a coffee shop. In 1980, the building was remodeled to include 155 rooms, a restaurant known as Bogie's, and a new lounge called Sam's Lounge, which seated 153 people. The building is now the Columbus Inns & Suites.

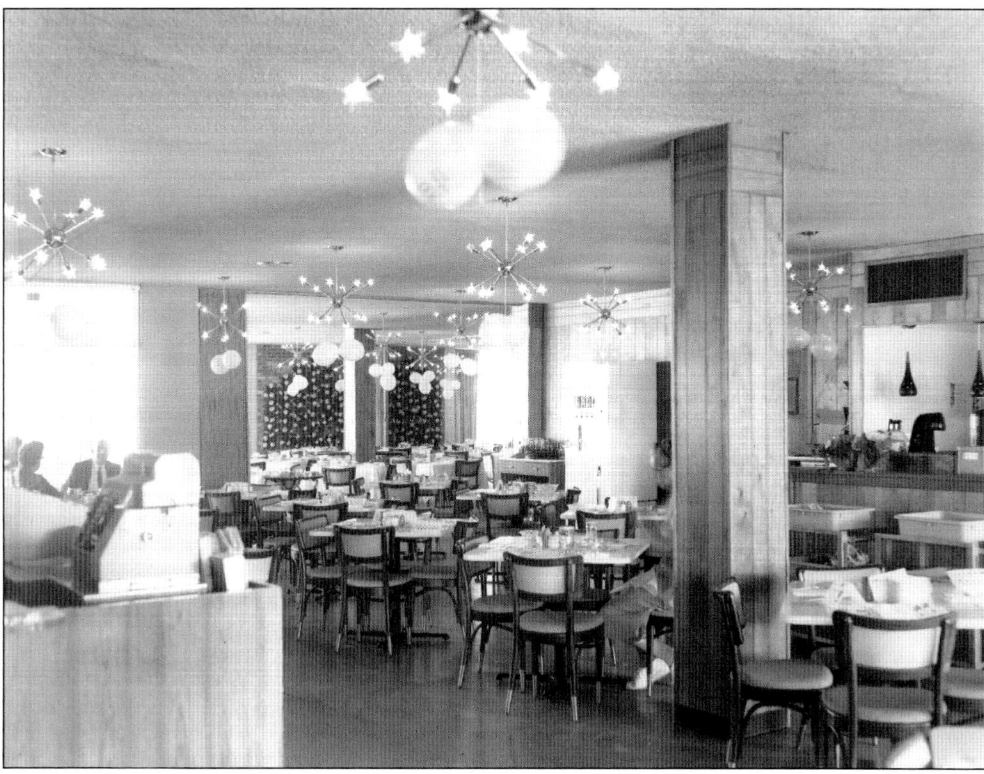

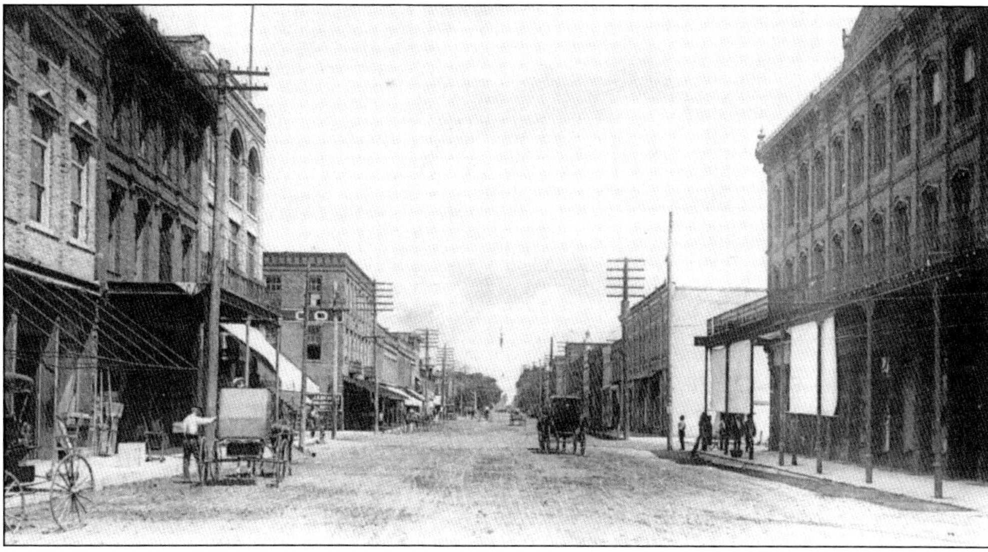

This postcard from around 1900 shows Fifth Street, formerly known as Market Street, looking north. The first building on the left is the grocery store Donoghue and Dee while the third building is Banks Hardware Company. Robertson and Company, a grocery store, is the fourth building on the left, facing R.E. Leigh Woman's Store across the street. The first building on the right is the dry goods store Simon Loeb and Brother. The Simon Loeb and Brother Building is now home to the WCBI television station.

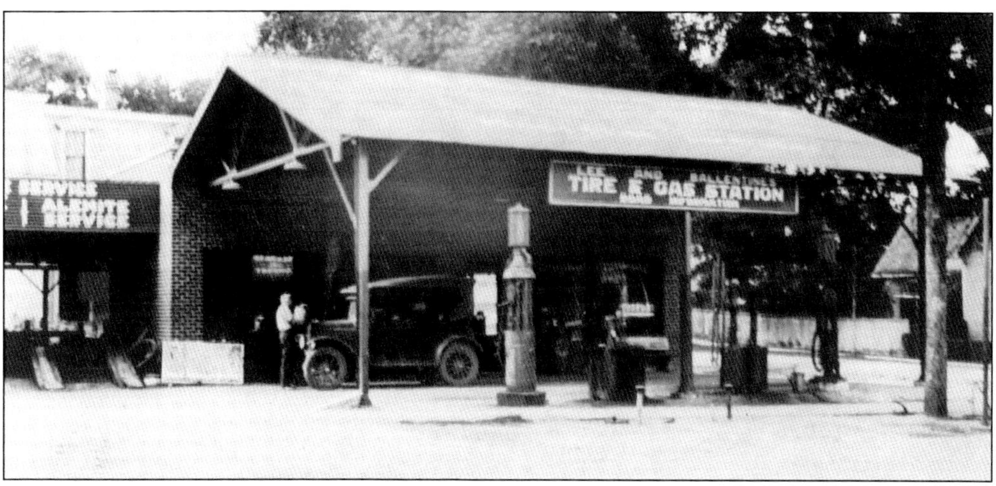

Lee and Ballentine's Tire & Gas Station, pictured here in 1923, was situated at 623 College Street and Seventh Street South. The service station was owned by Claude L. Ballentine.

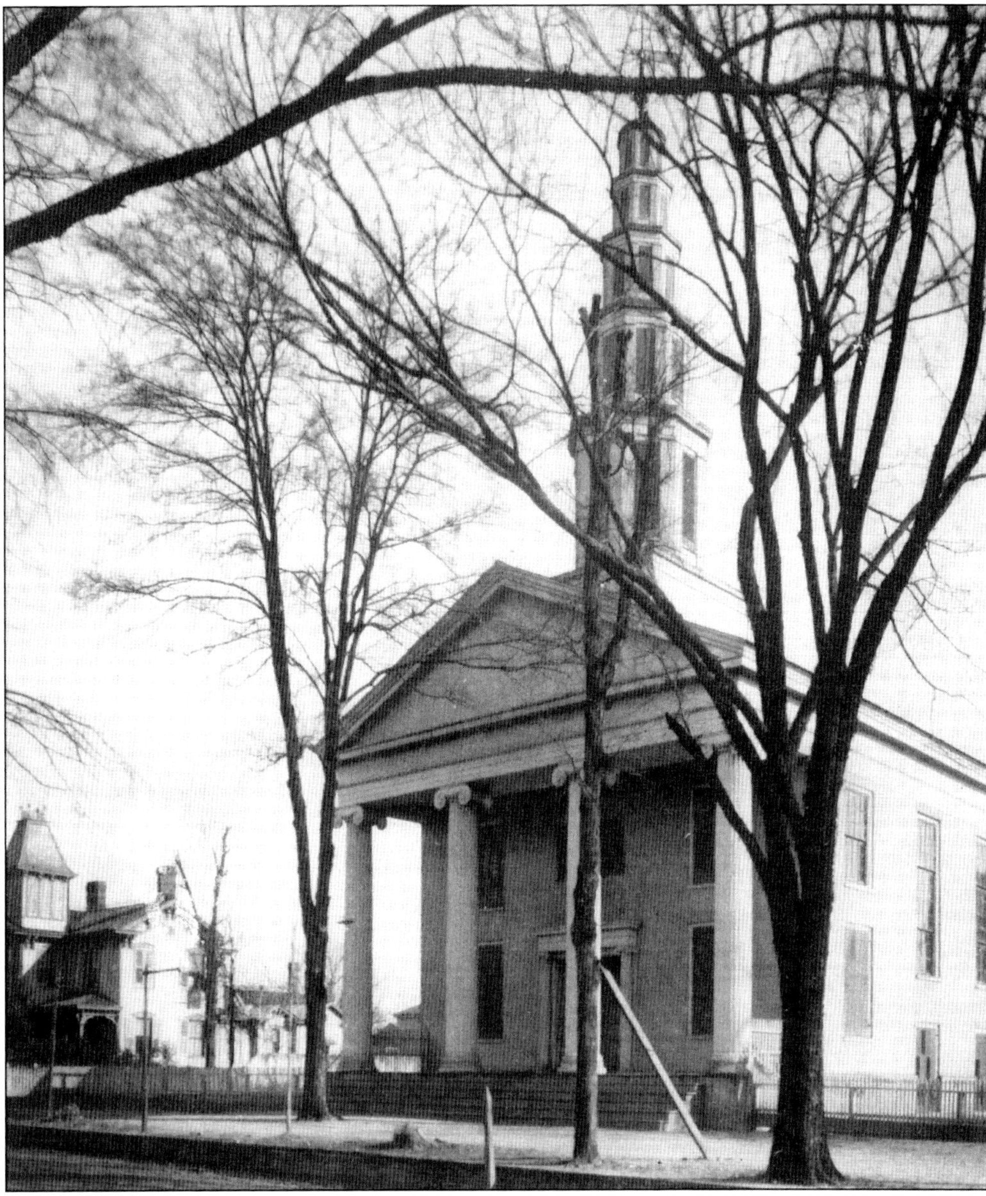

The residence to the left of the First Baptist Church was used as a hospital. Known as the Davis Infirmary, the hospital was owned and operated by both Dr. John E. Davis and Dr. Walter Russell McKinley. While the building was originally the residence of the McCabe family, the hospital opened there in 1886. This image of the hospital was captured around 1900. In 1905, Dr. Davis built a new hospital on Main Street and renamed it Columbus Hospital. That same year, Dr. McKinley also went on to open a hospital on Main Street, which was known as McKinley Sanitarium. The Davis Infirmary, on the corner of Third Avenue North and Seventh Street, was torn down in the late 1920s and replaced by the First Baptist Church Educational Building.

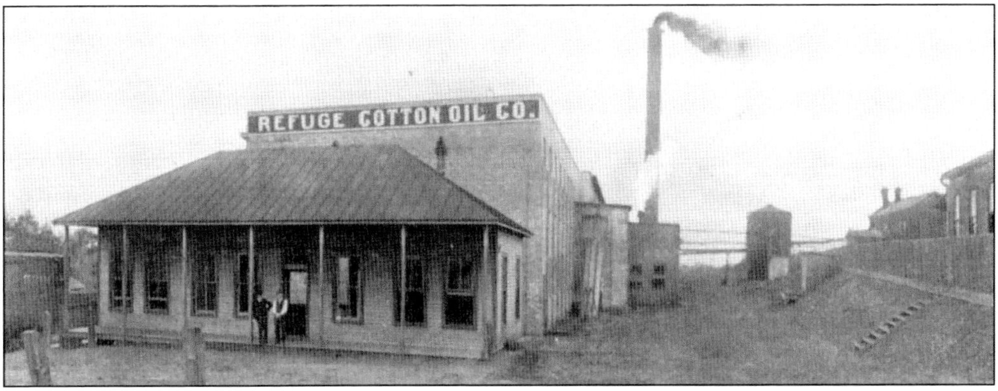

The Refuge Cotton Oil Company manufactured cottonseed oil, fertilizer, and meal and hull. Managed by W.C. McClure, the business included an eight-stand Munger gin with the capacity of 100 bales per day. The company crushed 75 tons of cottonseed and made and sold 2,000 tons of fertilizer in a year. It was located behind the present-day campus of Mississippi University for Women.

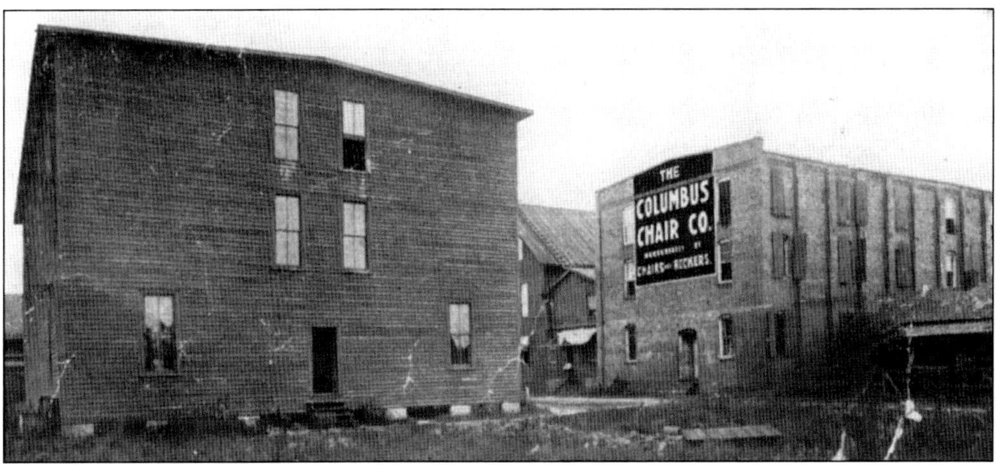

The Columbus Chair Company made medium-priced chairs and rockers from Mississippi white oak and other native hard woods. It was founded by Leopold Loeb and John Askew around 1900. Loeb handled the sales department while Askew focused on the factory. The plant contained electricity and was located along the lines of the Mobile and Ohio Railroad. A total of 75 workers turned out 35 dozen chairs and rocking chairs per day. The company's products were placed on exhibition throughout the country, including in Chicago and New York City.

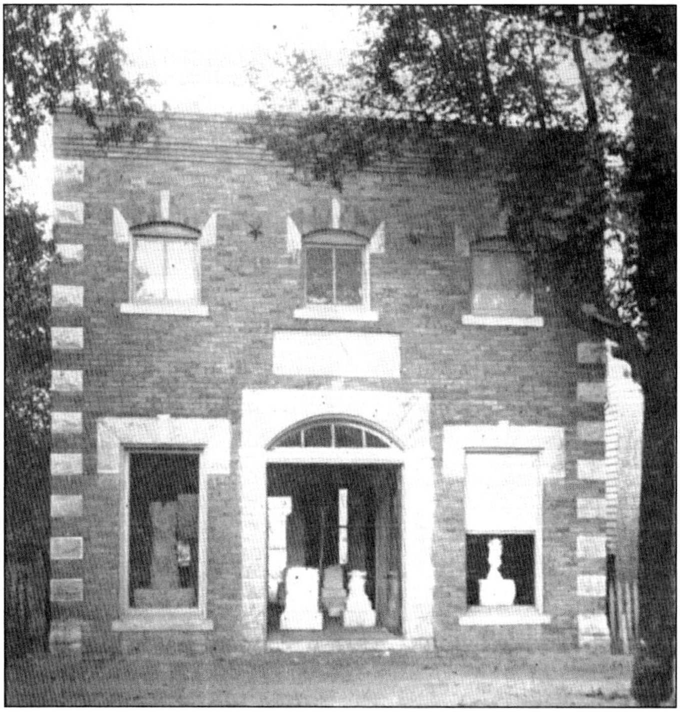

Columbus Marble Works began its operations in 1846. In 1891, it was purchased by John A. Stinson and operated with 14 employees. The salesroom, seen here, is located on Fifth Street South. Columbus Marble Works completed work on both the Merchants and Farmer's Bank and the current City Hall Building. The salesroom was later used as Laws Drugstore.

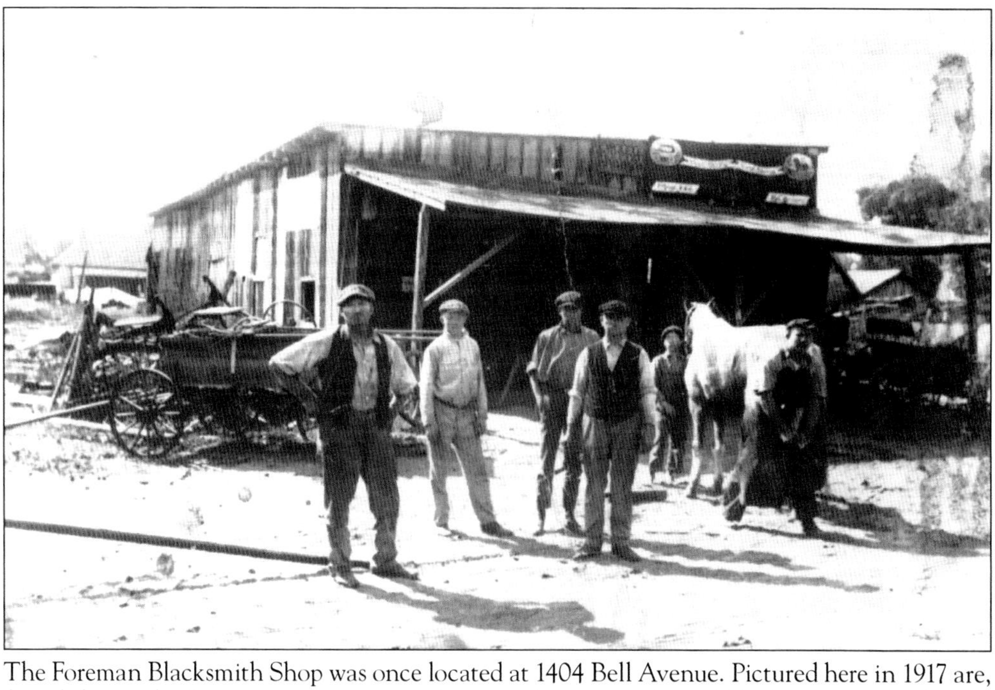

The Foreman Blacksmith Shop was once located at 1404 Bell Avenue. Pictured here in 1917 are, from left to right, Harvey C. Foreman, William P. Foreman, Johnny Ellis, Napoleon B. Wright, A.C. Foreman, Otho L. Taylor, and "Prince" the horse belonging to Samuel Kaye Sr.

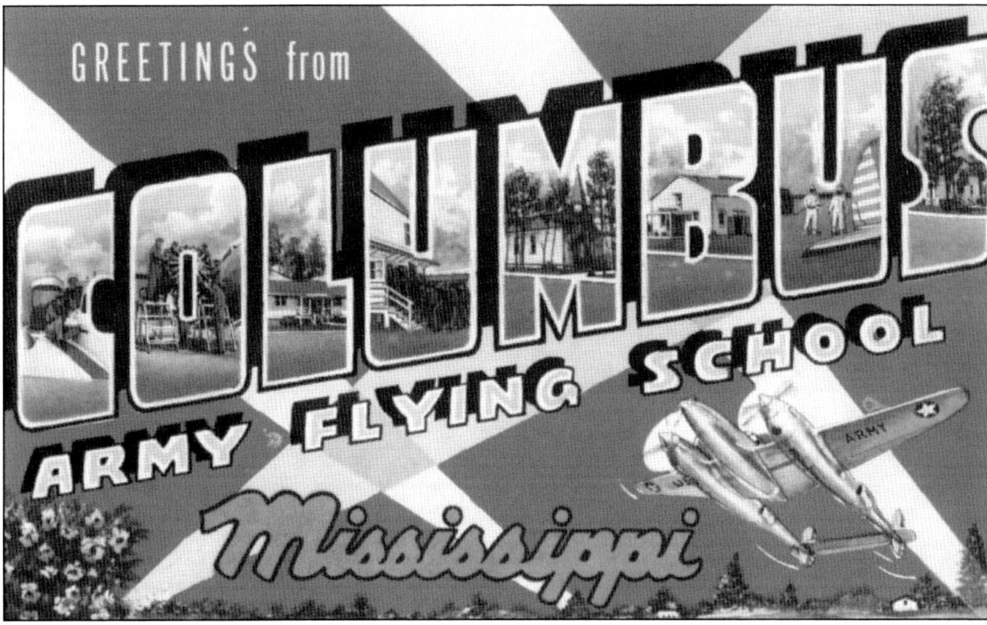

Established on June 26, 1941, as the Air Corps Advanced Flying School, the Columbus Air Force Base is a training base for US Air Force pilots and is located just north of Columbus. In 1942, it was named Kaye Field after Capt. Sam Kaye Jr., a decorated World War I pilot from Columbus. It was quickly changed to Columbus Army Flying School, however, when confusion arose over its similar sound to that of Key Field in Meridian, Mississippi. After World War II, the base remained inactive until 1951, when it was reopened for the Korean War and given its current name.

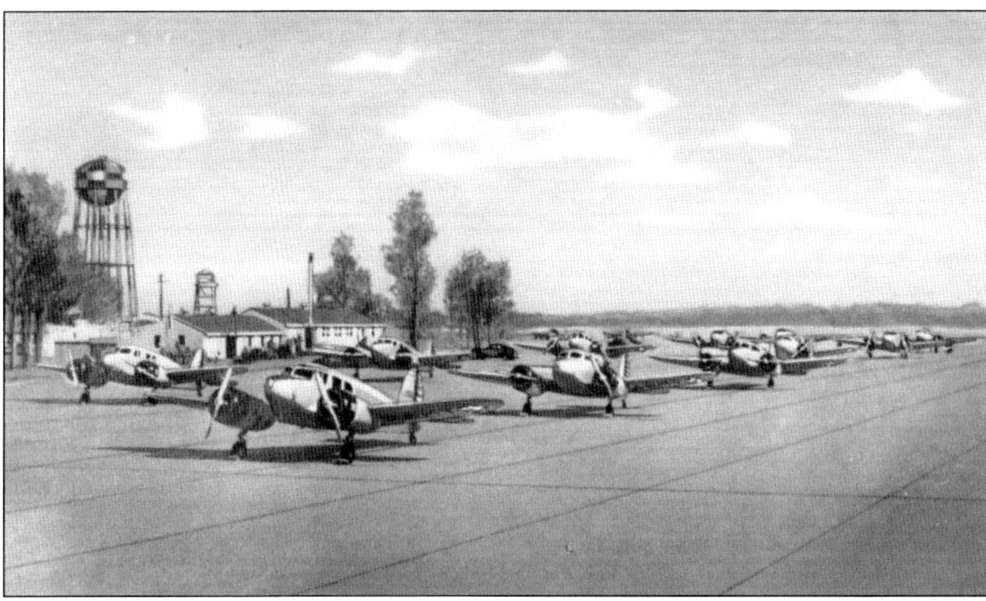

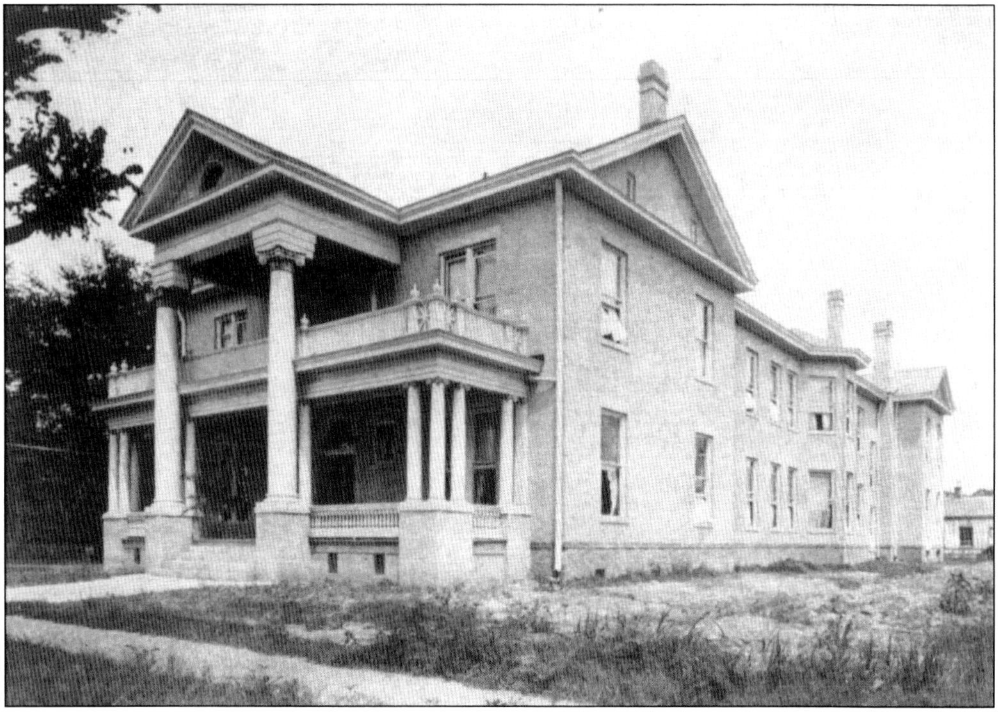

Opened in 1905, Columbus Hospital Inc. initially only housed between 40 to 50 patients. The first physicians to work at the hospital were Dr. John E. Davis, Dr. L.W. Crigler, and Dr. Rushton Clarke Molloy. The cost for a room varied from $2 to $5 per day. In 1980, the hospital opened a new 92-bed facility on Fifth Street North and Willowbrook Road, now known as Baptist Memorial Hospital-Golden Triangle. The original building on Main Street was remodeled and is now used by Community Counseling Services.

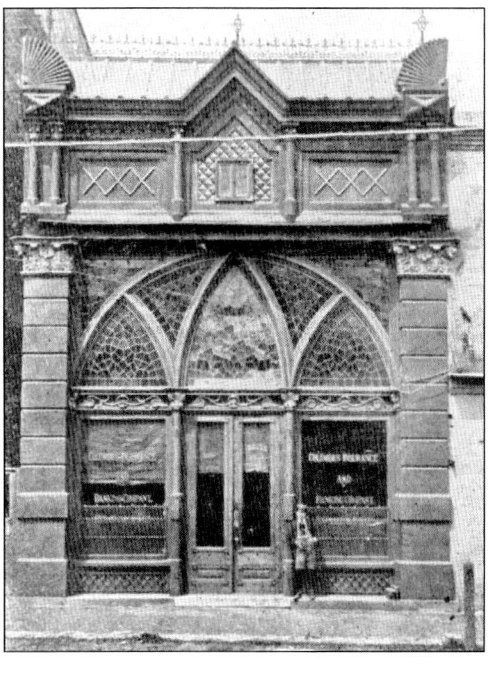

The Columbus Insurance and Banking Company, pictured in 1903, was chartered on February 14, 1852, and located at 507 Main Street. At the turn of the century, officers included T.B. Franklin, president; B.A. Weaver, vice-president; W.H. Lee, cashier; C.H. Ayres, teller; and E.R. Hopkins, bookkeeper.

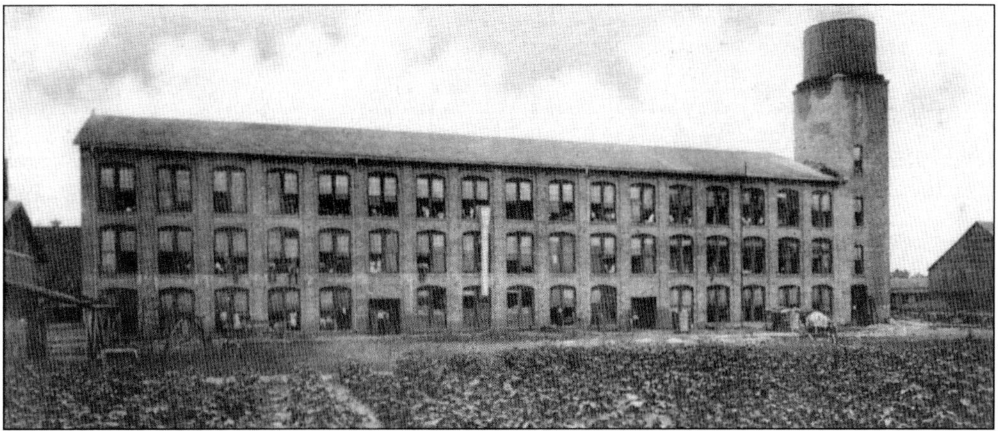

The Columbus Underwear Company, shown here shortly after it opened on February 1, 1905, made high-grade fleece-lined underwear. The factory, located at Eighteenth Street and Sixth Avenue South, was made of brick and touted a new sprinkler system and electric lights for its 110 employees. Owners were F.W. and J.R. Kavanaugh. John McGinnis worked as superintendent. The Kavanaugh brothers were proprietors of the Kavanaugh Knitting Company out of Waterford, New York. Their Egyptian Liste-thread mercerized and silk underwear was sold all over the world. The finishing room at the Columbus plant, below, contained 80 sewing machines assisting in the work of producing 250 dozen garments per day.

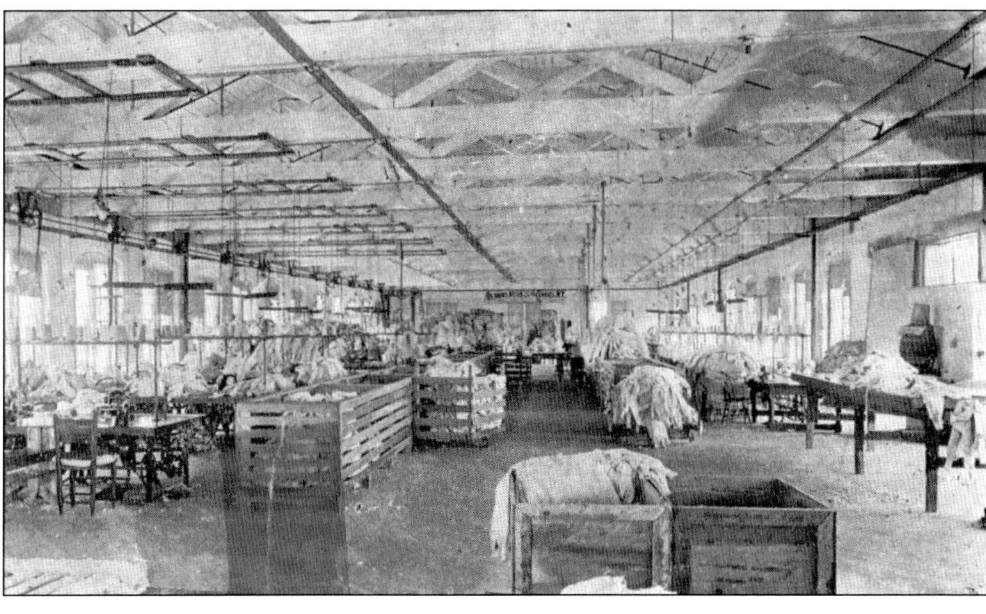

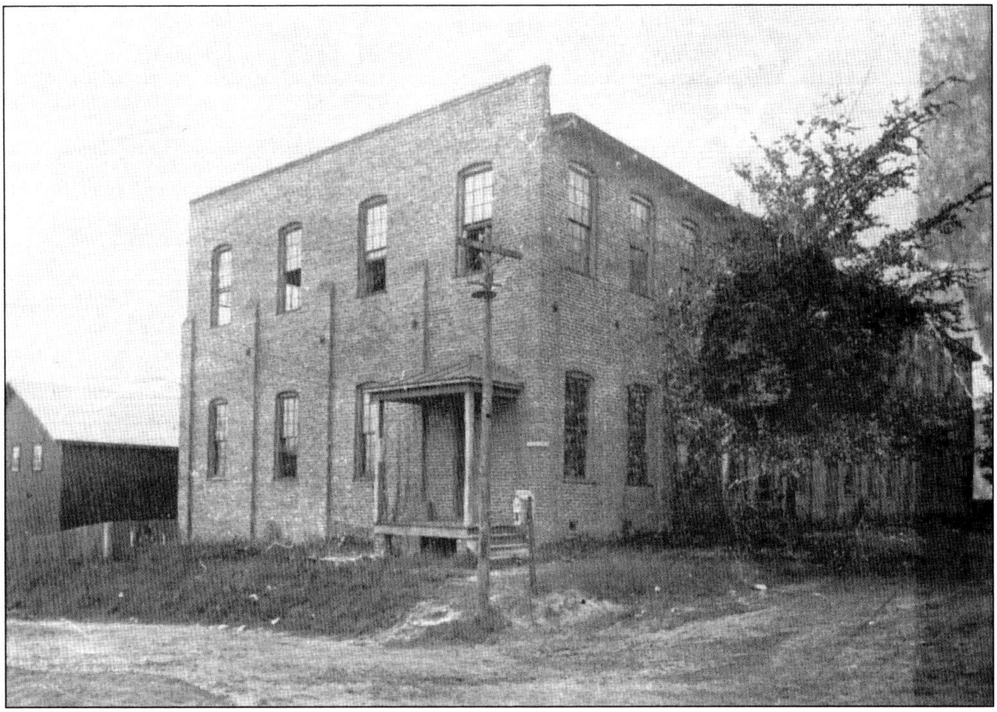

Built by the Southern Cotton Down Company in 1901, the corporation was rechartered in April 1902 as the Columbus Comfort Company. Located at 802 First Street South, the company was managed by V.D. Molloy. Nearly 100 men and women produced items of "comfort," such as sofa pillows and stair pads. The brick building included a quilting room, carding room, and a packing and cutting room.

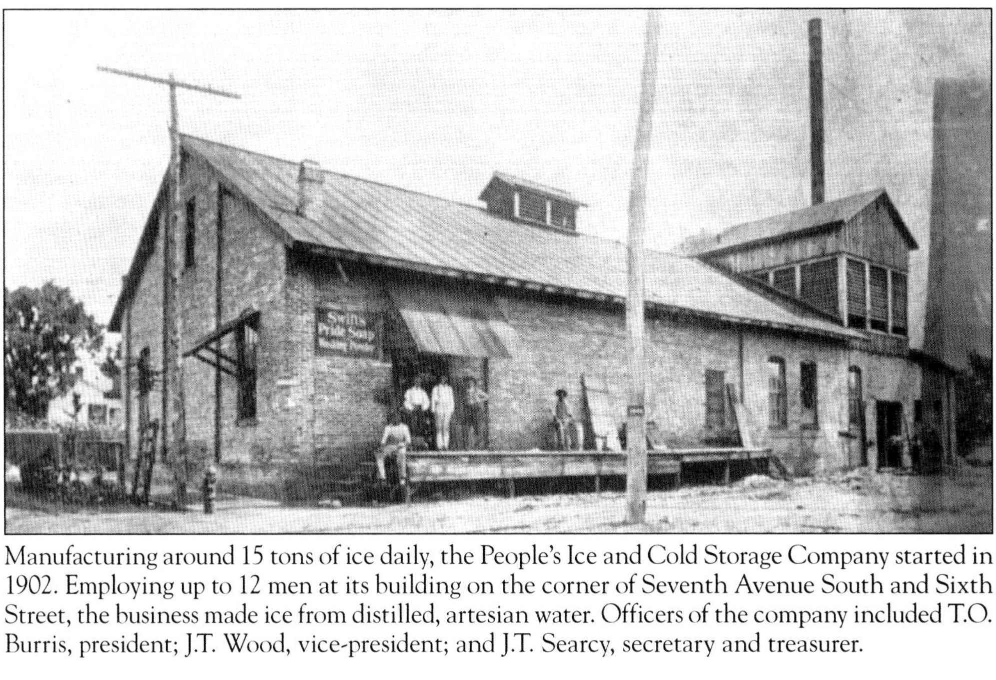

Manufacturing around 15 tons of ice daily, the People's Ice and Cold Storage Company started in 1902. Employing up to 12 men at its building on the corner of Seventh Avenue South and Sixth Street, the business made ice from distilled, artesian water. Officers of the company included T.O. Burris, president; J.T. Wood, vice-president; and J.T. Searcy, secretary and treasurer.

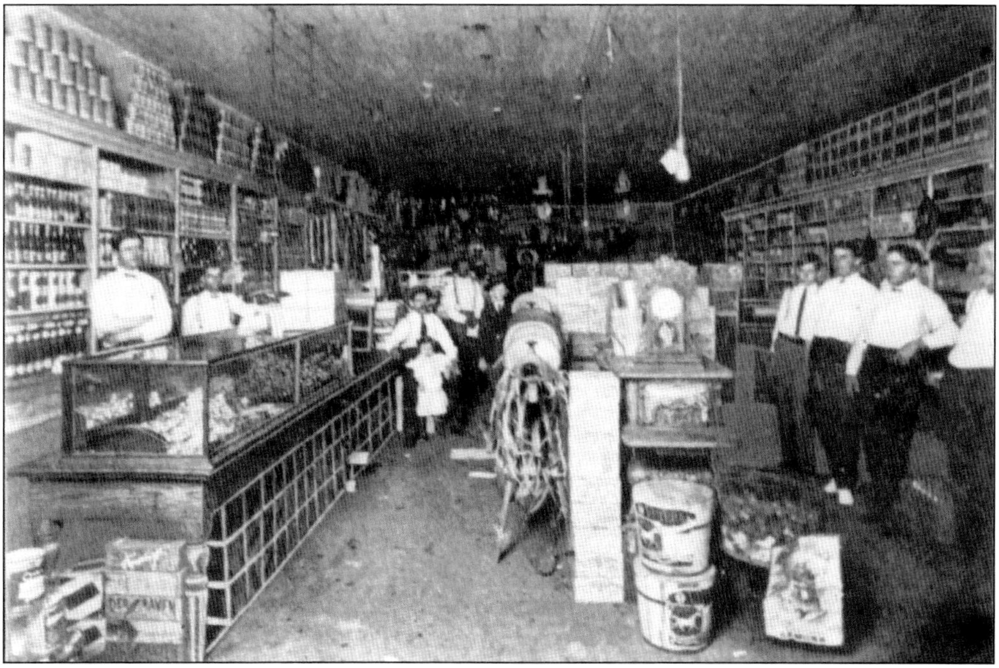

R.A. Mullins and Company was a wholesale and retail general merchandise store. Located at 406 Main Street, the dealers opened their business in 1901 and sold everything from groceries, dry goods, saddles, hardware, hats, plantation supplies, and shoes to different types of feed, such as oats, corn, and hay.

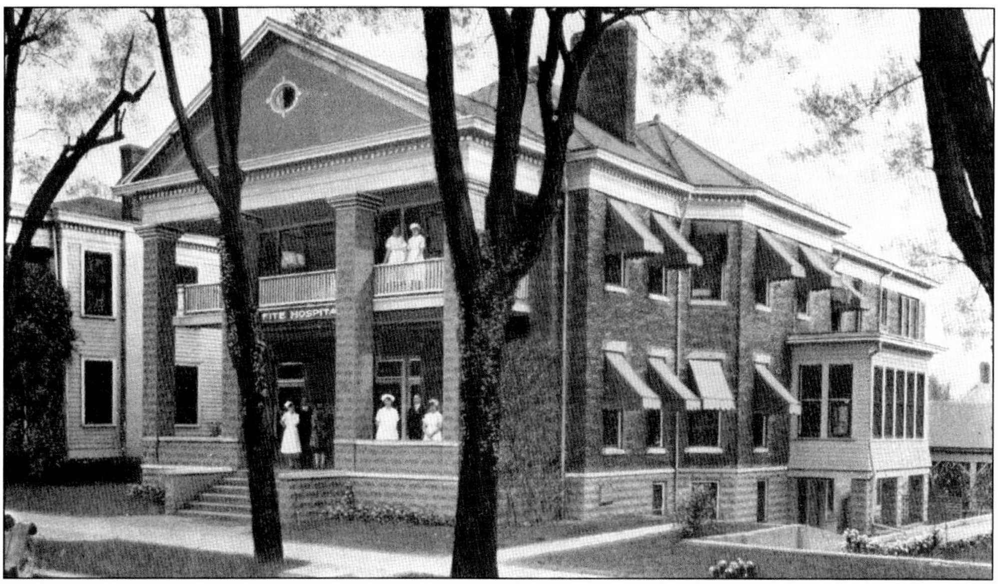

First opened as McKinley Sanitarium in 1905, this building, located at 618 Main Street, was sold in 1924 by Dr. Walter R. McKinley to surgeon Ped L. Fite. Dr. Fite renamed the sanitarium Fite Hospital and specialized in "Diagnosis, Surgery, and Gynecology." The hospital boasted a laboratory, operating room, an emergency room, an X-ray machine, and a delivery room. Playwright Thomas Lanier "Tennessee" Williams was born here on March 26, 1911. In 1935, Dr. James Doster bought the building, and it became Doster Hospital. The building was torn down in 1970.

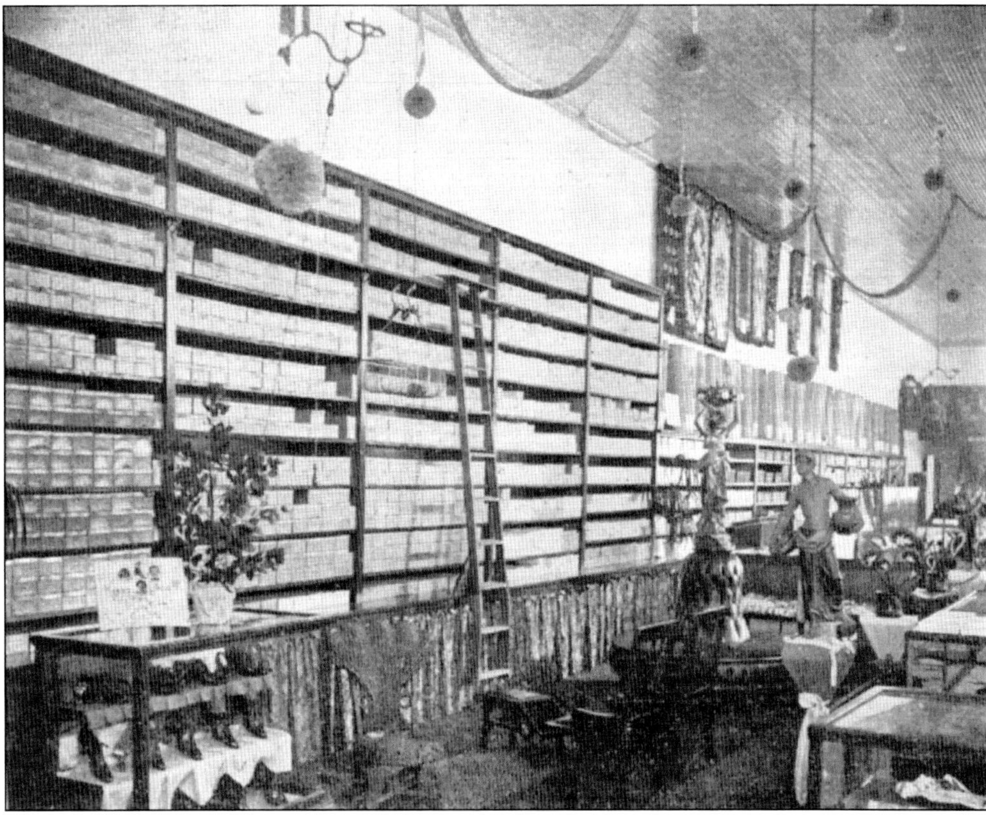

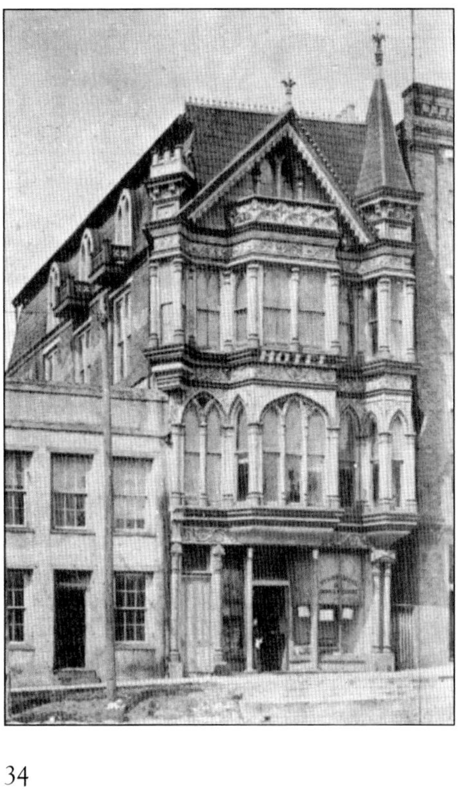

Opened in 1902, the Woman's Store carried dry goods, furnishings, millinery, and shoes. Owned and operated by R.E. Leigh, the store was located at 125 Fifth Street South. Students from the Industrial Institute and College (now Mississippi University for Women) could purchase materials from the Woman's Store for their once required uniforms.

The book and stationery business of William N. Munroe and Company was situated just left of the Gilmer Hotel on Main Street. Established in 1869, the store also sold pictures, picture frames, wallpaper, periodicals, school and artist's materials, and newspapers. The upper story was used as the River View hotel. Munroe sold the business just prior to his death in 1905.

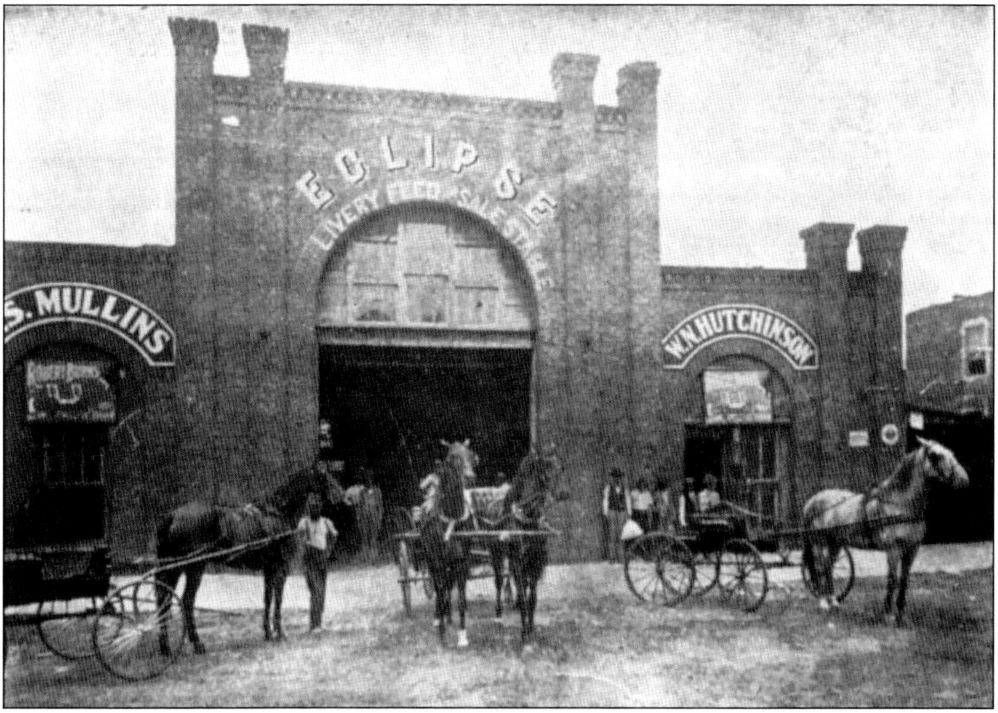

The Eclipse Livery, Sale and Feed Stable was one of several stables that operated in Columbus at the turn of the century. Located at 526 Main Street, proprietors included Ira Gaston and W.N. Hutchinson. Managed by Eugene Egger, the Eclipse Livery sold horses and mules and boarded horses by the day, week, or month. It also offered horses and carriages for those interested in pleasure driving around the city. The interior of the building is seen below.

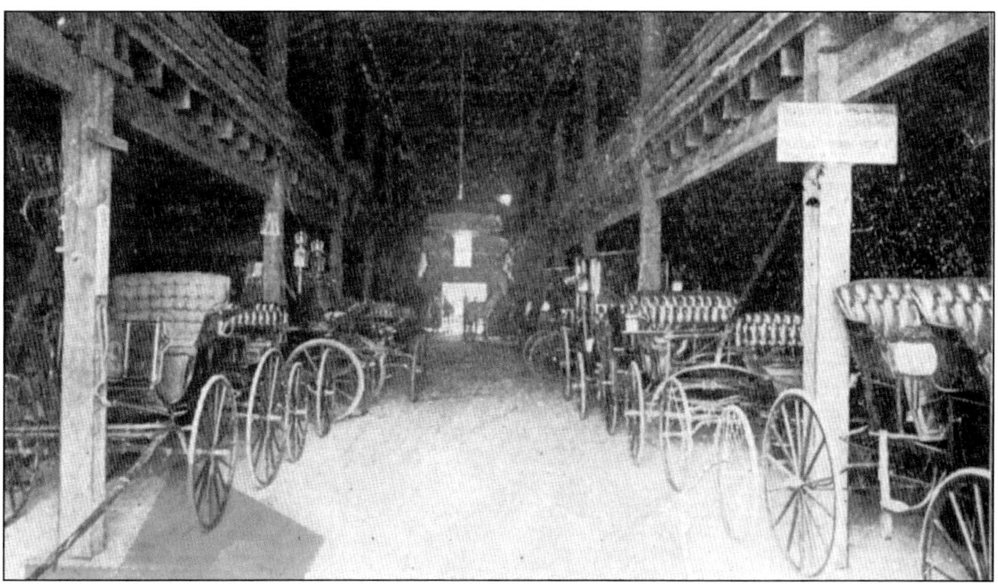

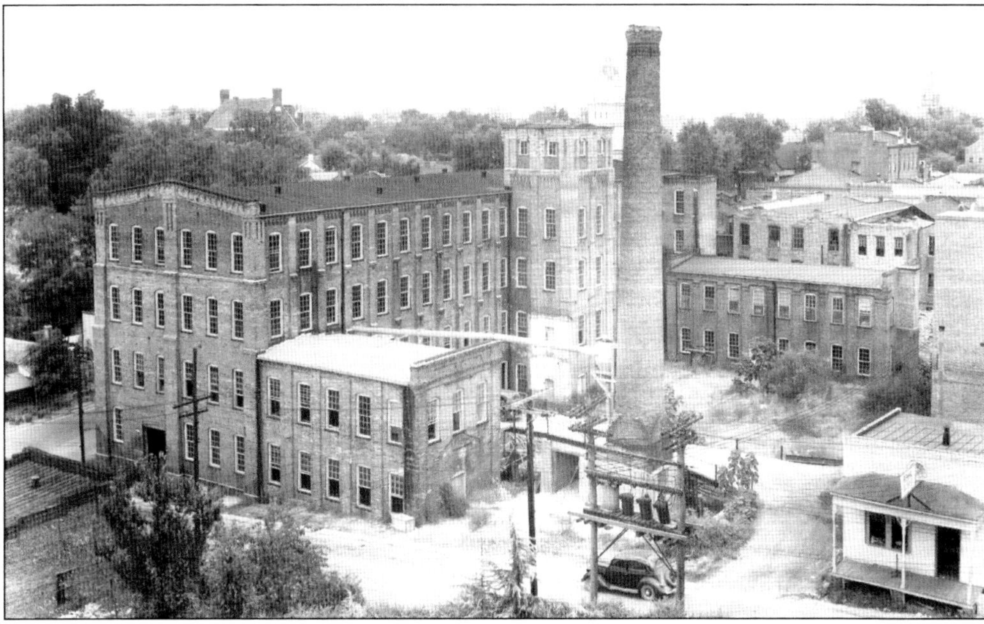

The Tombigbee Cotton Mill, seen above in the 1920s, was located on the corner of Fourth Street and Second Avenue North (site of present-day James M. Trotter Convention Center). Built in 1887 by Harrison Johnston, the mill chiefly produced cloth. On January 20, 1940, one of the biggest fires to hit Columbus started in the old Cotton Mill and destroyed over half a city block, seen below. At the time of the fire, the building operated as the Columbus Marble Works Casket Division, owned by Arthur McGahey. The fire struck during one of the coldest winters on record in Columbus. It was 15 degrees outside as the fire raged. (Courtesy of the Southern Historical Collection, Wilson Library, the University of North Carolina at Chapel Hill.)

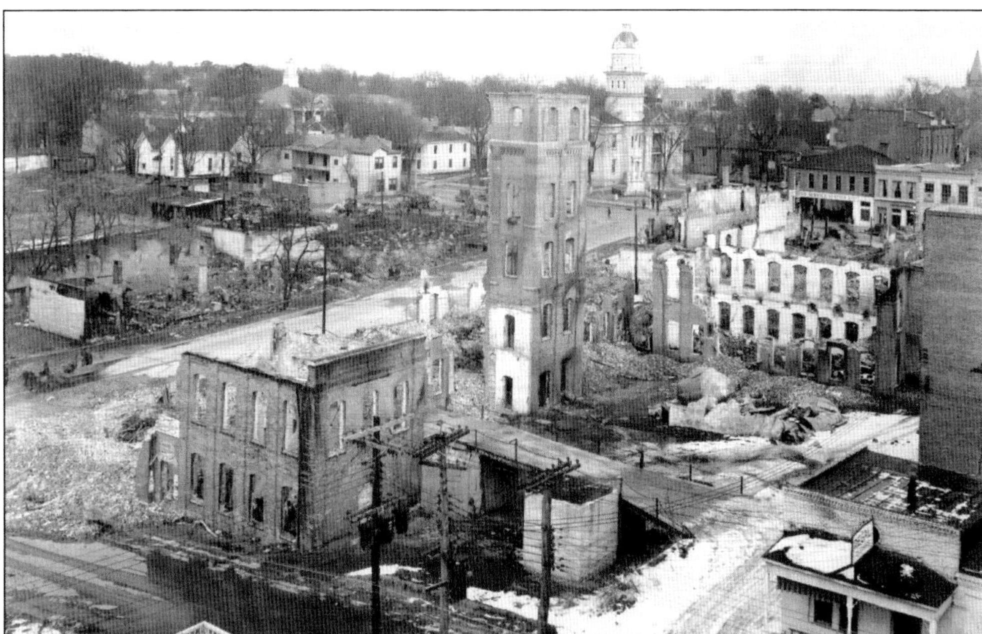

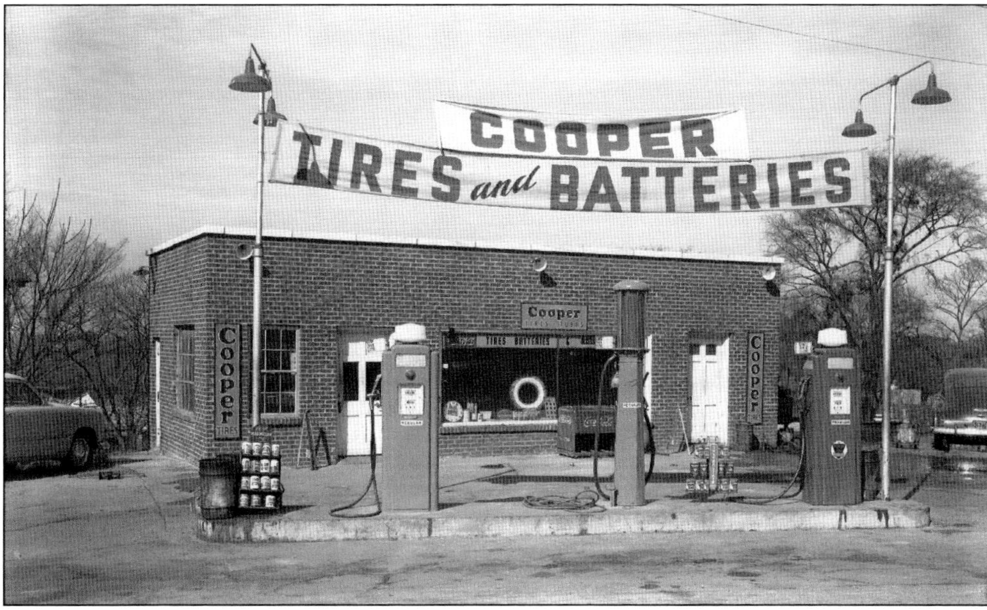

The Johnson Service Station, seen here in 1950, was located at 223 Main Street. The station was owned and operated by Thomas A. Johnson.

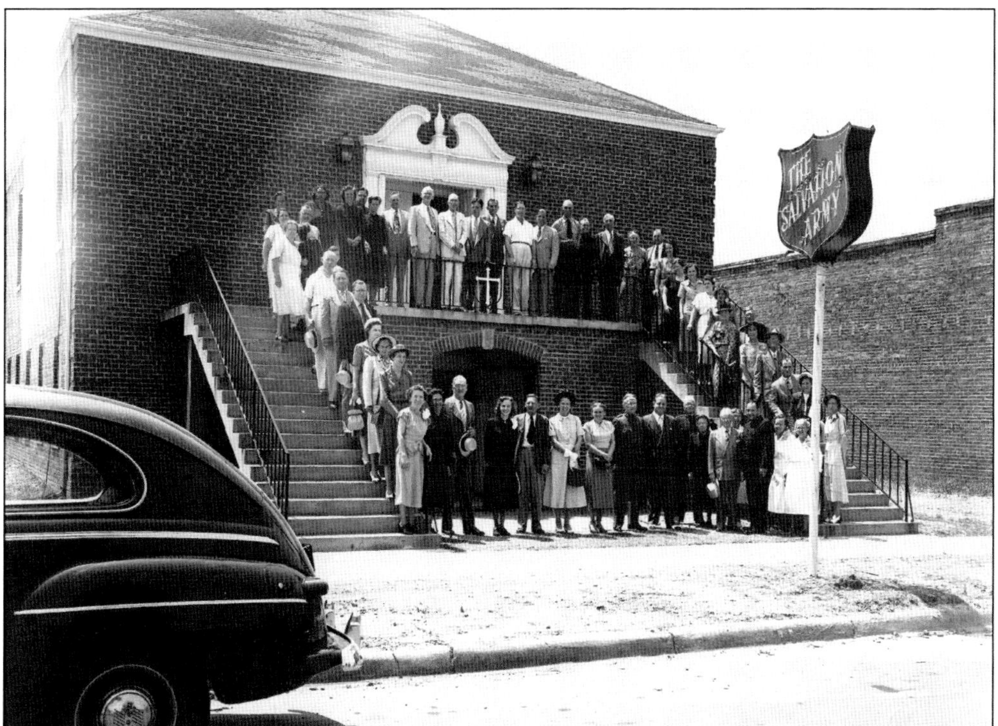

The Salvation Army, pictured here around 1950, was located at 116 Twenty-first Street South. This building was erected in 1948 and served the organization for over 30 years. While this structure still exists, the Salvation Army later moved to a new building a few blocks away.

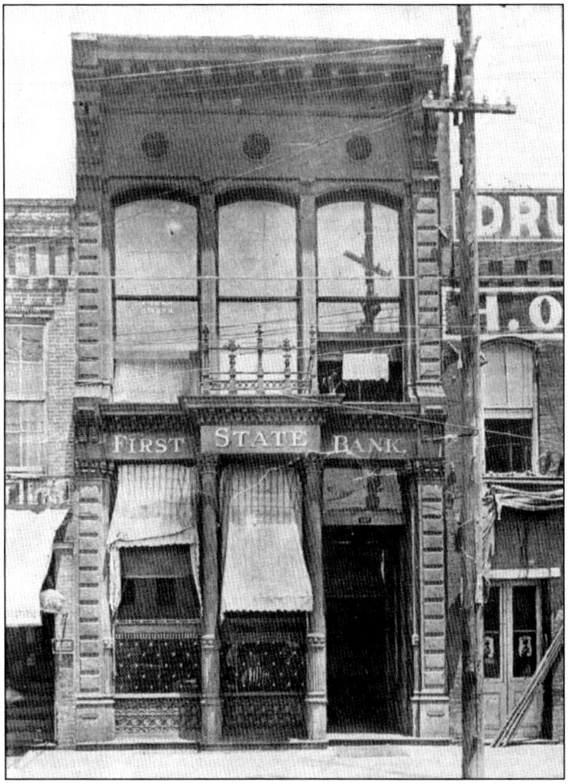

Organized in 1892, the First State Bank was located at 427 Main Street (present-day Bancorp South Building). While the first floor was used by the bank, the upper floor was divided into offices and suites used by business professionals. The bank included a vault built of chilled steel, eight inches thick.

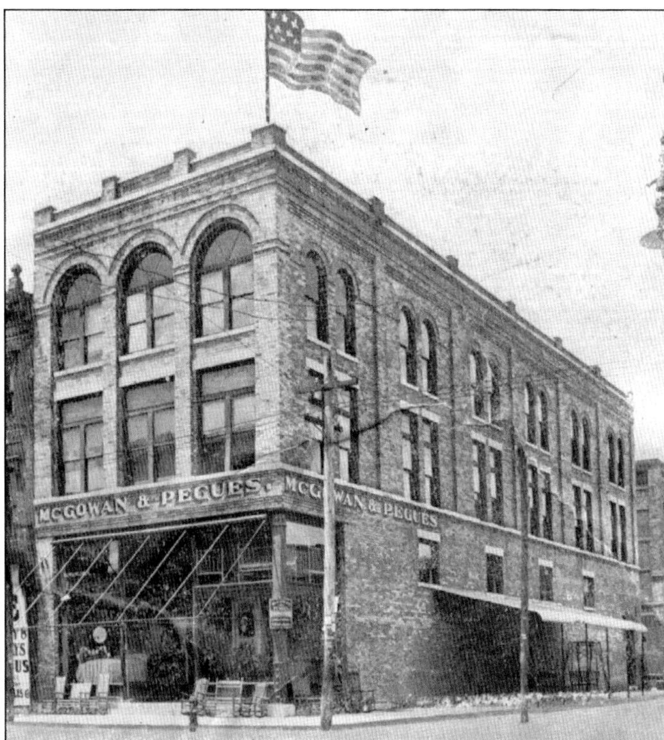

Now the site of Leadership Plaza, this three-story building belonged to the McGowan and Pegues Furniture Store and stood at 202 Fifth Street South (to the right of present-day Hollyhocks Gift Shop). Established in 1891 by Leopold Loeb as Loeb and McGowan Furniture Store, the building included steam heat, electricity, and a freight elevator. The first floor contained the sales room, the second floor was the undertaking and upholstering departments as well as a show room, and the third floor and basement housed reserve stock.

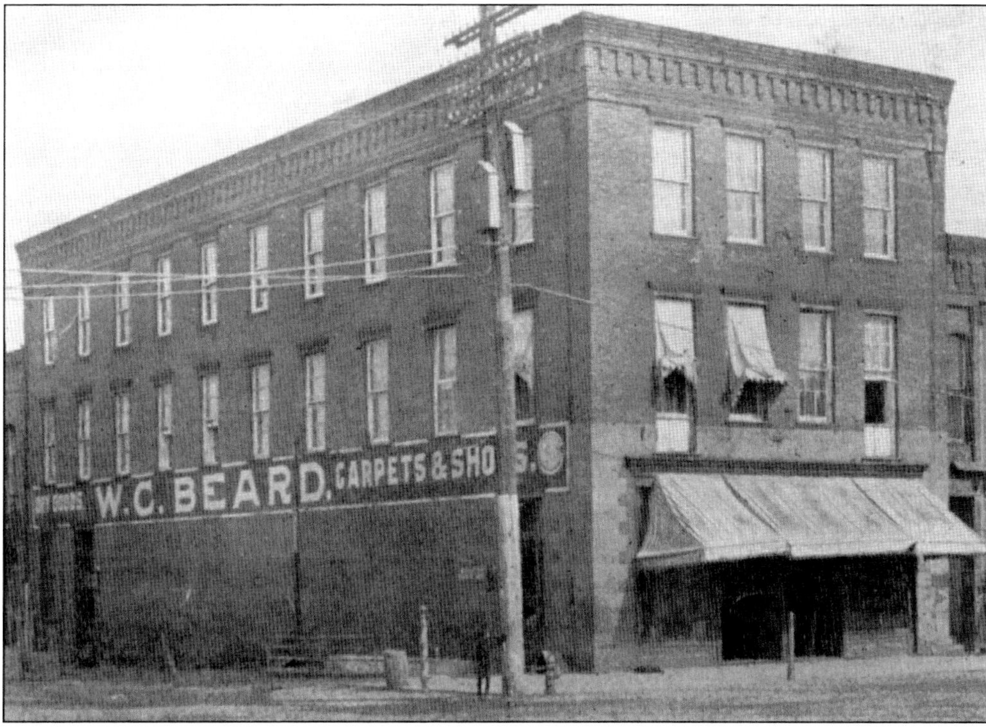

Advertised as the largest dry goods and furnishing business in the region, W.C. Beard's store was located on the southeast corner of Main and Market Streets. At W.C. Beard's, one could find dry goods, dress goods and trimmings, draperies, floor covers, and house furnishings. W.C. Beard, owner, was assisted by his sons E.N. and J.H. Beard along with 15 other employees.

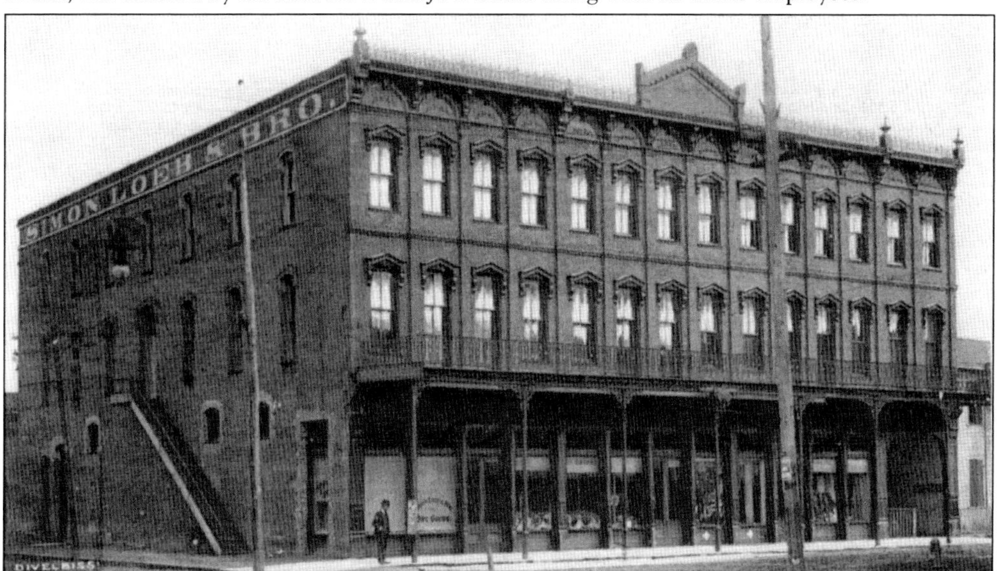

The Simon Loeb and Brother Store opened in 1874 and is now home to the WCBI television station. The three-story brick structure included modern conveniences such as electric lights and hot air furnaces for heating. In 1902, the second floor also housed a public library. Simon Loeb Sr. and Julius Loeb owned and operated the business, while Simon's son J. Albert Loeb was an associate.

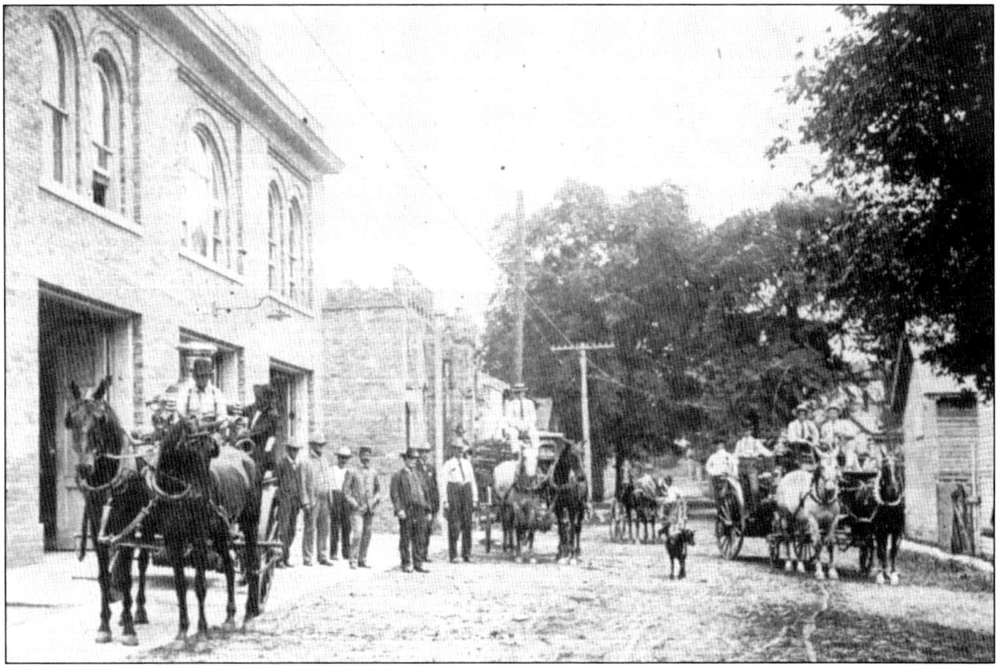

On the left is the old fire station building, known as Fire Station No. 1, completed in 1903. The second building on the left is the 2,062-square-foot Armory. Built prior to the 1880s, the Gothic-style Armory was used to store artillery for the Columbus-area troops of the Mississippi state militia, which later became the National Guard. It is the only documented 19th-century militia armory remaining in Mississippi and is listed as both a Mississippi Landmark and in the National Register of Historic Places.

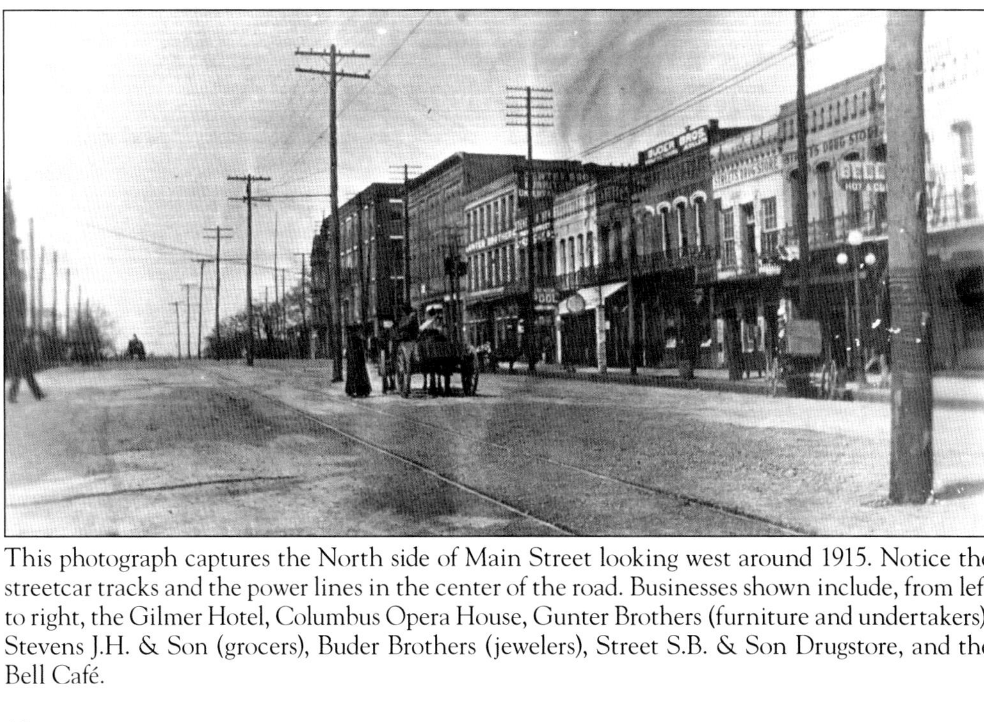

This photograph captures the North side of Main Street looking west around 1915. Notice the streetcar tracks and the power lines in the center of the road. Businesses shown include, from left to right, the Gilmer Hotel, Columbus Opera House, Gunter Brothers (furniture and undertakers), Stevens J.H. & Son (grocers), Buder Brothers (jewelers), Street S.B. & Son Drugstore, and the Bell Café.

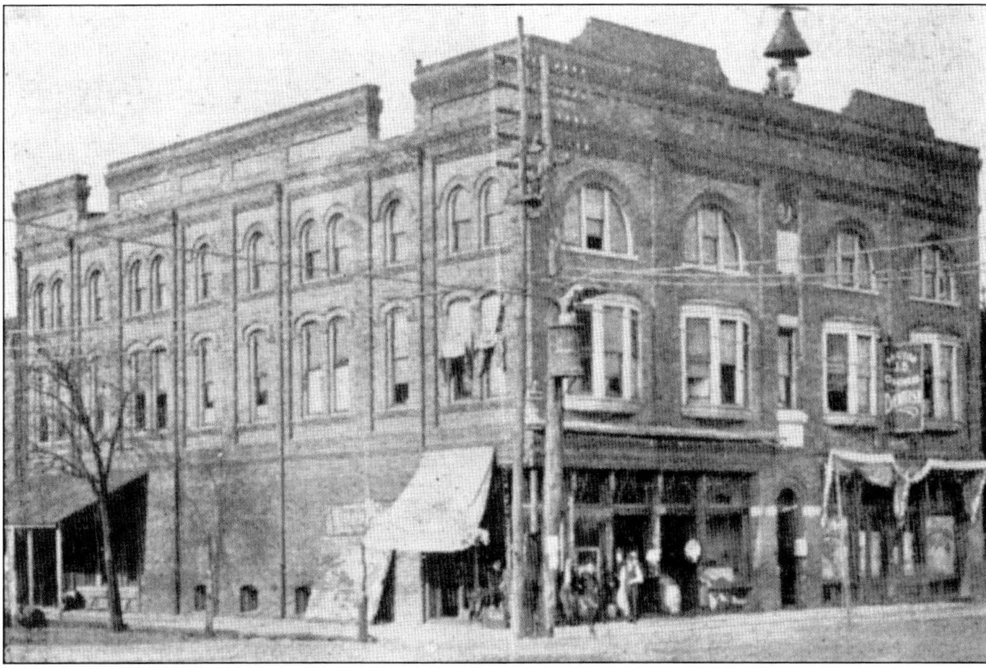

This image from 1903 shows the three-story structure on the southeast corner of Main and Market Streets when druggists John P. Mayo and Blanche A. Weaver occupied it. On the second story, John Dearing Odeneal operated his dental practice. The building was destroyed by fire in 1919. The site is now the location of the Rosenzweig Arts Center and the Columbus Arts Council.

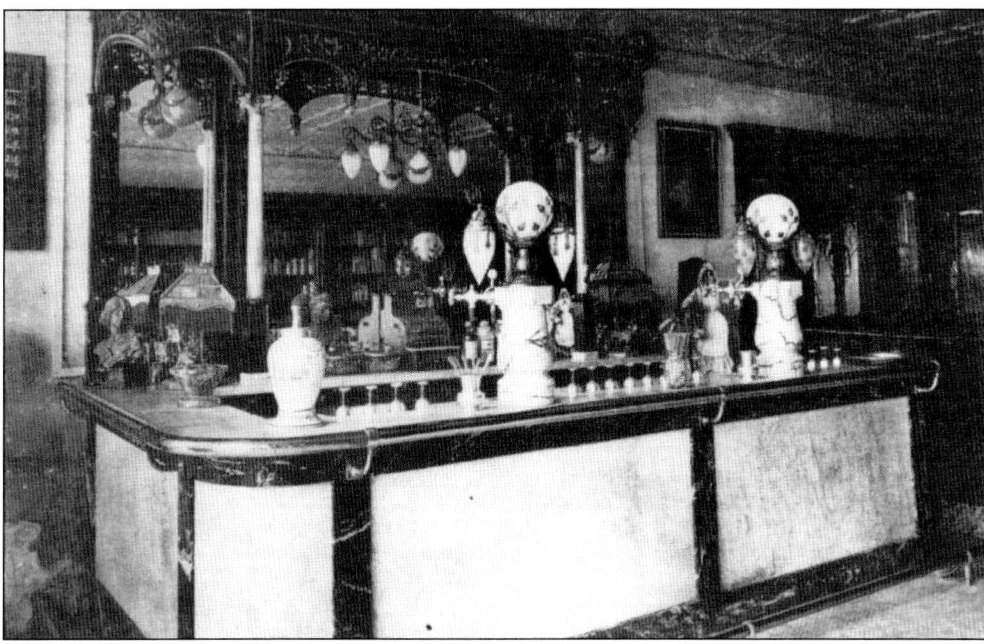

At the turn of the century, drugstores across America purchased soda fountains for customers to enjoy a variety of drink concoctions. In Columbus, Lide's Drugstore had such a fountain, seen here around 1913. It was operated by druggist Leighton E. Lide and located at 116 Market Street South.

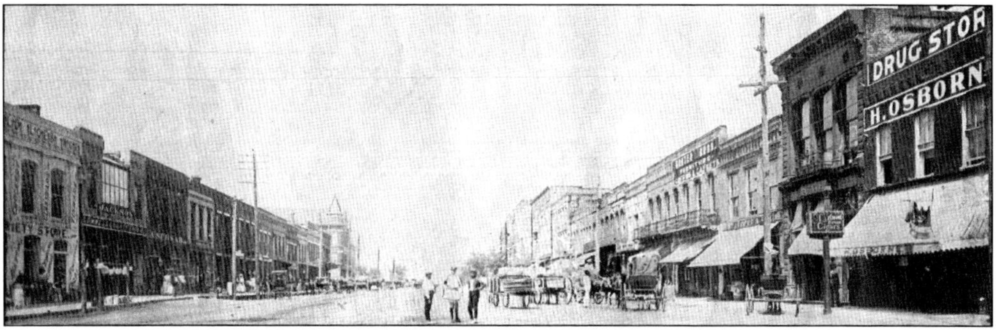

This image shows both the north and south sides of Main Street looking west around 1905. One can see the glass roof (left) of Jackson's Photography Studio (now the clothing store The Globe). Other businesses identified include (left) Loeb Variety Store and A. Schwab Dry Goods; (right) Gunter Brothers Furniture store, T.J. Locke and Son grocery store, and H. Osborne's Drugstore.

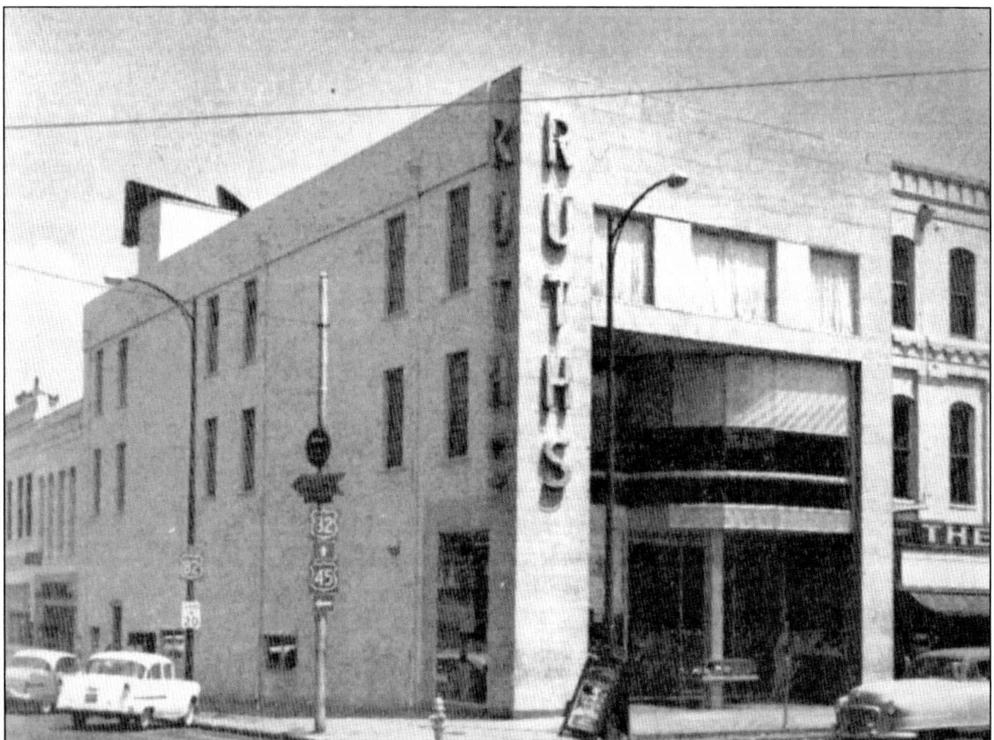

For over 60 years, Ruth's Department Store was a landmark in ladies clothing and jewelry. Opened in 1940 by Aaron Bernstein, it moved to the southeast corner of Main and Market Streets in 1948. In 1992, Bernstein's grandson, Bill Strauss, became president. Strauss operated the department store until it closed in 2003. The building was then converted into apartments and retail space. The first floor of the building is now home to the Café on Main restaurant.

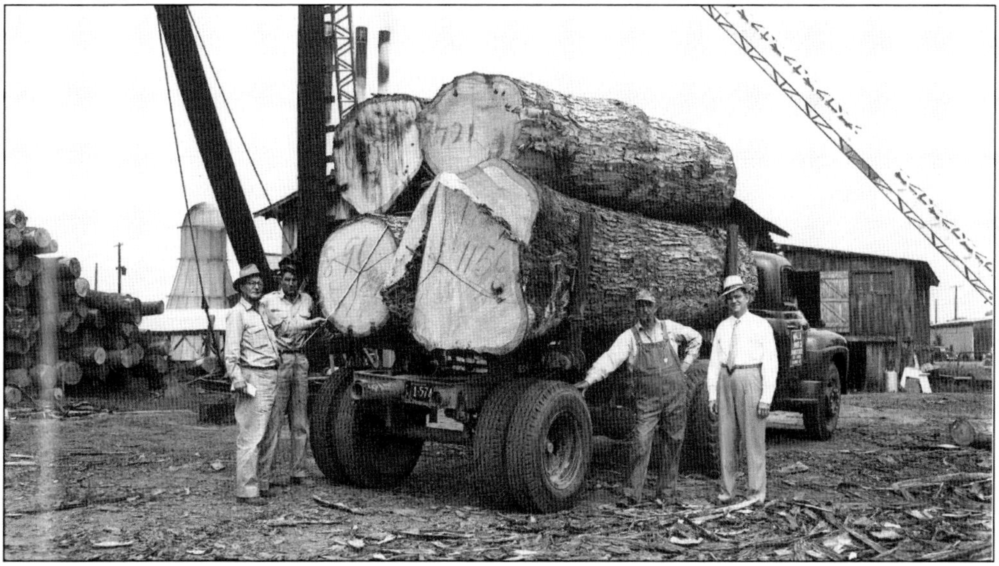

The Wallin Lumber Company, seen here around 1950, was located at 724 Fifteenth Street South and offered southern hardwood, cypress, and pine lumber.

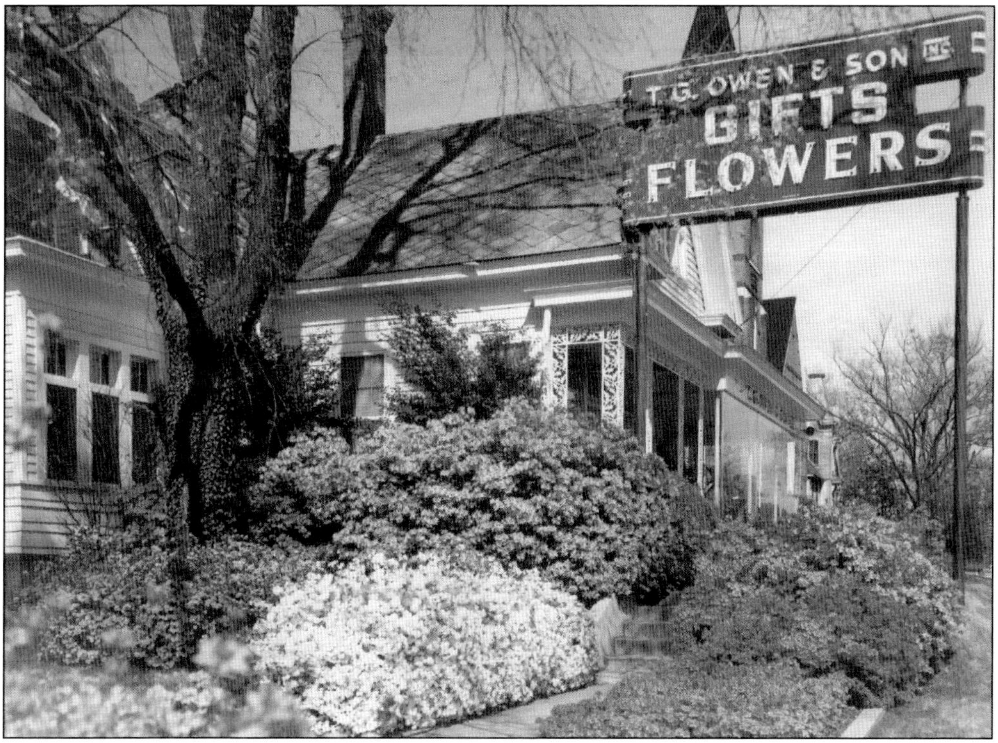

T.G. Owen and Son Inc. was a nursery as well as a flower and gift shop. Thomas G. Owen (1861–1935) founded a nursery that covered over 950 acres and shipped all over the nation. Located at 1700 Ninth Street South, the home is now the Jackie O' House Bed and Breakfast. The flower shop (seen here) was located at 623 Main Street and was known for its elaborate window displays. It was operated by Herman Mohr, T.G.'s son, and Hazel Reynolds Owen until the late 1960s. This building was torn down in 2010.

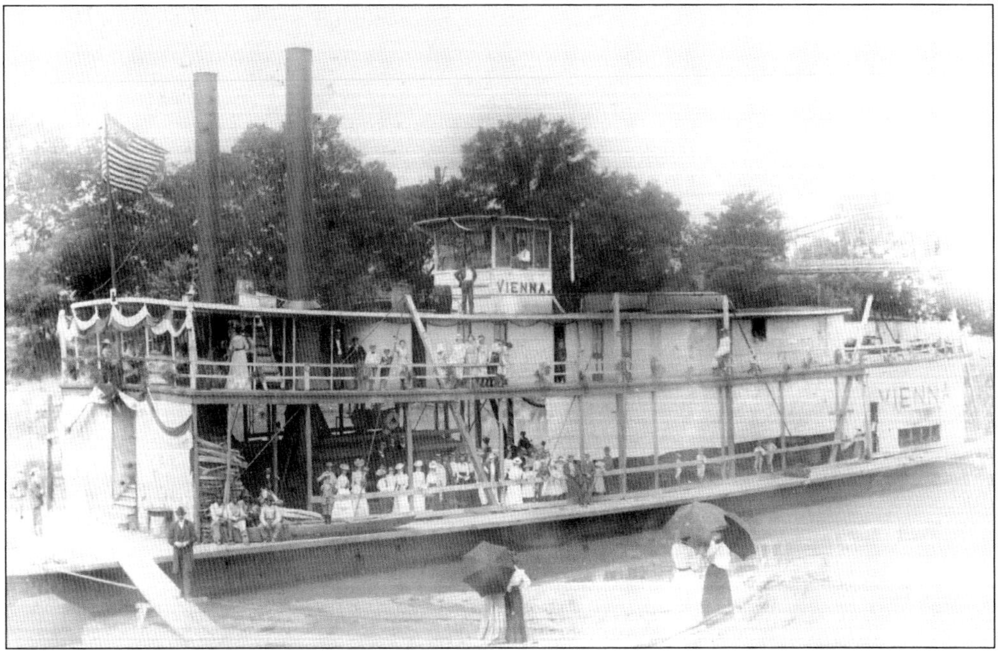

One of many steamboats that traveled the Tombigbee River was the *Vienna*. Built in Columbus in 1898 by William Pentecost, it was designed specifically for the Demopolis and Columbus River trade. The stern-wheeler measured 176 tons and measured 155 feet by 276 feet by 4.5 feet. Capt. Samuel A. Cosper designed the boat and oversaw its construction. On January 19, 1906, the steamboat sank at Moore's Bluff with over 250 bales of cotton and 2,200 sacks of cottonseed.

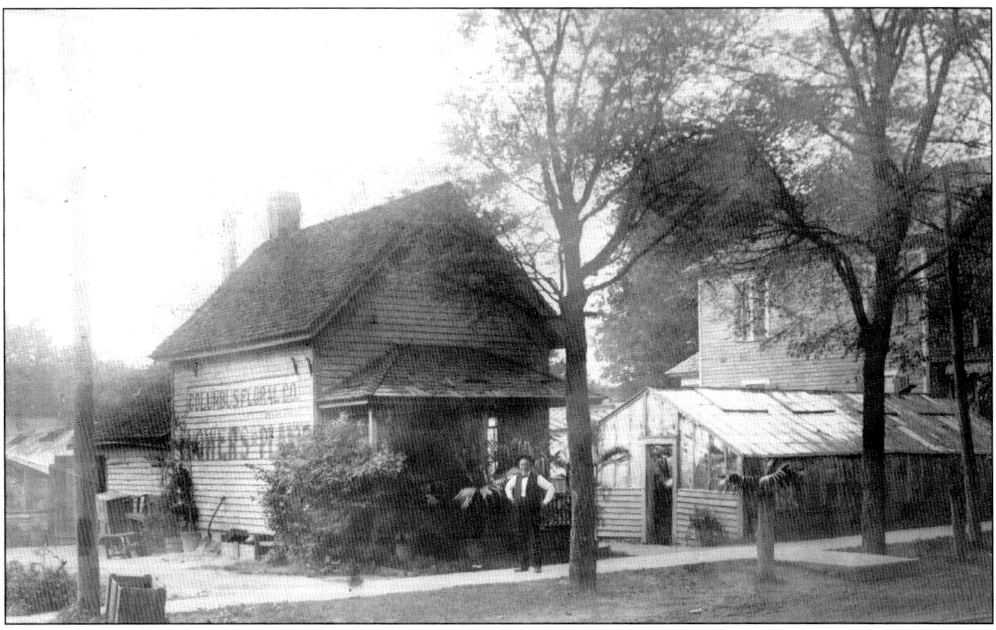

The Columbus Floral Company was located at 410 Seventh Street South. In 1912, it was owned and operated by architect and restaurateur George Benjamin "Ben" Cline and his wife, Lucy. Ben Cline was the son of one of Columbus's pioneer families, Jacob and Ferraby Cline. Bessie Laws operated the company in 1918, but by 1925, the business no longer existed.

The Straight Eight Café, seen here in 1954, was opened by W.H. Hunter around 1941. Located at 511 Main Street, it was managed by A.C. Williams. The cafeteria was later owned by Wendell T. and Virginia A. Haynes and advertised steaks, chicken, and chops in an air-conditioned restaurant. By 1971, the café was located on Highway 82 West and renamed the Straight Eight Junior Restaurant by M.F. Dick.

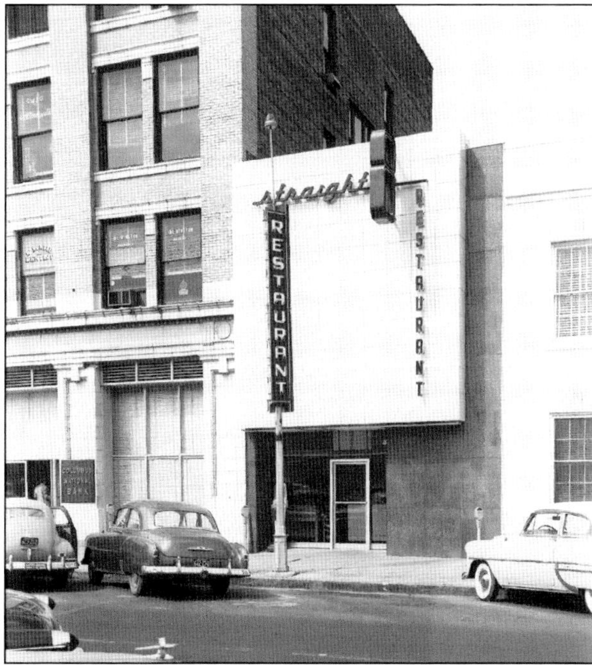

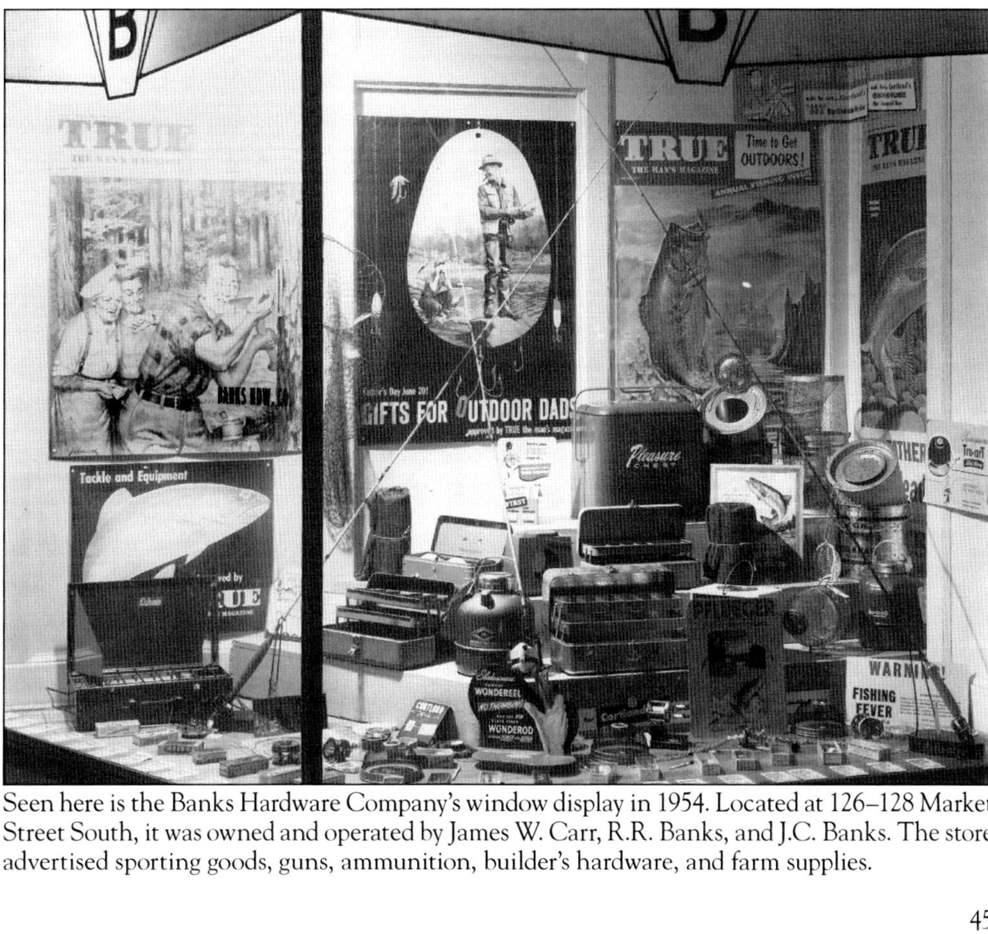

Seen here is the Banks Hardware Company's window display in 1954. Located at 126–128 Market Street South, it was owned and operated by James W. Carr, R.R. Banks, and J.C. Banks. The store advertised sporting goods, guns, ammunition, builder's hardware, and farm supplies.

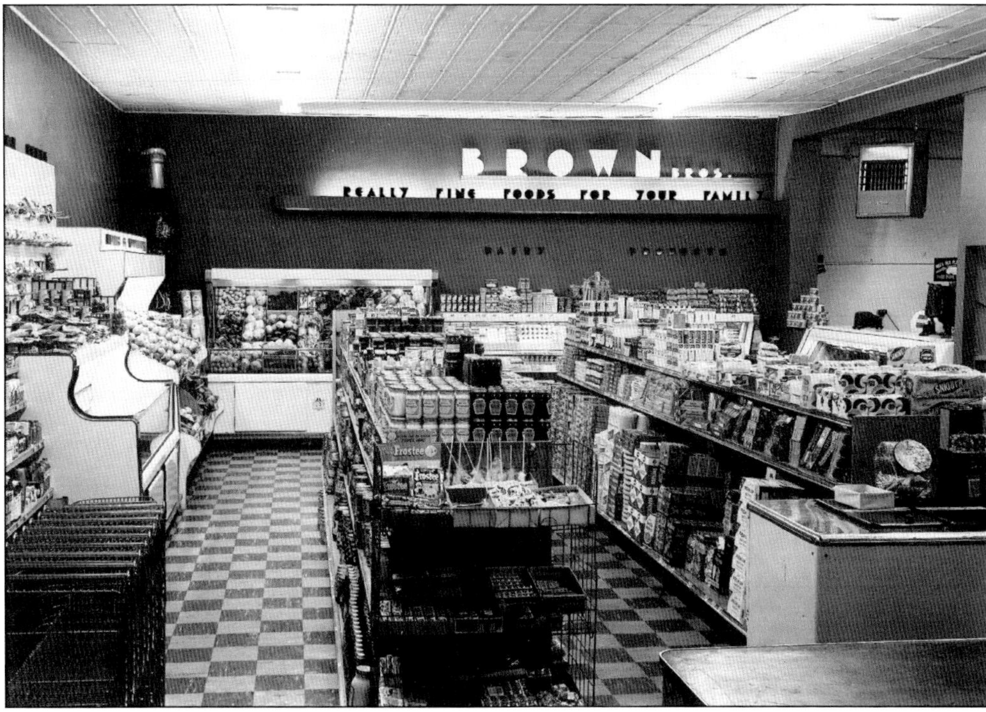

The Brown Brothers Grocery Store, located at 2008 Seventh Avenue North, was owned and operated by O. Franklin and Walter L. Brown. This image shows the interior of the grocery store in 1953.

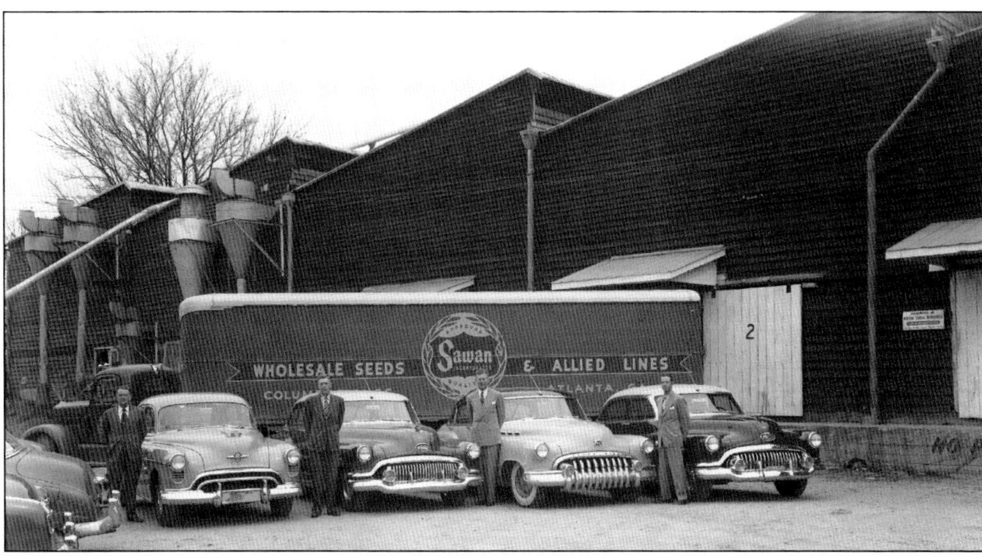

Around 1950, Sawan Inc. of Columbus was a wholesale grain, seed, and feed store located at 925 Second Street South. Wilburn E. Tidwell was president and general manager. Tidwell was also president of Dixie Cottonseeds Inc. and vice-president of Columbus Milling Company.

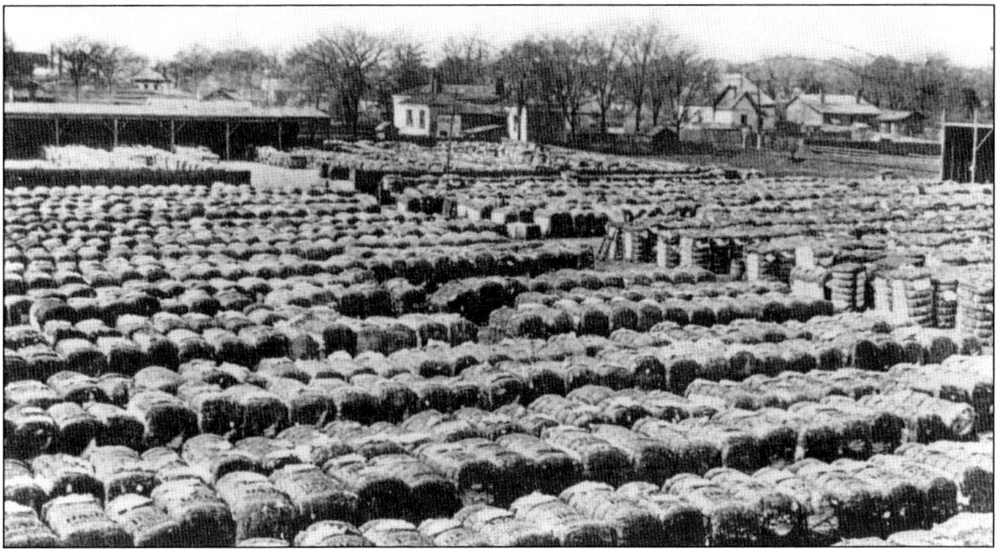

Originally located on the east bank of the Tombigbee River, the Columbus Compress and Warehouse Company (above) moved to Tenth Street South around 1897. The company stored and compressed cotton, seen here around 1920, to standard density at a cost of 60¢ per bale. The company handled 35,000 to 45,000 bales per year; half of which was produced in Lowndes County. The cotton was then loaded, at around 100 bales per car, onto the railroad, as seen below in November 1903.

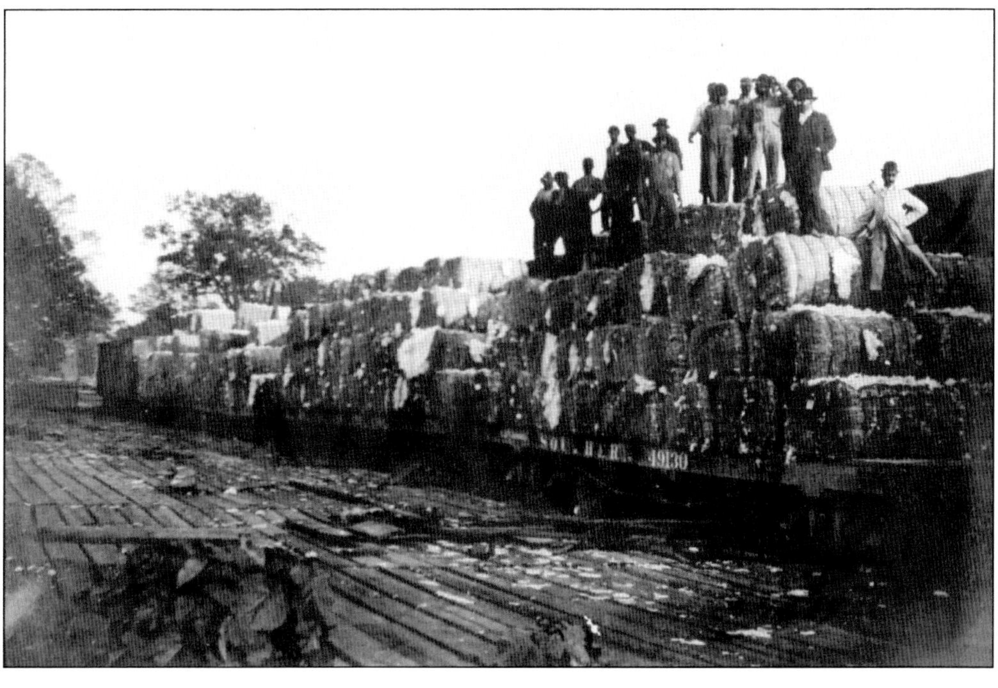

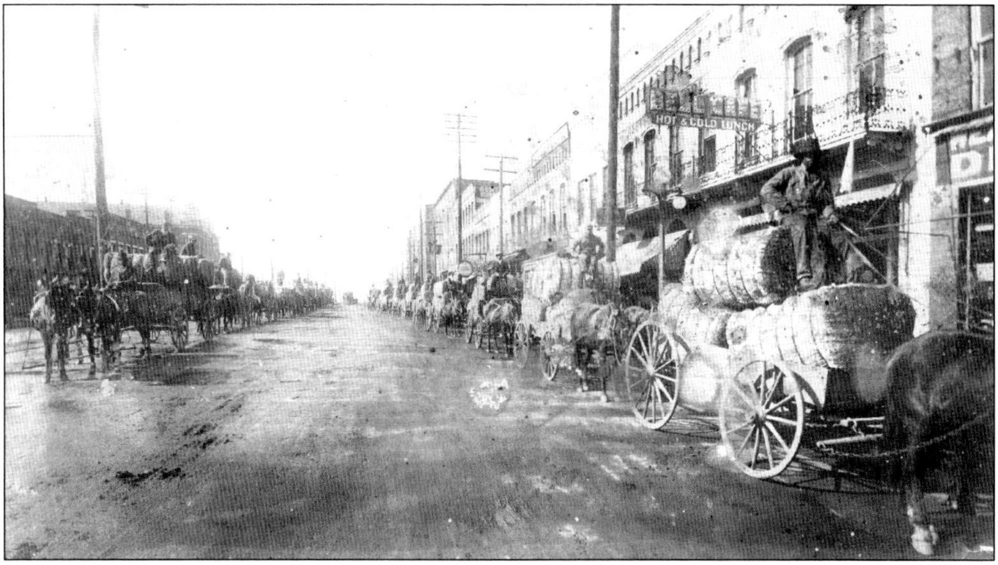

With the photographer facing west, this picture shows bales of cotton lining Main Street on November 28, 1914.

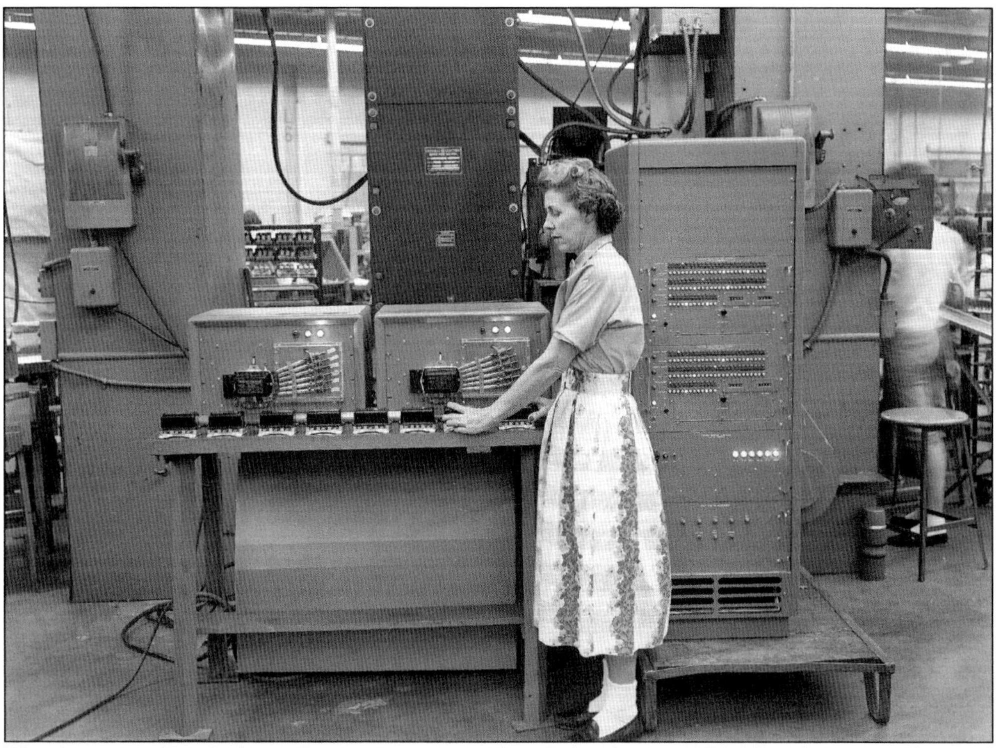
The American Bosch Arma Corporation opened in Columbus in 1954. The plant manufactured motors, including those used in cars for electric door locks, window lifts, and windshield wipers. At one time, the plant covered 43.5 acres and employed over 1,700 people, including this woman seen working at one of the machines in February 1959. In 1978, the business was bought by United Technologies Corporation and operated until 2001, when the company, then owned by Johnson Electric, closed.

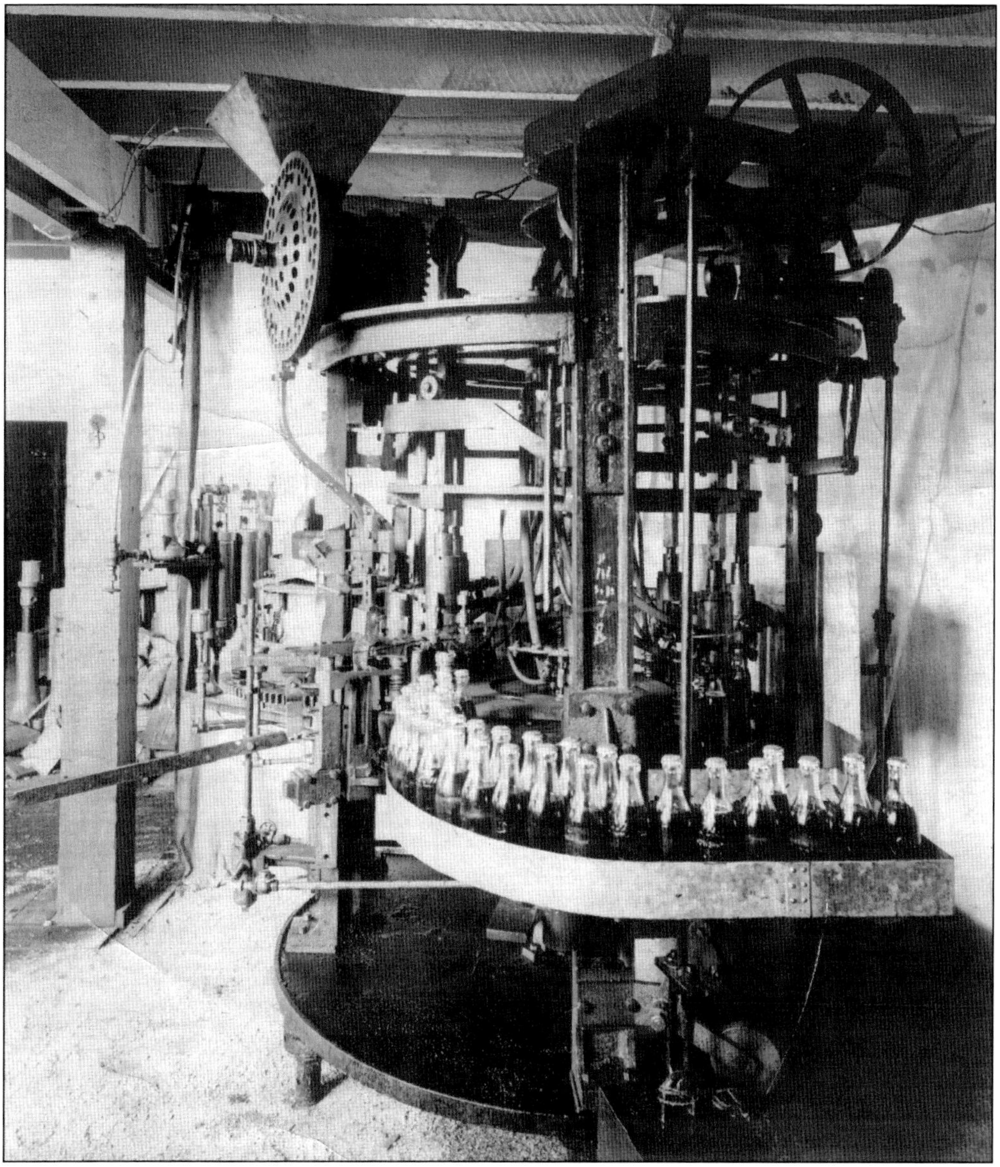

This is a bottling machine from the Columbus Ice and Bottling Works, which was once located on the southeast corner of Second Avenue North and Third Street. Samuel Kaye Sr. operated ice and bottling companies in West Point and Columbus. He worked on this machine for eight years before perfecting it. While the bottles, moving on a carrier belt, were filled with syrup and carbonated water, the machine could automatically register when the water was sufficiently carbonated. It filled 28 bottles per minute, as opposed to previous machines that bottled only 10 per minute.

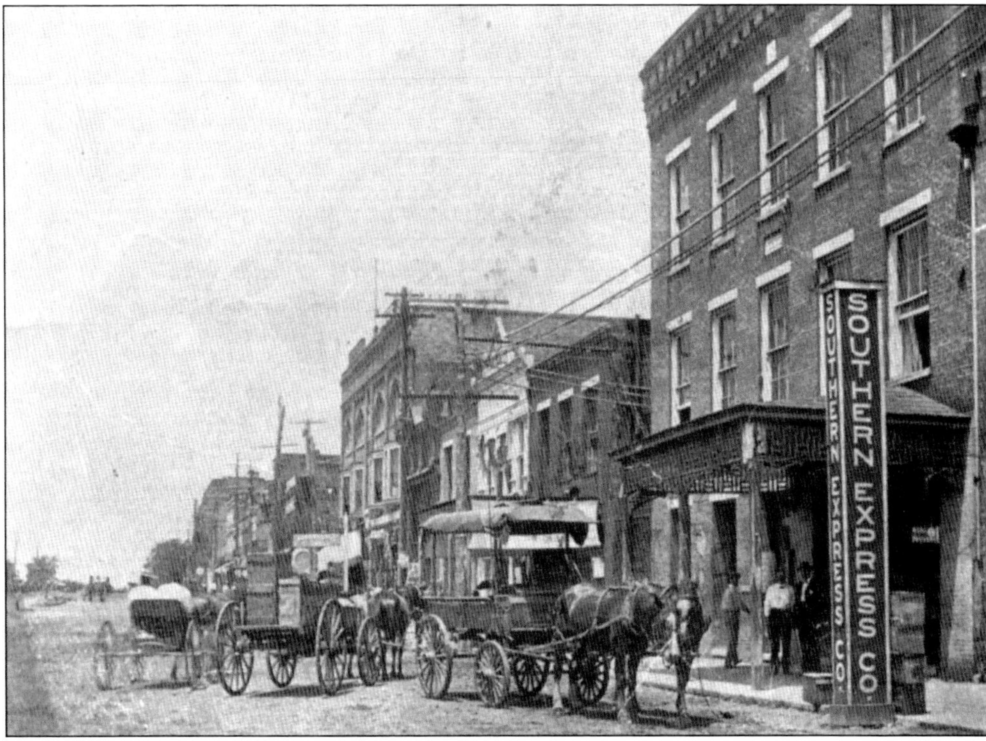

This 1905 photograph of Main Street looking west shows the Independent Order of Odd Fellows Building (right) prior to its renovation the following year. The three-story brick building also housed the Southern Express Company, a subsidiary of the Adams Express Company. Prior to the 1920s, the Southern Express Company operated as a freight and transport company. The building now houses retail space.

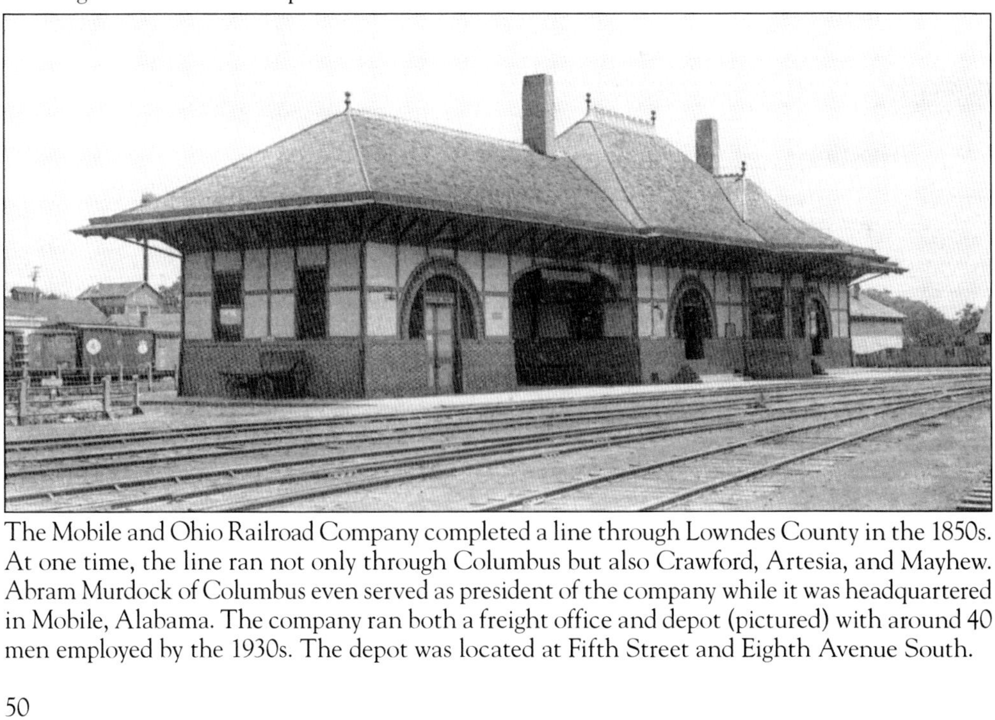

The Mobile and Ohio Railroad Company completed a line through Lowndes County in the 1850s. At one time, the line ran not only through Columbus but also Crawford, Artesia, and Mayhew. Abram Murdock of Columbus even served as president of the company while it was headquartered in Mobile, Alabama. The company ran both a freight office and depot (pictured) with around 40 men employed by the 1930s. The depot was located at Fifth Street and Eighth Avenue South.

Three

CELEBRATIONS

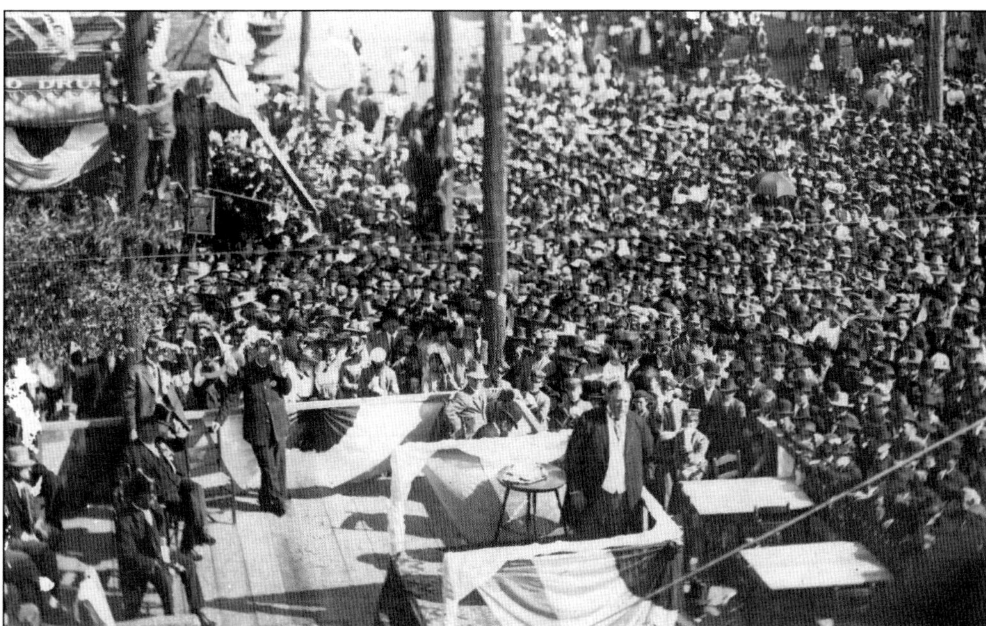

On November 2, 1909, Pres. William Howard Taft spoke to the citizens of Columbus from a stand on the corner of Main and Market Streets (now Fifth Street). As part of a national tour, the visit was arranged by Secretary of War Jacob McGavock Dickinson (1909–1911), a Columbus native. President Taft participated in a parade, ate at a barbeque, visited the home of Blewett Lee (now the Stephen D. Lee Home and Museum), and spoke at the Industrial Institute and College (now Mississippi University for Women.)

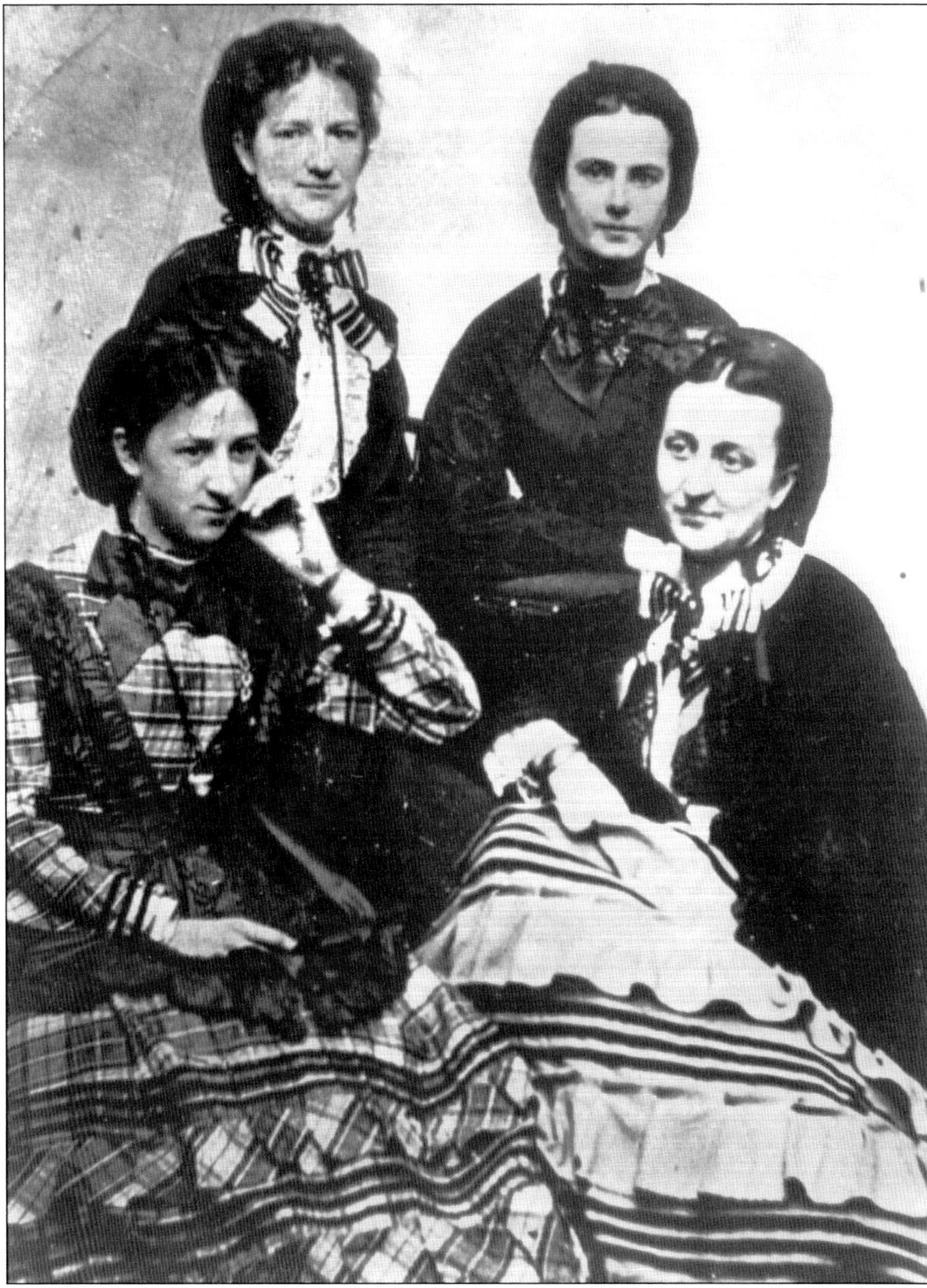

Pictured are, from left to right, (sitting) Jane T. Fontaine and Matilda "Matt" Elizabeth Morton; (standing) Kate M. Hill and Augusta M. Sykes Cox. On April 25, 1866, these four women placed flowers on the graves of both Confederate and Union soldiers in Friendship Cemetery. Originally called Decoration Day, modern-day Memorial Day traces its roots back to this event. It was out of this observance that New York lawyer Francis Miles Finch drew the inspiration for his famous poem, "The Blue and the Gray."

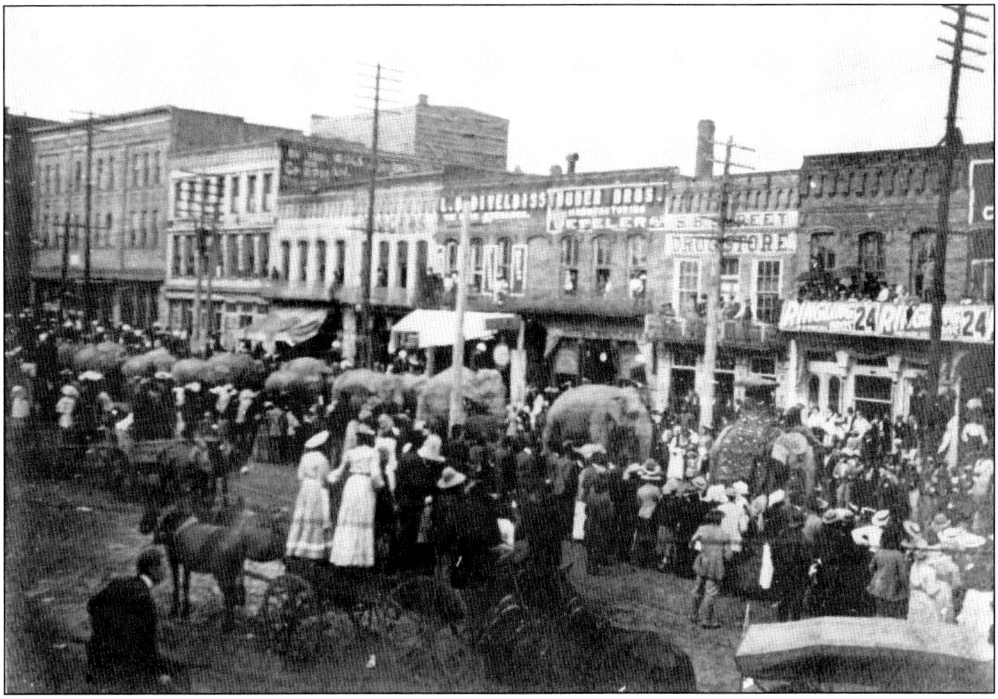

The world-renowned Ringling Bros. Circus came to Columbus around 1908. The circus held a three-mile-long street parade on Main Street that included 40 elephants, 20 camel, mounted soldiers, cavalry bands, clowns, gymnasts, tableaux floats, and many exotic animals. Over 1,280 circus men, women, and children were in the show.

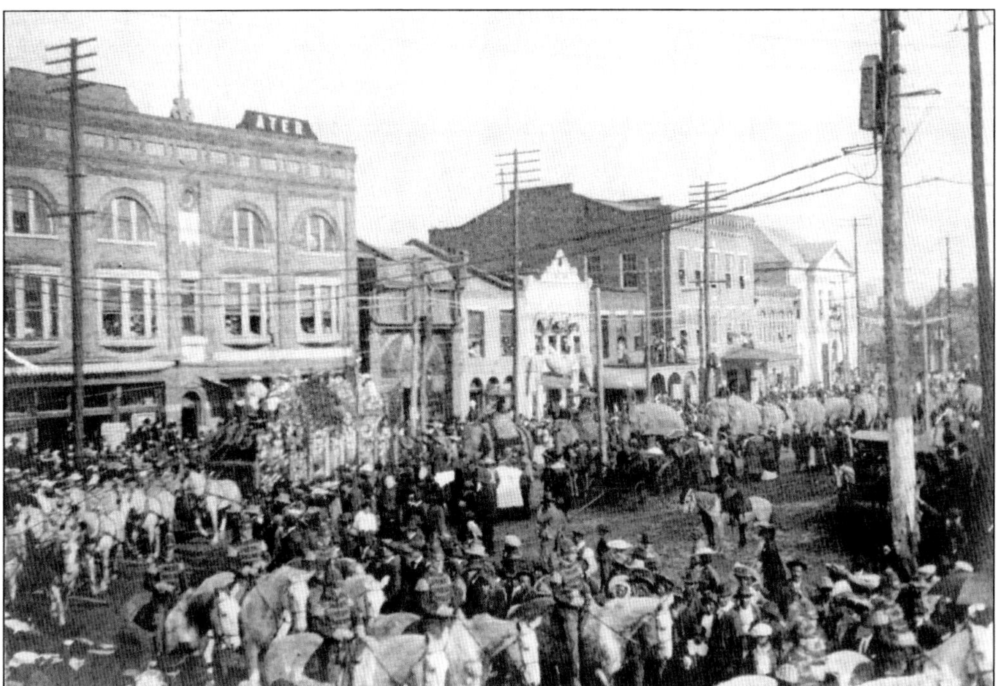

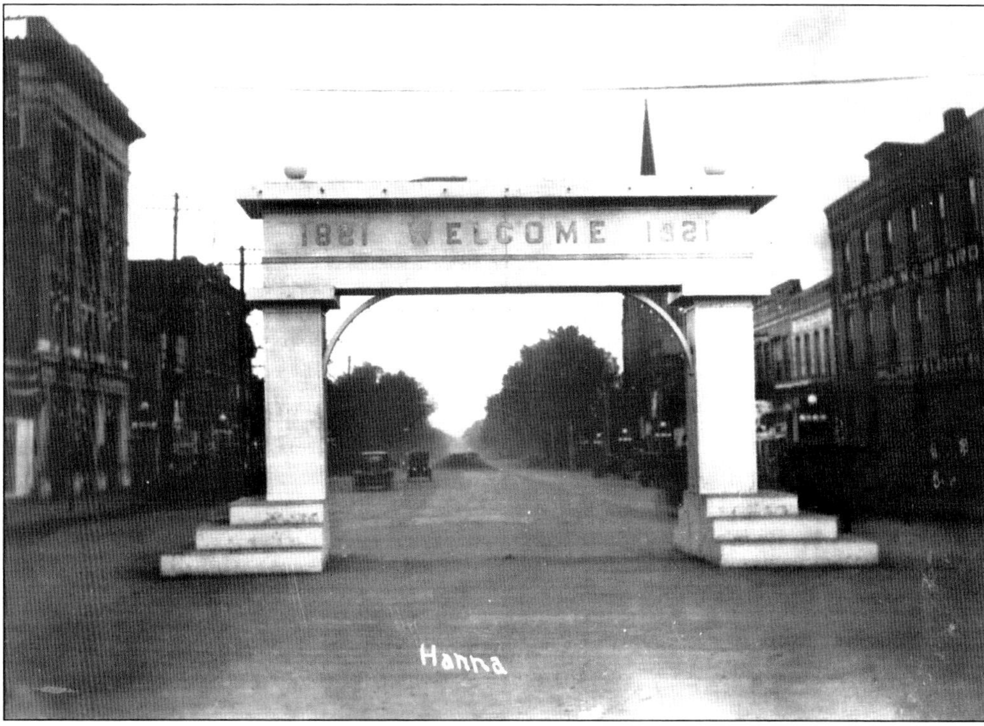

Columbus celebrated its 100th birthday during a centennial celebration held October 17–22, 1921. The city held parades, speeches, dances, concerts, and much more in honor of the occasion. The parade on Main Street, seen below, shows a float made by the Shuk-ho-ta Tom-a-ha chapter of the Daughters of the American Revolution. The float is passing in front of the Presbyterian Church. The house to the right of the church no longer stands.

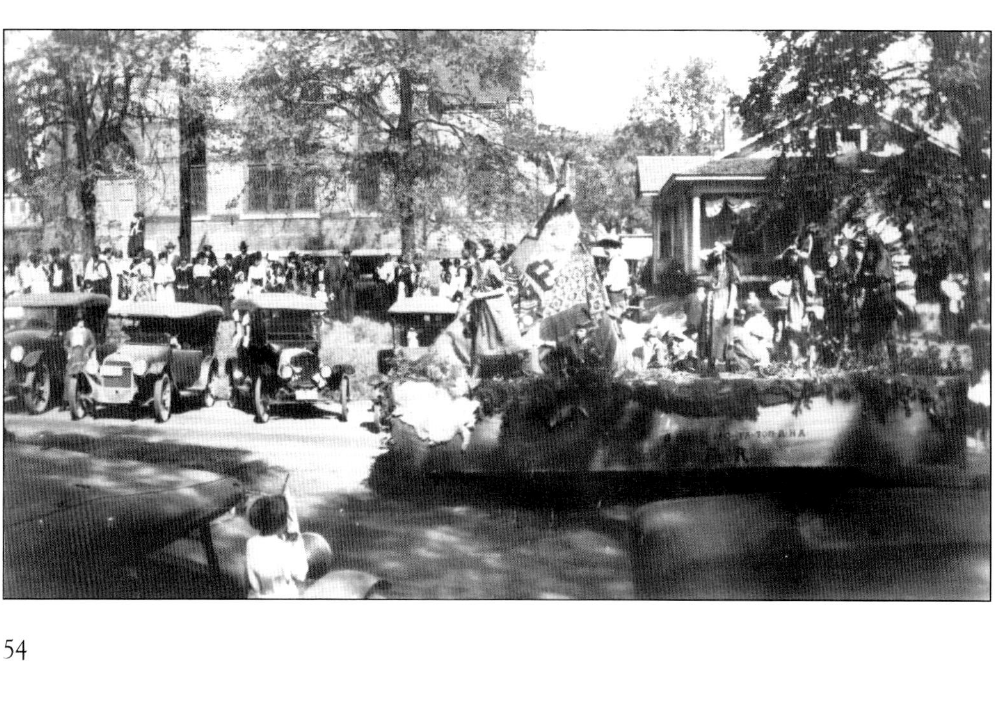

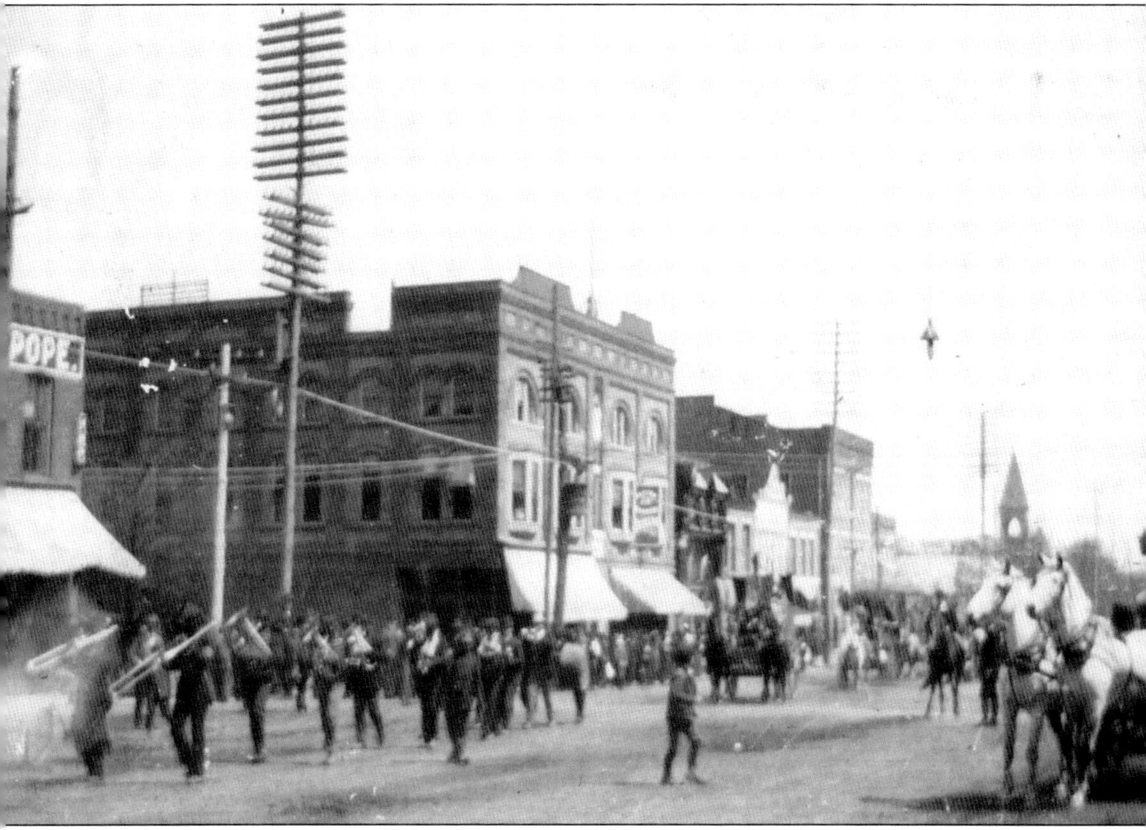

Here is an African American "Eight-O-May" parade at the intersection of Main and Market Streets facing east around 1900. The exact origins of and reasons behind the Eight-O-May celebration are a source of debate. Possibilities include the surrender of Gen. Nathan B. Forrest on or around May 8, 1865, or perhaps the surrender of Confederate lieutenant general Richard Taylor, commander of some 10,000–12,000 troops, on May 4, 1865. It was on May 8 that Taylor delivered his epilogue on the event. Either way, May 8, also known as "Emancipation Day," became a holiday celebrated with parades, barbecues, and picnics in honor of the freeing of African American slaves. The Union Band, a band formed of former slave musicians, is shown marching in one of the parades.

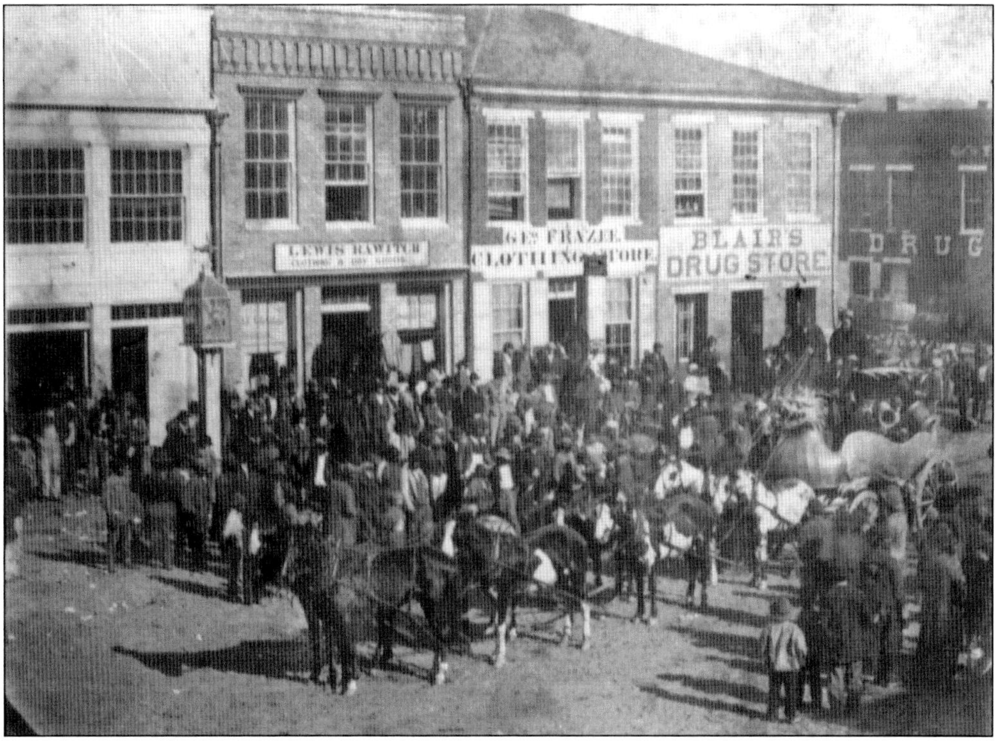

Columbus has held many parades, including this one at the southern intersection of Main and Market Streets (now Fifth Street) in the 1860s. On the right is a float shaped like a dragon pulled by eight horses. Notice Blair's Drugstore (fourth building from the left). Dating to as early as 1852, it was owned and operated by brothers James and David P. Blair. The store not only sold medicine but also paints, oils, garden seeds, and dentist's supplies as well.

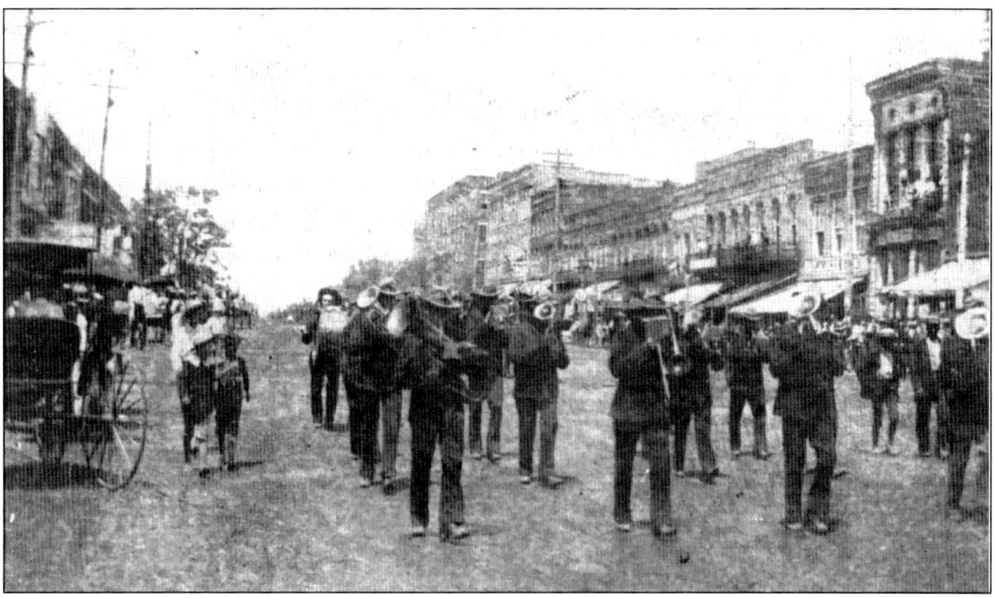

This image shows an unknown parade on Main Street marching east around 1900. Notice how many of the buildings contained balconies and awnings.

Four

GOVERNMENT

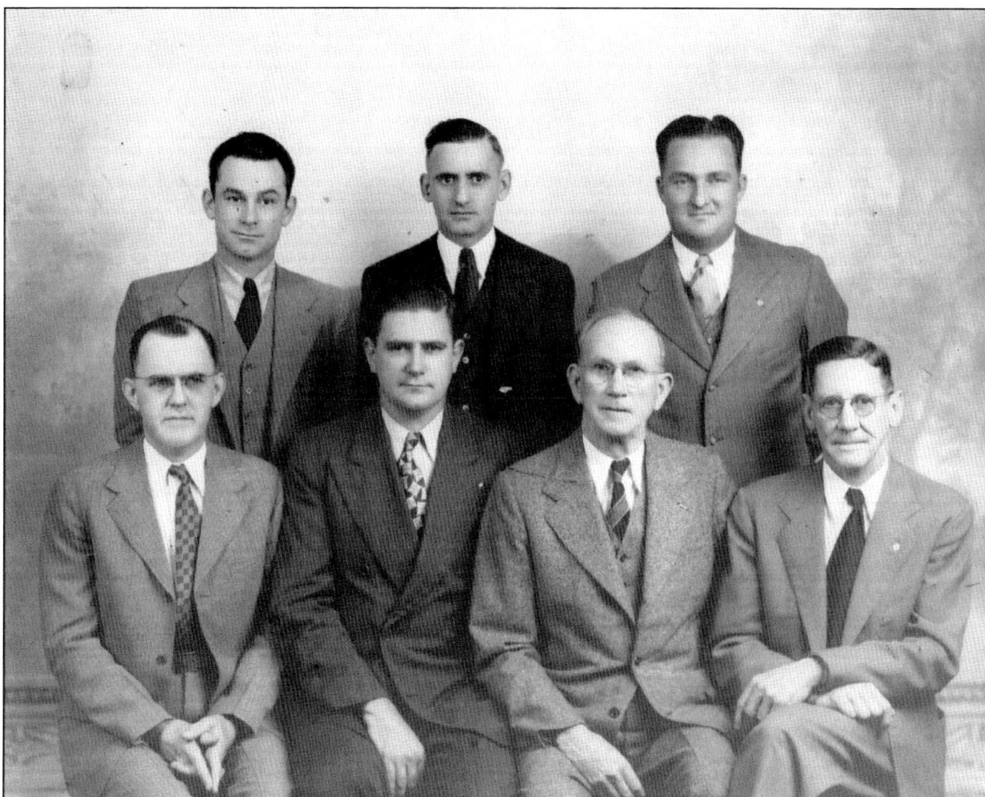

Seen here are Columbus city officials from around 1948. Pictured are, from left to right, (first row) Mayo Ellis, Ward 5; Robert D. Harmon, Ward 1; P.C. "Doc" Hairston, Ward 2; and William Gray Hairston, mayor; (second row) Herbert J. Perry, Ward 4; Sidney F. Nash, Ward 6; and Roy R. Lawrence, Ward 3.

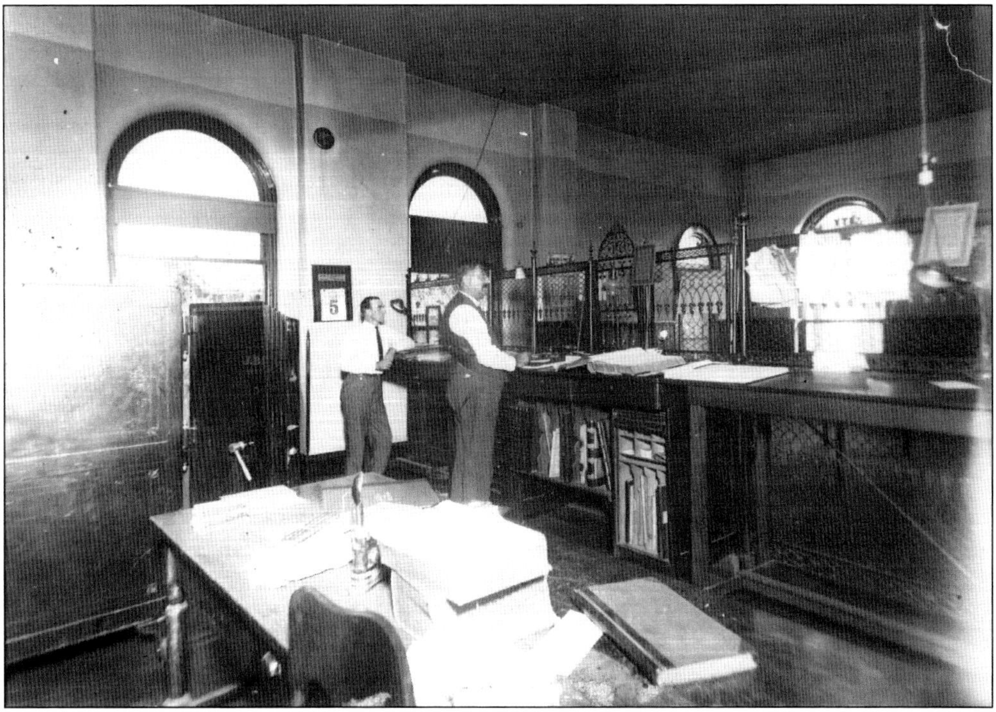

The office of the city marshal and tax collector was housed in city hall around the 1910s. Shown here are M.C. Vandiver (1866–1925), marshal and tax collector, with Charles A. Wakefield (1878–1916), assistant inspector of water and sewage. Vandiver was mayor-elect when he died after a long illness.

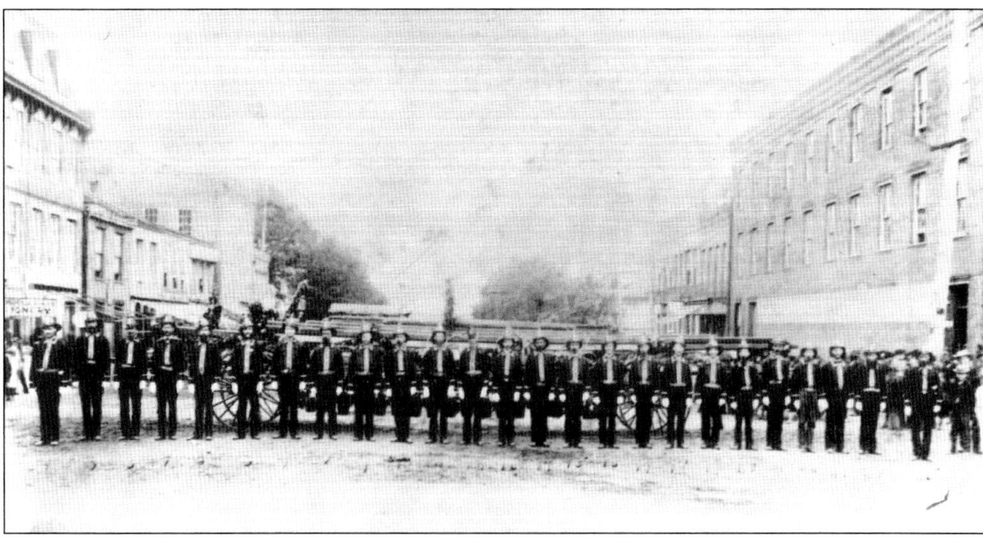

During the late 19th century, there were five volunteer fire departments in Columbus: the Lurline Steam Fire Company No. 4; the Luxapallila Steam Fire Company No. 1, named for the river in east Columbus; the Hercules Hook and Ladder Company No. 1; the Coal Cart; and the Rough and Ready Hand Fire Company No. 2, an African American company. Seen here standing on Main Street just east of Market Street are members of the Hook and Ladder Company posed in their uniforms (black hats, blue shirts, and black pants) on May 19, 1885.

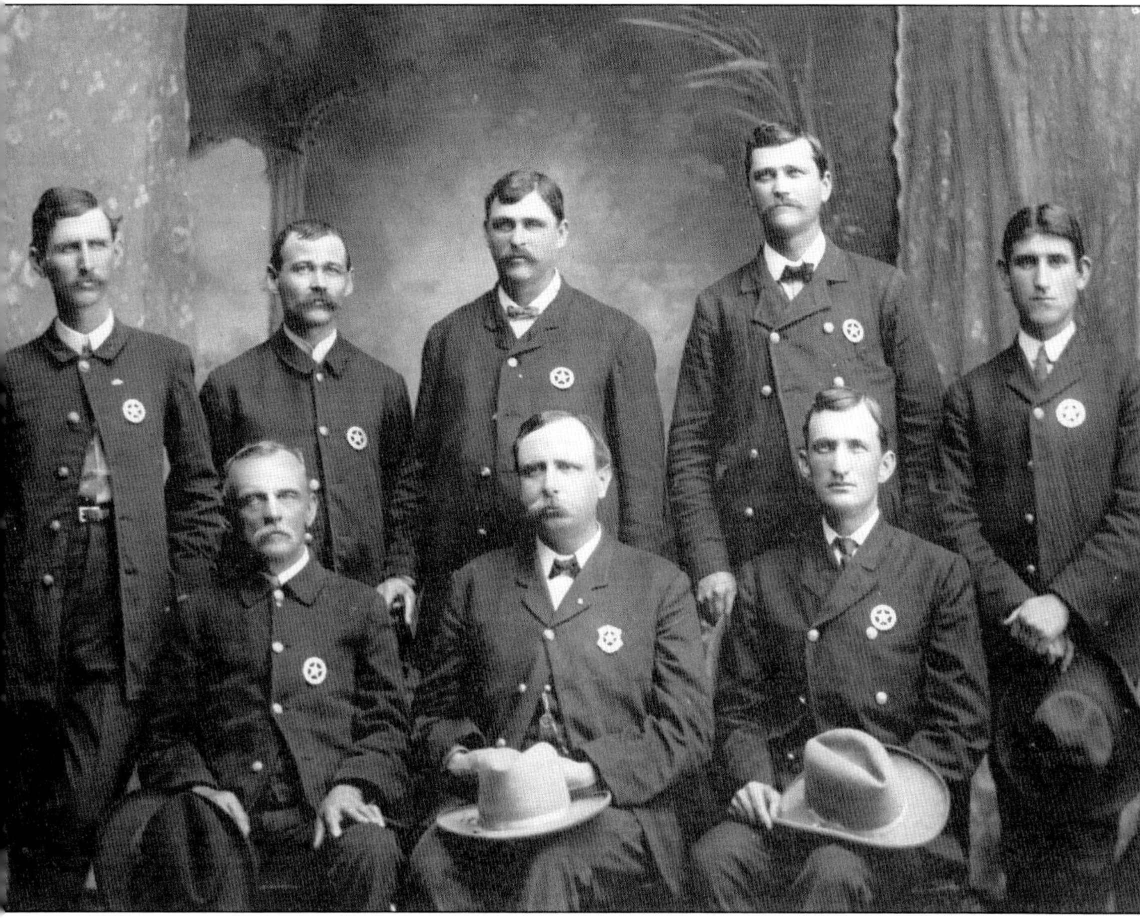

The Columbus Police Department had this photograph taken around 1909. The members are, from left to right, (first row) Captain G.N. Smith, Chief T. Grey Munger, and J. Will Shackelford; (second row) W.D. Reeves, John Morton, Thad Brazeale, W.M. Brazeale, and Henry S. Noland.

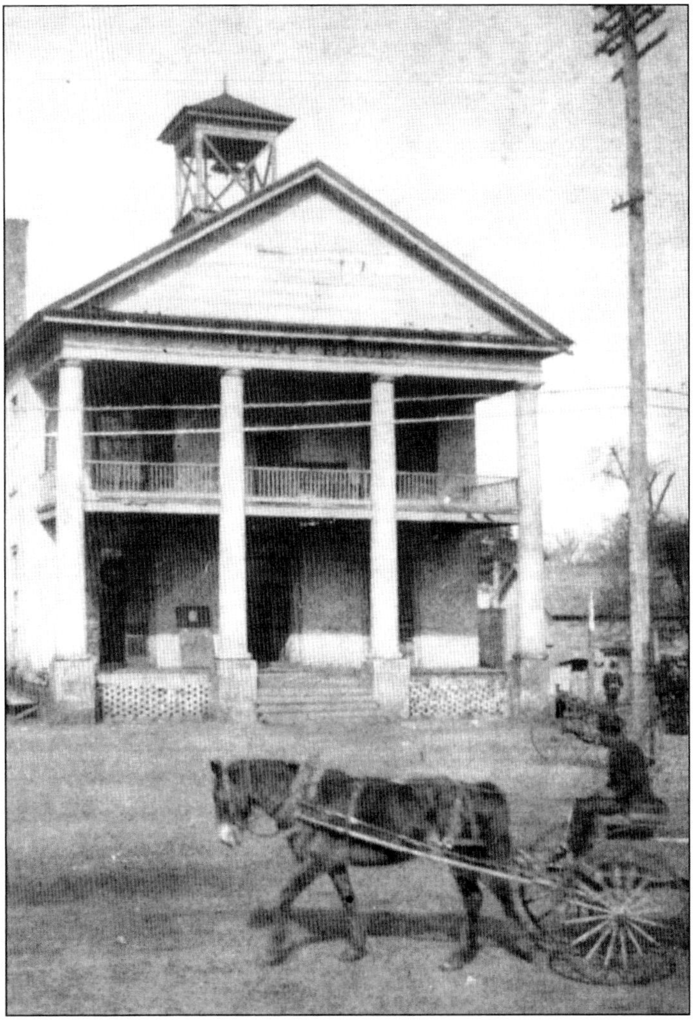

These two images show Columbus City Hall. The first city hall, located on the current site of First United Methodist Church, burned in 1854. The second city hall (left) was built around 1871 on the corner of Main Street and Sixth Street South. It was built as a bank, but then used as a school, hotel, private residence, and then the home for city government. The existing city hall (below) was completed in 1903. Notice the smaller building extending from the left of city hall. This building was used as a jail. Also, the Frank P. Phillips home can be seen across Sixth Street to the right. The home was demolished in 1977 to make way for an expansion of the YMCA. (Courtesy of the Southern Historical Collection, Wilson Library, the University of North Carolina at Chapel Hill.)

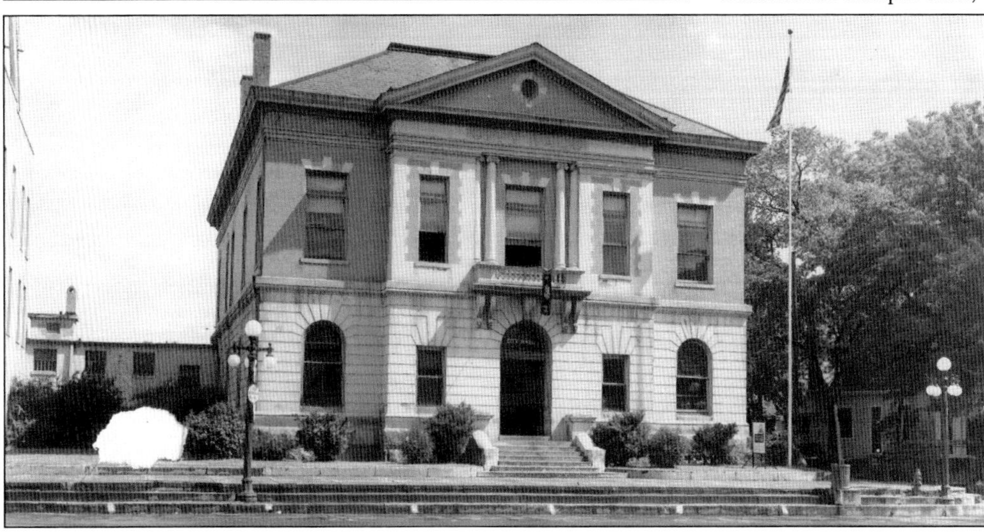

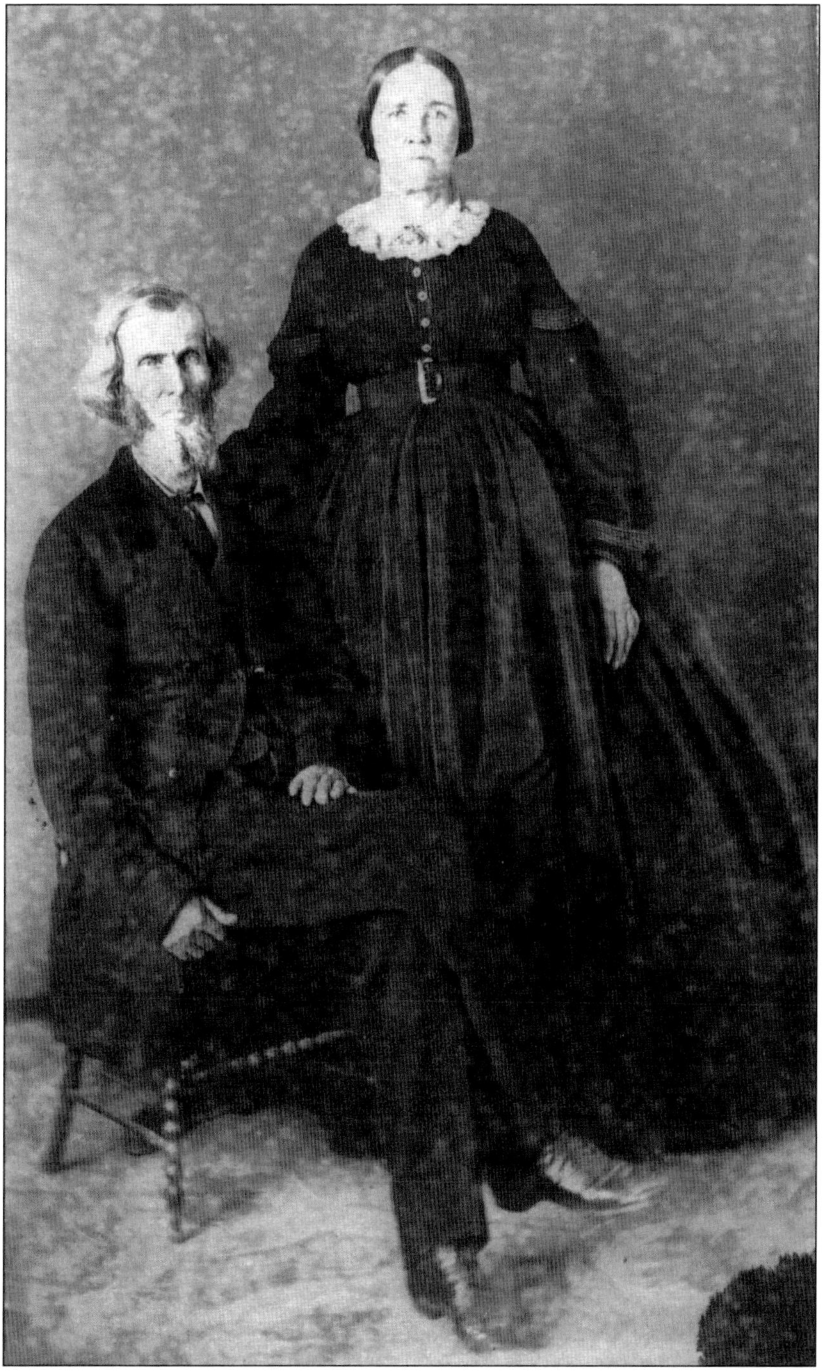

Mayor Levi Donnell and his wife, Elizabeth, the sister of Columbus photographer Hiram T. Sherrill, were commemorated on tintype around the 1860s. Donnell served as mayor for over 20 years from 1845 to 1869. He was also one of the founding members of the Cumberland Presbyterian Church in Columbus. Donnell's son William P. Donnell was editor of the *Columbus Whig* newspaper in 1847, and his grandson Emmett S. Donnell also served as mayor in 1896 and then again from 1909 to 1913.

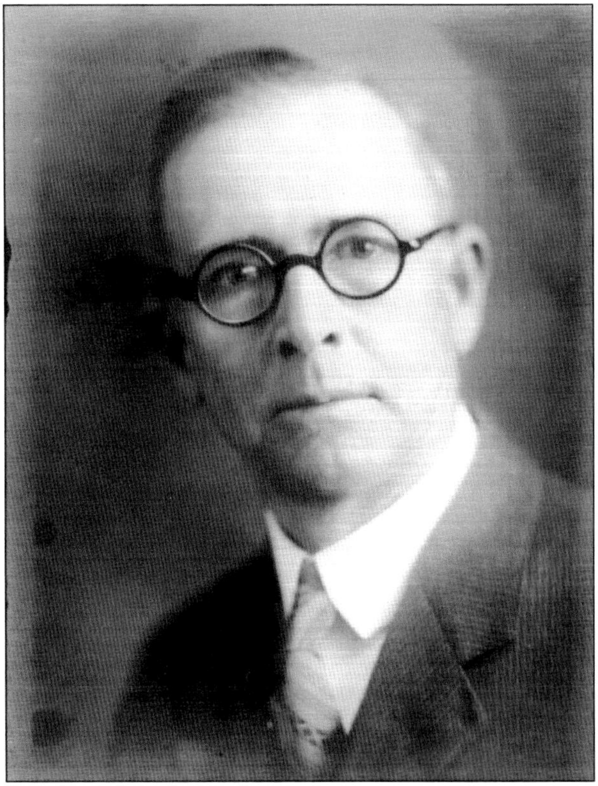

Mayor Thomas William Harris (1869–1950) served as mayor of Columbus from 1929 to 1933 and then was reelected from 1935 to 1945. Prior to becoming secretary-treasurer of the Columbus Compress, he worked in the hardware business. During his administration, the Tennessee Valley Authority came to Columbus, bringing cheaper power to the region.

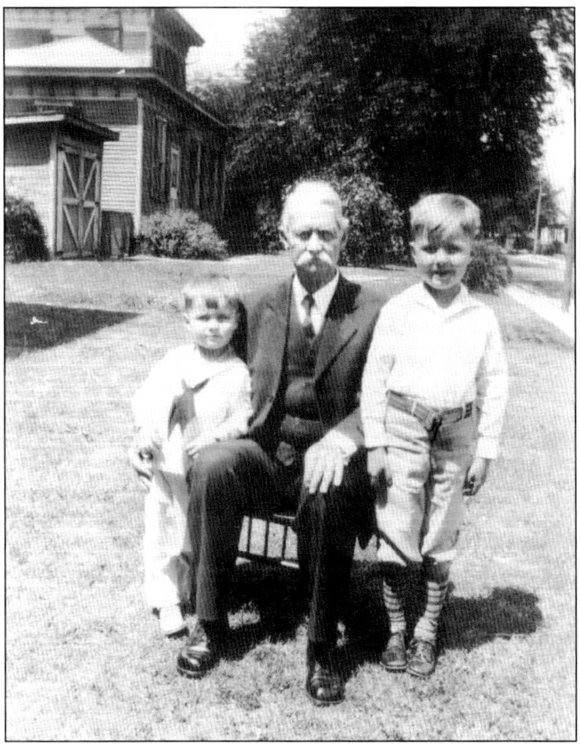

Col. Cicero L. Lincoln, seen here with his grandchildren Atwell and Lee Lincoln III, was a local attorney and politician. He served as deputy sheriff from 1869 to 1885, sheriff from 1885 to 1896, chancery clerk from 1896 to 1900, and mayor of Columbus from 1901 to 1902. Lincoln was a veteran of both the Civil War and the Spanish-American War. He married Tessie Alexander, and they had eight children. He died on January 28, 1939, at the age of 94.

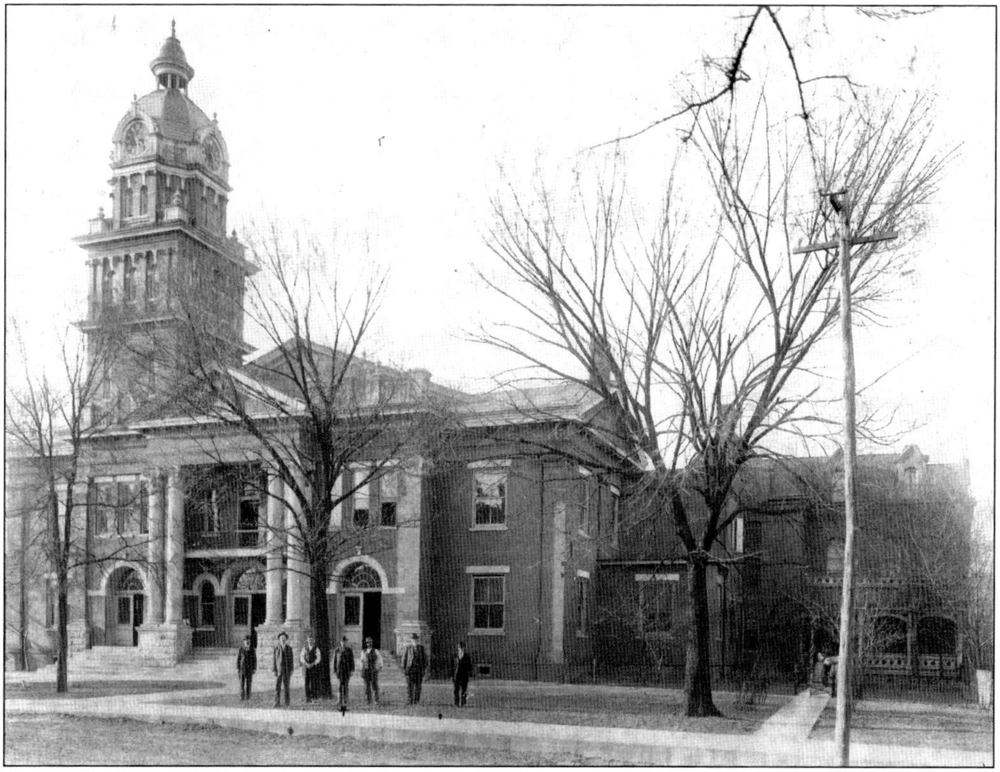

The first Lowndes County Courthouse was built in 1832 and then replaced by the current structure in 1849. The image above shows the building, built by local architect James S. Lull, after a remodeling of the clock tower in 1901. The building with the porch to the right of the courthouse was the county jail, constructed around 1890. By 1975, the jail was torn down, and an east wing was added with renovations to the main building completed the following year. The image below shows the courtroom on the second floor prior to the 1976 renovations. The state government operated out of the Lowndes County Courthouse during the Civil War in 1864.

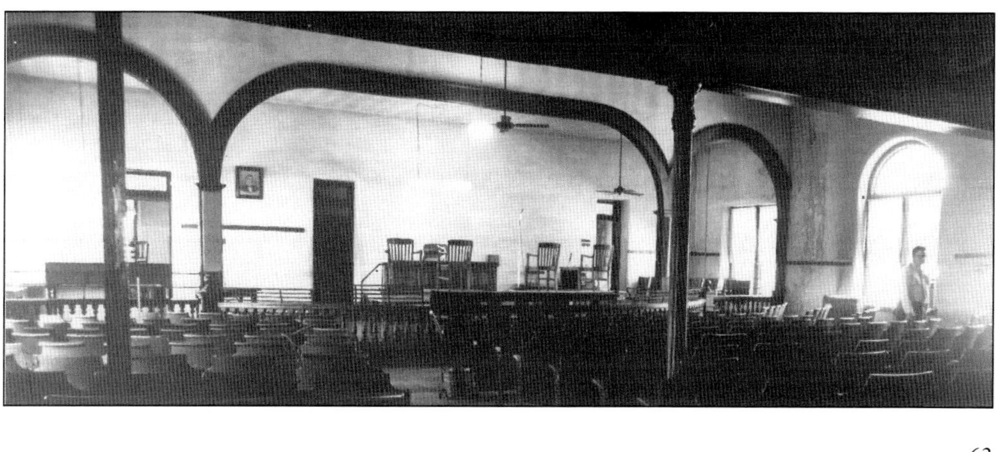

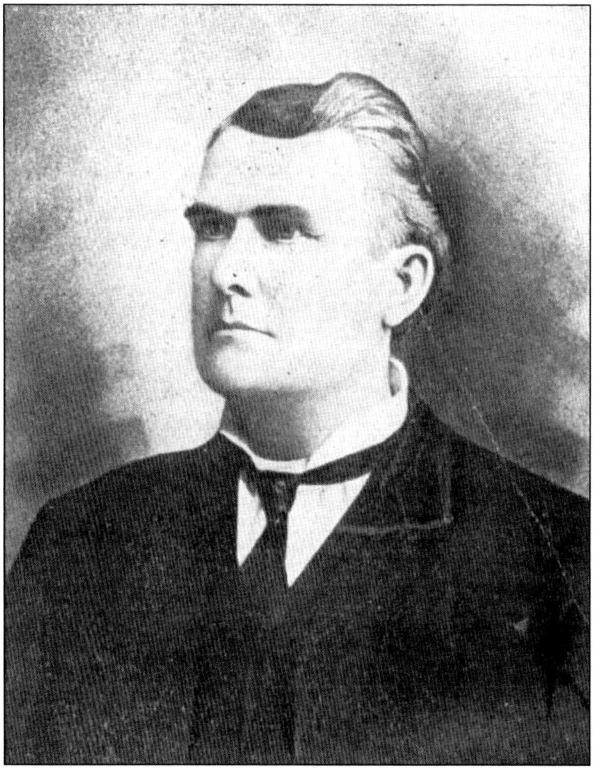

Mayor James Thomas Gunter served as Columbus mayor from 1902 to 1907. Born in 1852, he later became involved in the warehousing business and, in 1898, built the Commercial Hotel. Under Gunter's mayorship, Columbus constructed an additional public school building, extended the sewage and water system, and built parks. Gunter was also instrumental in securing the street railways. He died in 1907 before being able to run for a third term.

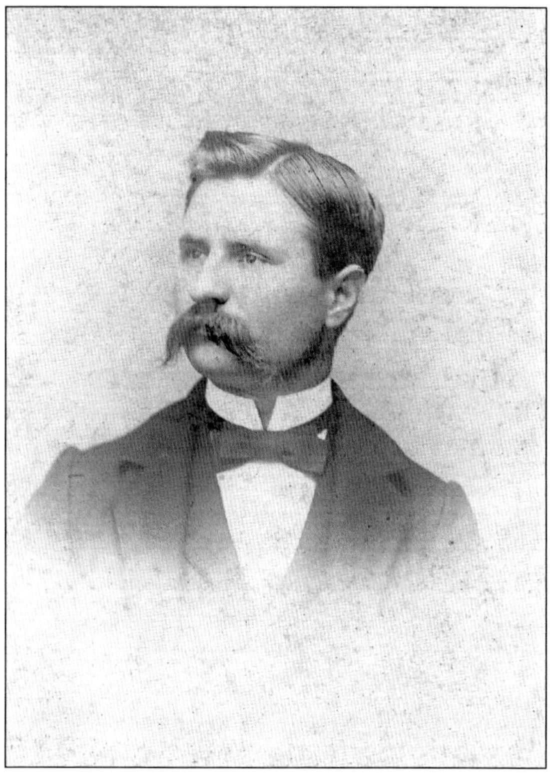

John B. Williams served as Lowndes County sheriff from 1916 to 1920 and again from 1928 to 1932. Up to that time, he was the only man to serve two terms in this office. In addition, Williams served as director of the Merchants and Farmers Bank, Lowndes County tax assessor, and a member of the Lowndes County Board of Supervisors for 16 years.

Five

CHURCHES

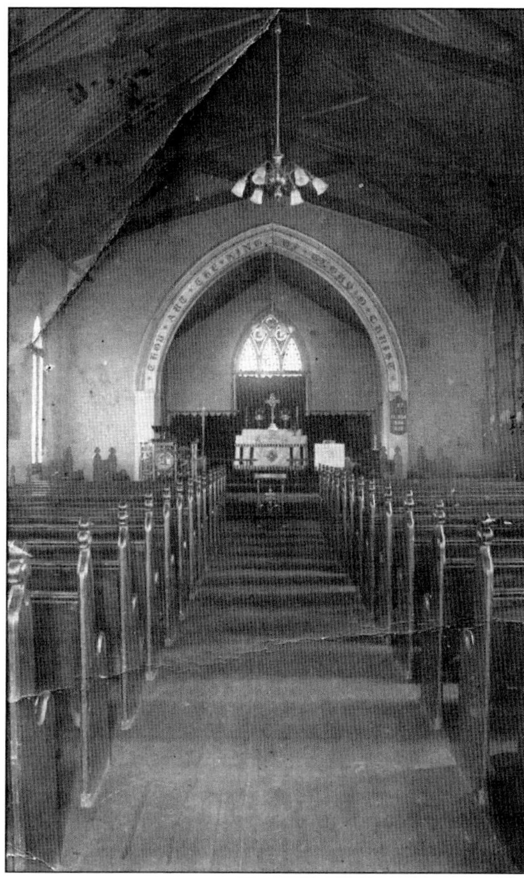

This image shows the interior of St. Paul's Episcopal Church, founded in 1836. The Gothic Revival–style church was completed in 1860, and the organ room added in 1889. Located at 318 College Street, the church is the second oldest Episcopal parish in Mississippi. In this postcard, the words "Thou Art the King of Glory O Christ" appear above the altar.

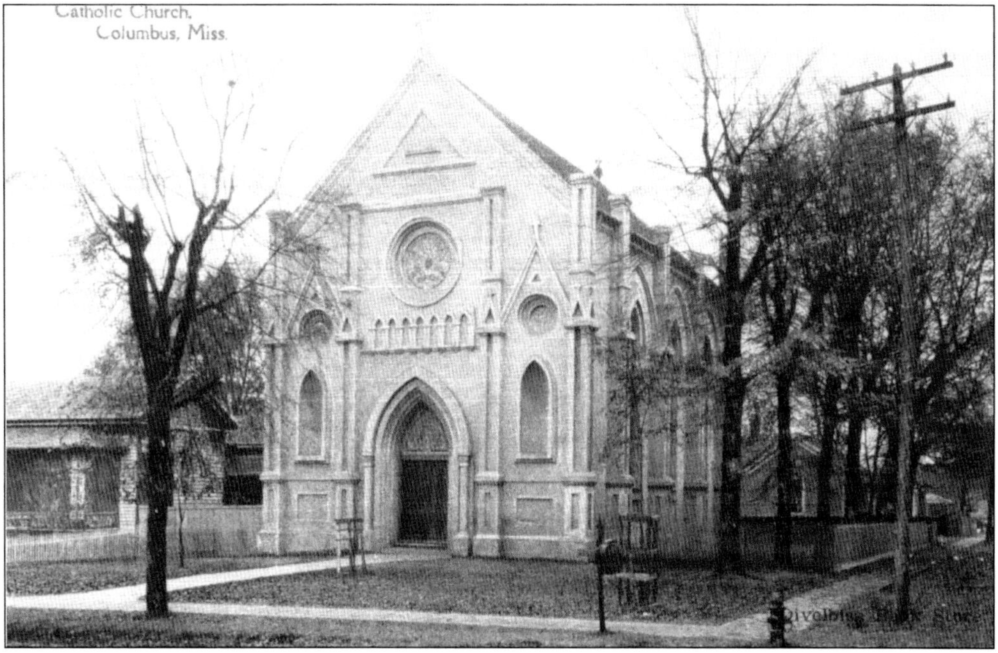

The cornerstone for Annunciation Catholic Church, located on College Street, was laid on May 4, 1863. Completion, however, was delayed due to the Civil War. The congregation, meeting as early as 1857, was part of a parish that once covered 12,000 square miles. The building's interior color scheme of umber, blue, and gold was painted by artist Joseph Kadich in 1963. That same year, the church opened its first parochial school, St. Mary's Elementary School (now Annunciation Catholic School). The new sanctuary was dedicated in 2000.

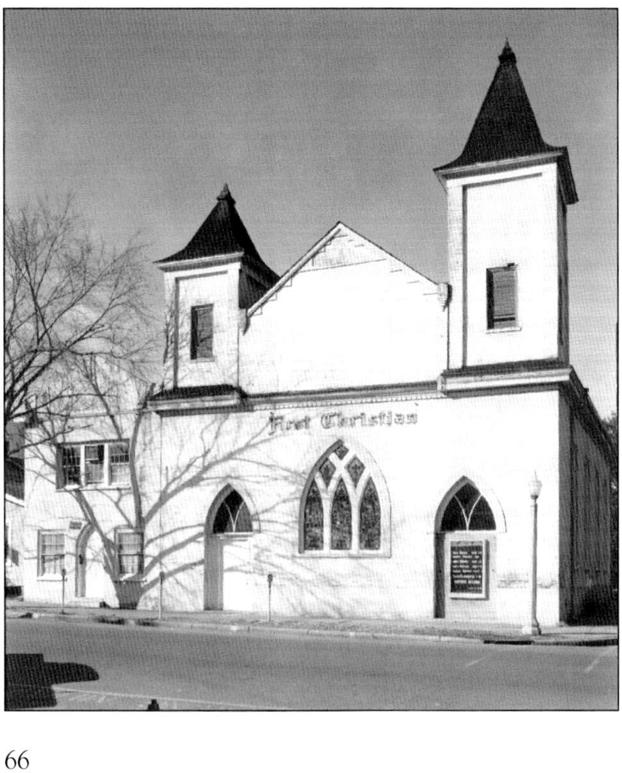

The First Christian Church was organized in 1839, and the church building was erected around 1850. The building, on Second Avenue North, served as the meeting place of the Mississippi House of Representatives during the Civil War. In 1958, the Tennessee-Tombigbee Waterways Agreement was signed there. The site is now a parking lot.

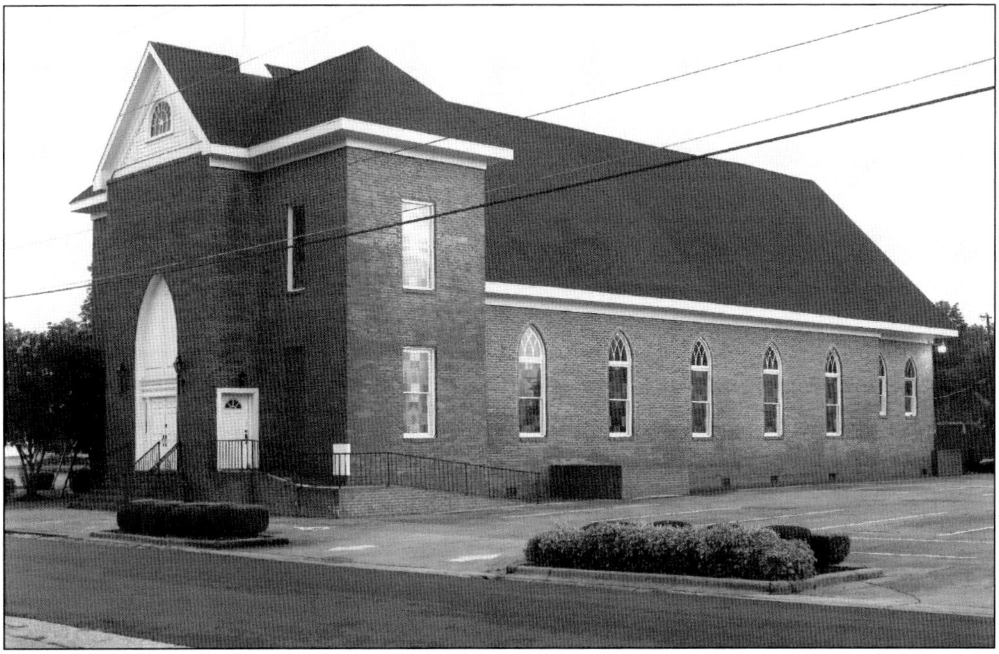

The Missionary Union Baptist Church was organized in 1833, making it the oldest African American church in northeast Mississippi. The church was chartered in 1867, but members continued to meet in the basement of First Baptist Church until 1871, when they moved to their current location at 1207 Fifth Avenue North. Soon afterwards, they built the structure seen here that is still used by its members today.

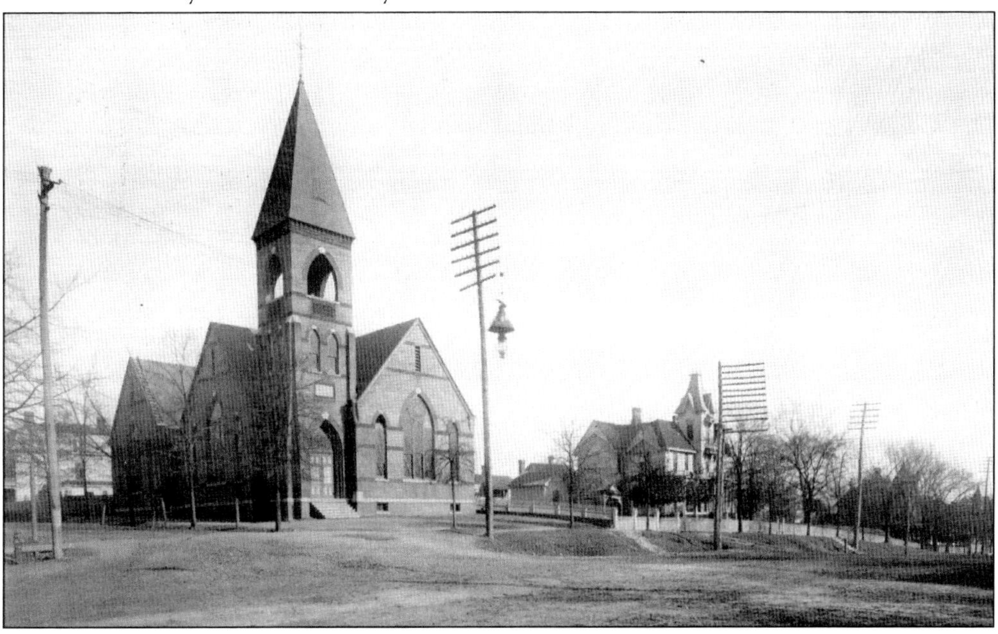

The Presbyterian Church of Columbus was organized in May 1829, and Rev. David Wright served as the first pastor in 1834. The first church was built in 1838 and used for almost 50 years. This brick structure was completed in 1885 on the corner of Main Street and Seventh Street North. The house on the right belonged to Bessie Tucker and no longer stands.

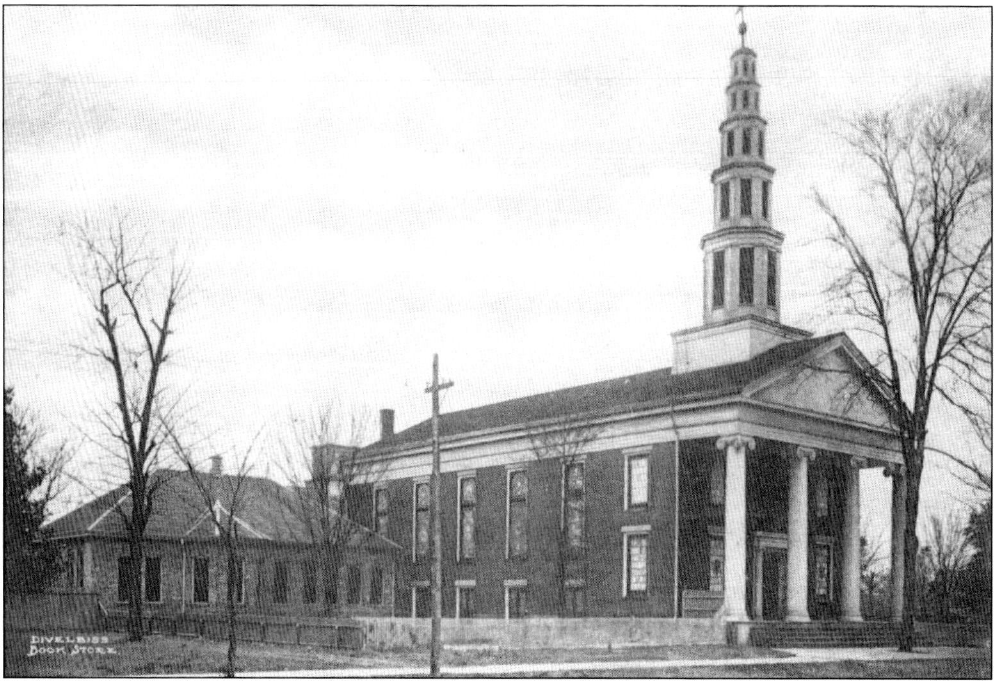

The First Baptist Church was organized in 1832 by Maj. Thomas G. Blewett, Thomas McGee, and the Gibson and Warren families. Under the leadership of Rev. George Tucker, the congregation constructed their first church; it was completed in 1838 by local architect James S. Lull. Following the Battle of Shiloh during the Civil War, the church was used as a hospital. The current structure was built in 1908, and the educational facilities were added in 1930.

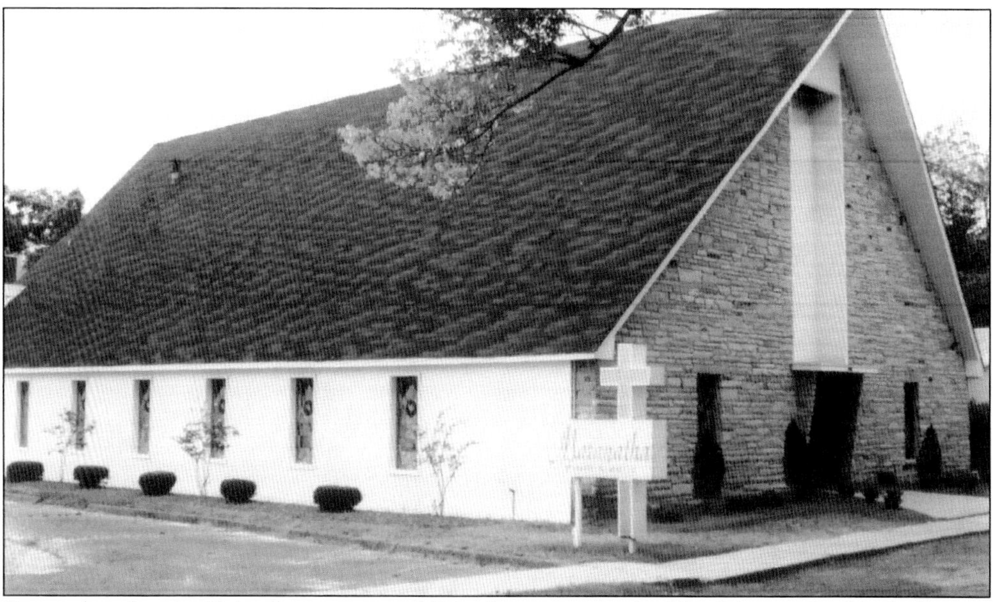

Some churches in Columbus were established more recently. The Maranatha Faith Center, founded by Pastor Steve M. Jamison, held its first service in September 1980. For many years, congregants met in a building on Nineteenth Street before moving to their current location at 716 Waterworks Road in 1988.

Organized in 1831, First United Methodist Church built its first brick church in 1844. The current structure was started in 1860 but not completed until 1867. During the Civil War, the building was used as a hospital for wounded soldiers, and portions of the tin roof were removed to make canteens. An annex was built in 1912, and an education building was added in 1950. The Marguerite Tennille Family Life Center, completed in 1988, includes a multipurpose room, recreational facilities, and educational space.

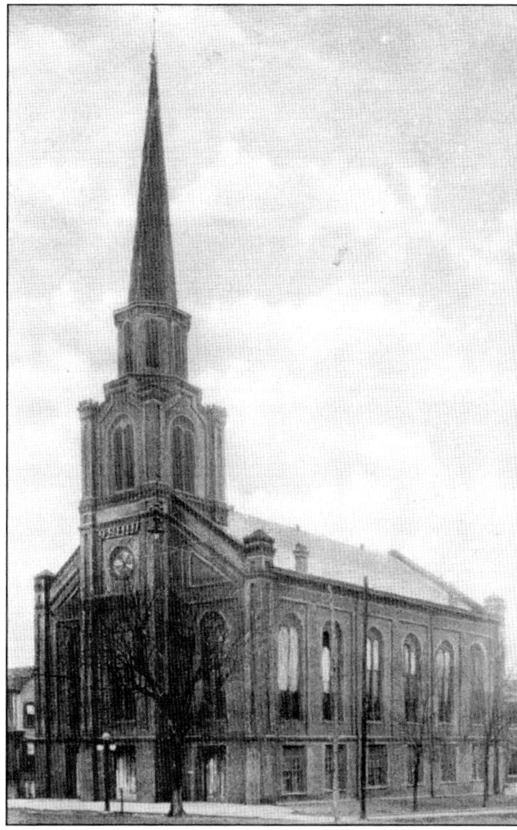

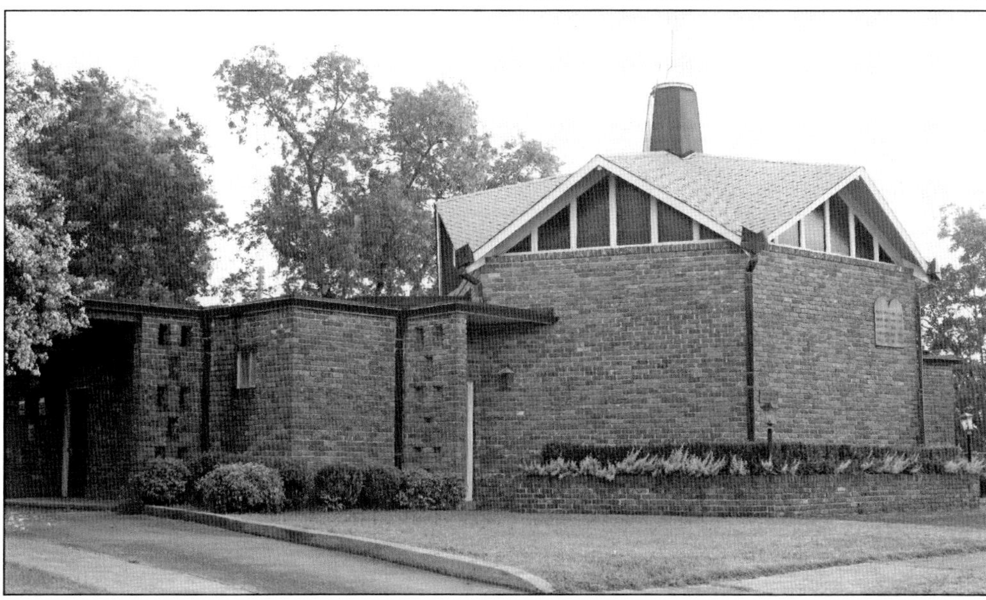

The Temple B'nai Israel, located on Second Avenue North, was organized in July 1879, although services were held in private homes as early as 1848. Members acquired their first temple, formerly used by the Methodist Church, in 1907. The building served the congregation until 1960, when it was torn down and the current structure (seen here) was constructed.

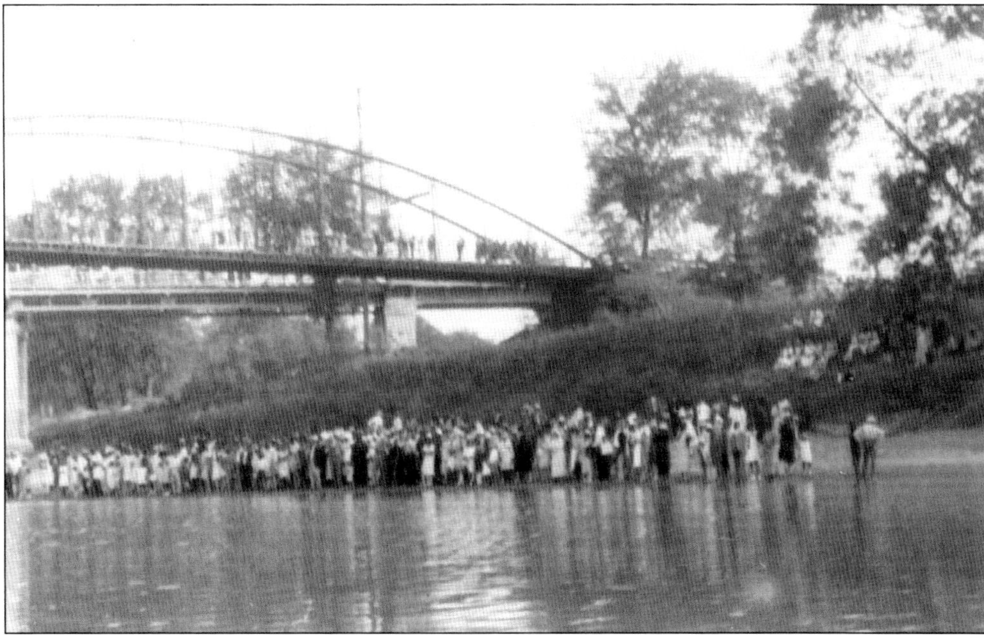

A large group gathered in 1927 to witness a baptism along the banks of the Tombigbee River.

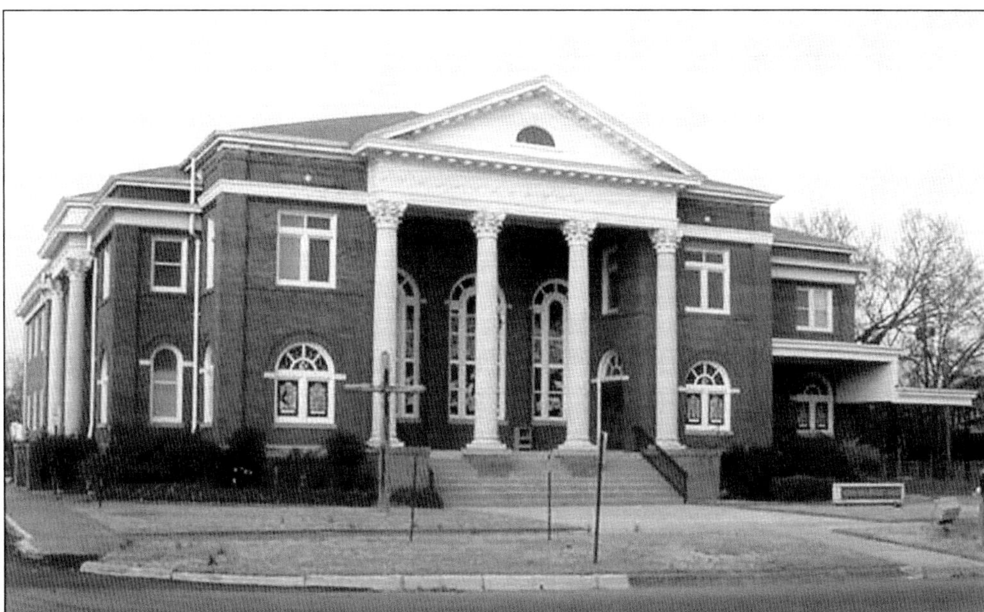

The Central United Methodist Church, first named Second Methodist Church, was organized by Rev. A.P. Leech as a Sunday school group in his home on Third Avenue North in 1899. In 1903, a church building was constructed on Bell Avenue. The cornerstone to the current structure, located on College Street, was laid in December 1921.

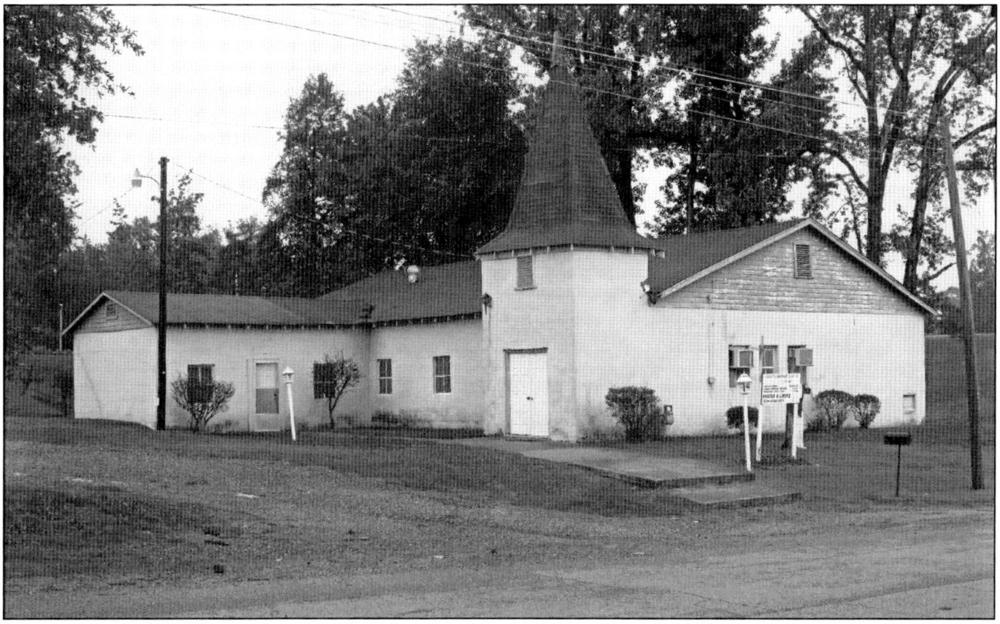

The Shiloh Missionary Baptist Church first chartered land for a church in 1821. Members met at an area known as Burns Bottom at Second Avenue and Second Street North. They met under what was called a "brush arbor" or a collection of limbs and bushes woven together to construct a roof over several poles stuck into the ground. By 1886, the church had constructed a more permanent building. A new structure, seen above, was completed in 1959 but is now used by the Christ Missionary Baptist Church.

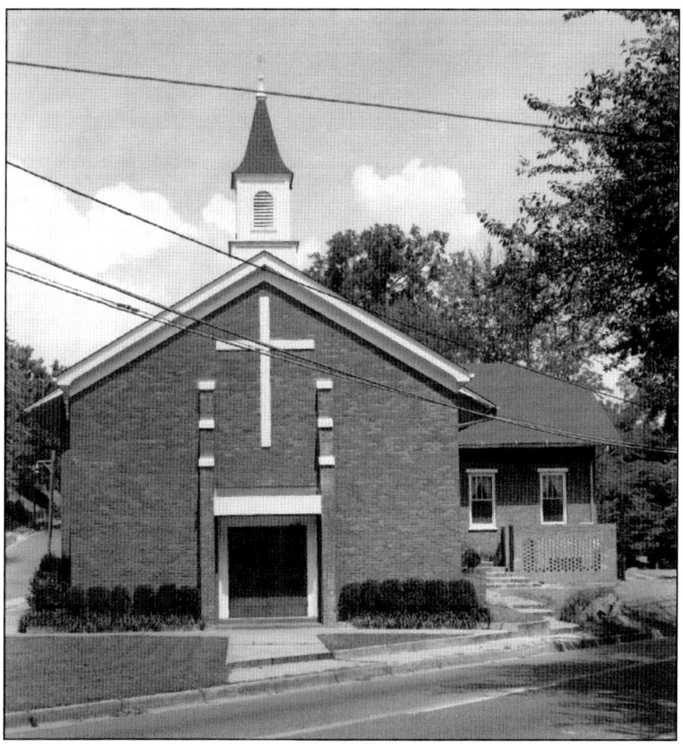

Here is the former home of the First Cumberland Presbyterian Church of Columbus, organized in June 1832. The church erected its first building in 1837. In 1926, this brick structure was completed on the corner of Military Road and Ninth Street North. The land for the congregation's current location on Ridge Road was purchased in 1987.

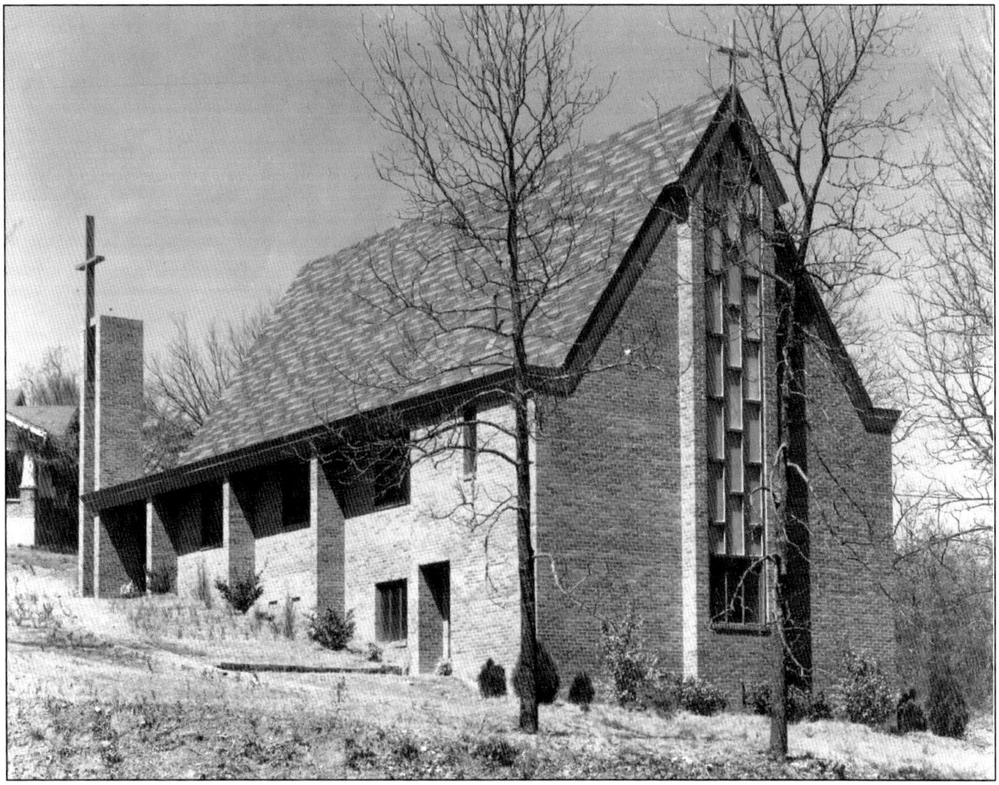

Our Savior Lutheran Church was constructed in 1954 on Eighteenth Avenue North. The land to build the church was donated by Dr. S.C. Matson. Architect William I. Rosamond constructed the building. The congregation was organized just two years prior, with Rev. David W. Friedrichs serving as its first minister.

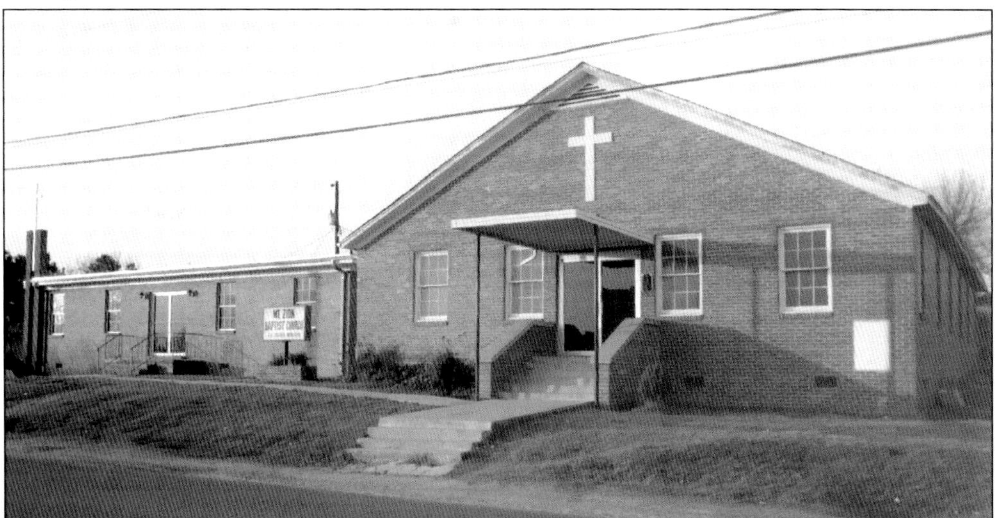

Mount Zion Missionary Baptist Church, located at 2221 Fourteenth Avenue North, is seen in the early 1970s. At the time of the photograph, Rev. Edward E. Heard served as pastor. In 1993, the church underwent a renovation and expansion of its facilities.

Six

People and Places

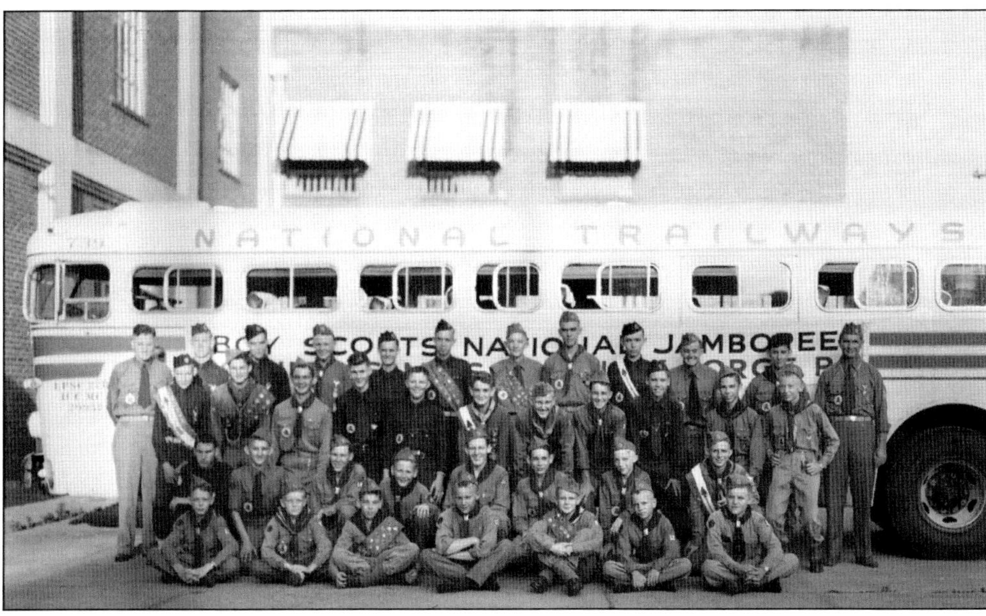

Boy Scouts and scoutmasters of the Pushmataha prepare to leave from the Columbus Trailways Bus Station for the Boy Scout Jamboree in 1950. Normally held every four years, this was the first Jamboree since before World War II. Held at Valley Forge, Pennsylvania, from June 30 to July 6, the Scouts witnessed a Fourth of July speech by Gen. Dwight D. Eisenhower.

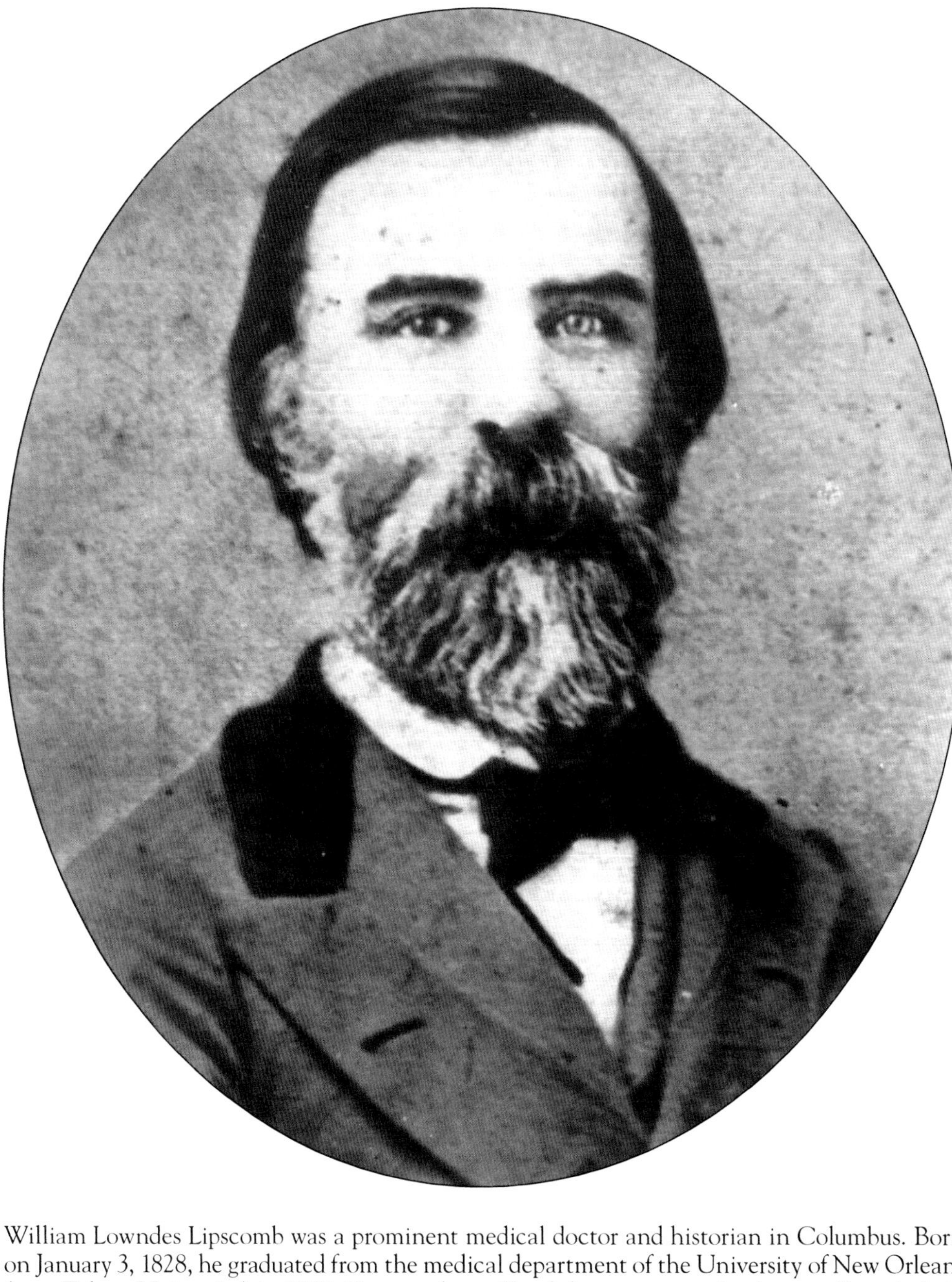

William Lowndes Lipscomb was a prominent medical doctor and historian in Columbus. Born on January 3, 1828, he graduated from the medical department of the University of New Orleans (now Tulane University) in 1850. He served as a Confederate surgeon in charge of hospitals in New Orleans and Columbus as well as medical director of the army under Gen. Stephen D. Lee. After the war, he helped establish and edit the *Columbus Democrat* newspaper. In 1870, Lipscomb served on the board of trustees of the Columbus Female Institute (now Mississippi University for Women) and as county superintendent of education for 10 years. He compiled the city's first comprehensive history, *A History of Columbus Mississippi During the Nineteenth Century*. Blind at the time, he dictated his memories to his daughter Laura Lipscomb Beard before his death on May 22, 1908.

During the 19th and early 20th centuries, many African American women, such as this unidentified woman from around the 1870s, worked as domestic servants in Columbus homes. She was employed in the home of the Billups family.

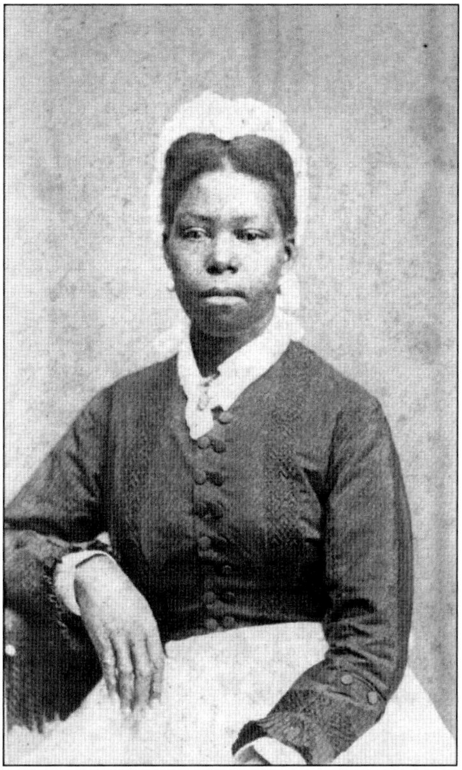

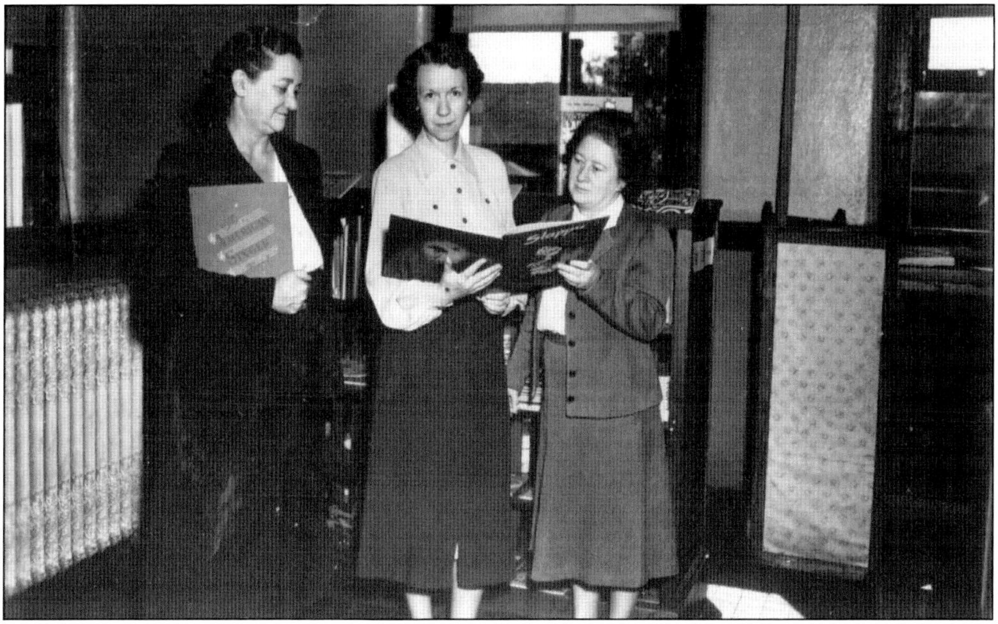

In celebration of Teacher's National Recognition Week, held in October 1950, Barrow Memorial School published this image of several of their teachers in the *Commercial Dispatch* newspaper. Those pictured are, from left to right, Elise Lipscomb, music; Maud Walker, first-grade teacher and chairman of the visual-aid committee; and Velma Stewart, sixth-grade teacher and chairman of the library committee.

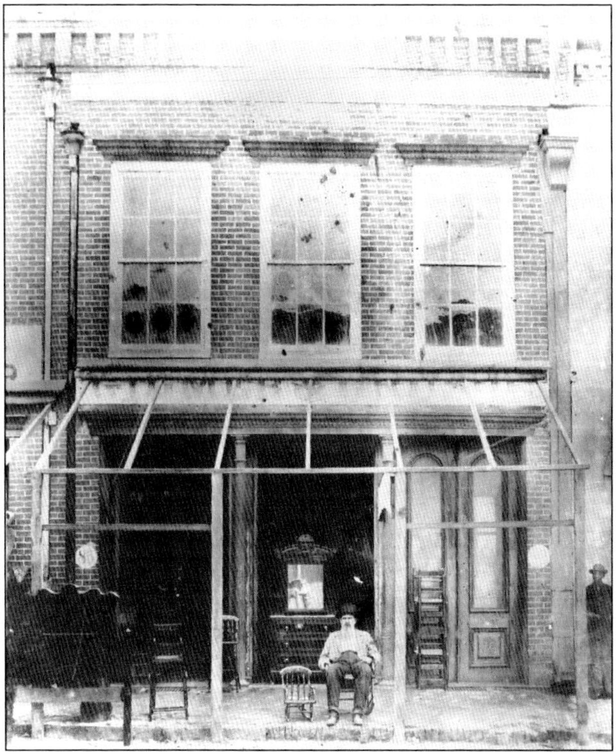

Here is Mr. Gaston in front of his furniture store, located at 83 Market Street (now 114 Fifth Street North). Notice the photographer reflected in the dresser mirror in the center of the photograph.

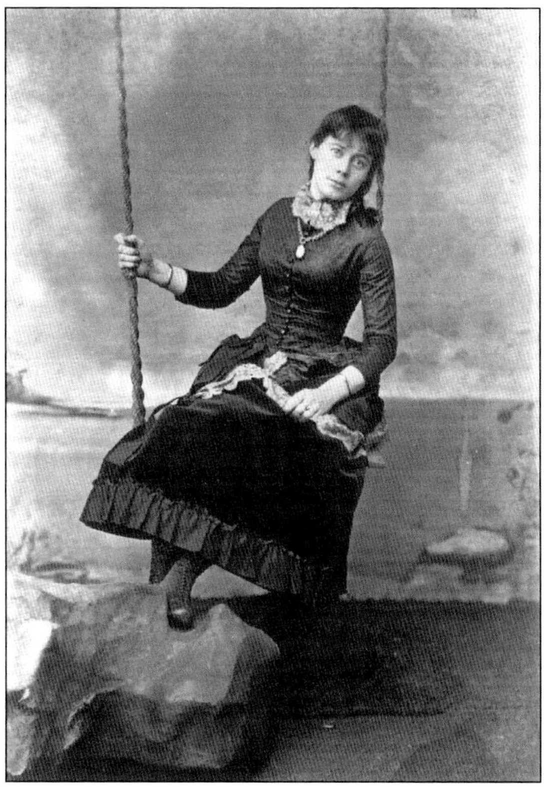

Many Columbus residents enjoyed getting their photograph taken in studios that offered a variety of backgrounds and props. Seen here is Bettie Whitfield, who went to W.C. Echard's Photography Studios in March 1883 to pose in a swing. Echard's studio was located in buildings 64 and 66 Main Street (only 64 still stands as 424 Main Street) and included a large skylight in the roof to provide natural light. The skylight can still be seen today.

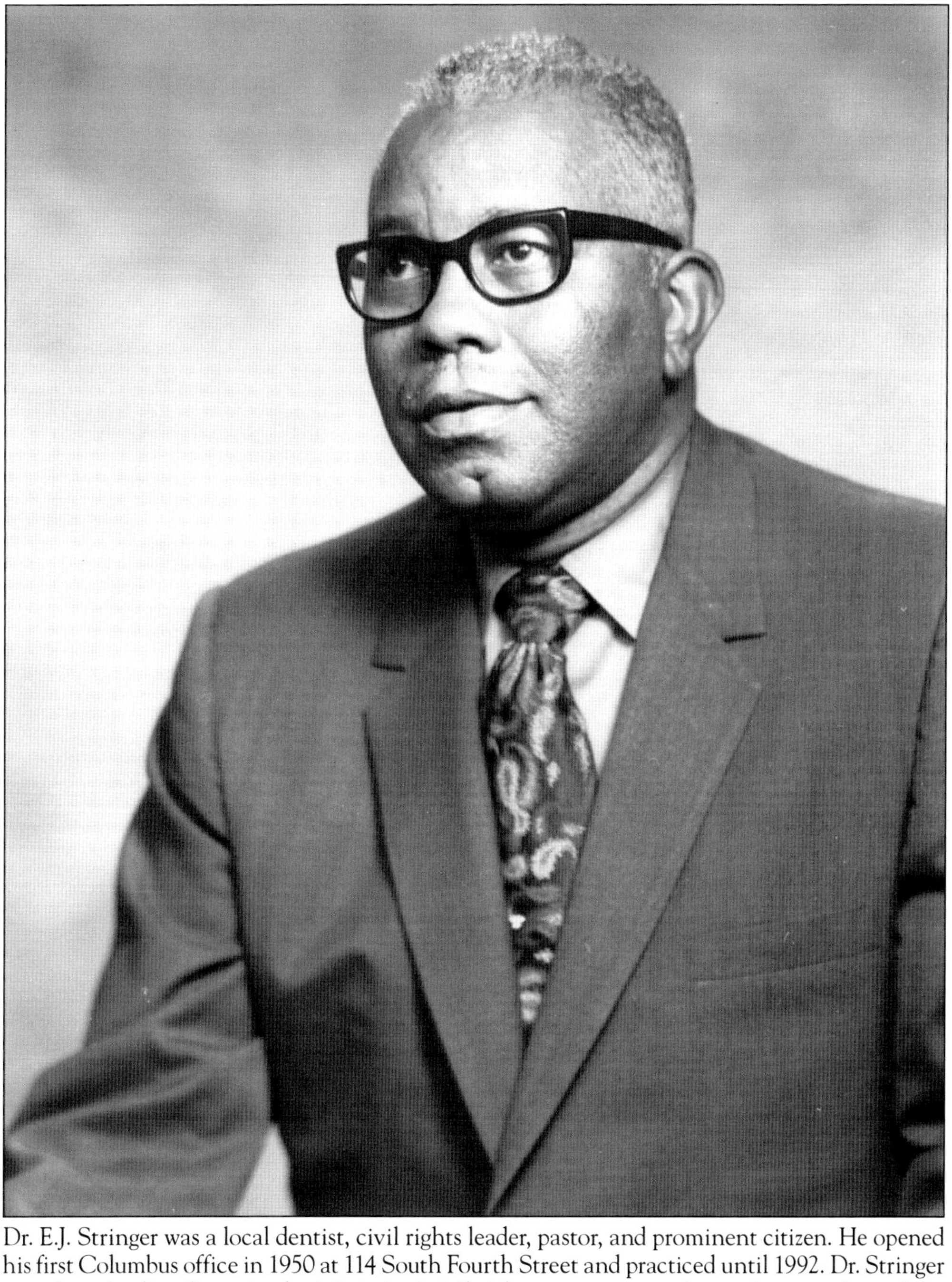

Dr. E.J. Stringer was a local dentist, civil rights leader, pastor, and prominent citizen. He opened his first Columbus office in 1950 at 114 South Fourth Street and practiced until 1992. Dr. Stringer was also a leading figure in the Mississippi civil rights movement and served as president of the Mississippi State Conference of the National Association for the Advancement of Colored People (NAACP) branches from 1953 to 1954. He also organized the Columbus branch of the NAACP and the Lowndes County Voters' League. Dr. Stringer served as the first chairman of the Biracial Advisory Committee to the Columbus Municipal School Board as well as president of the North Mississippi Medical, Dental, Pharmaceutical, and Nurses Society. Dr. Stringer passed away on September 6, 1995, at the age of 75.

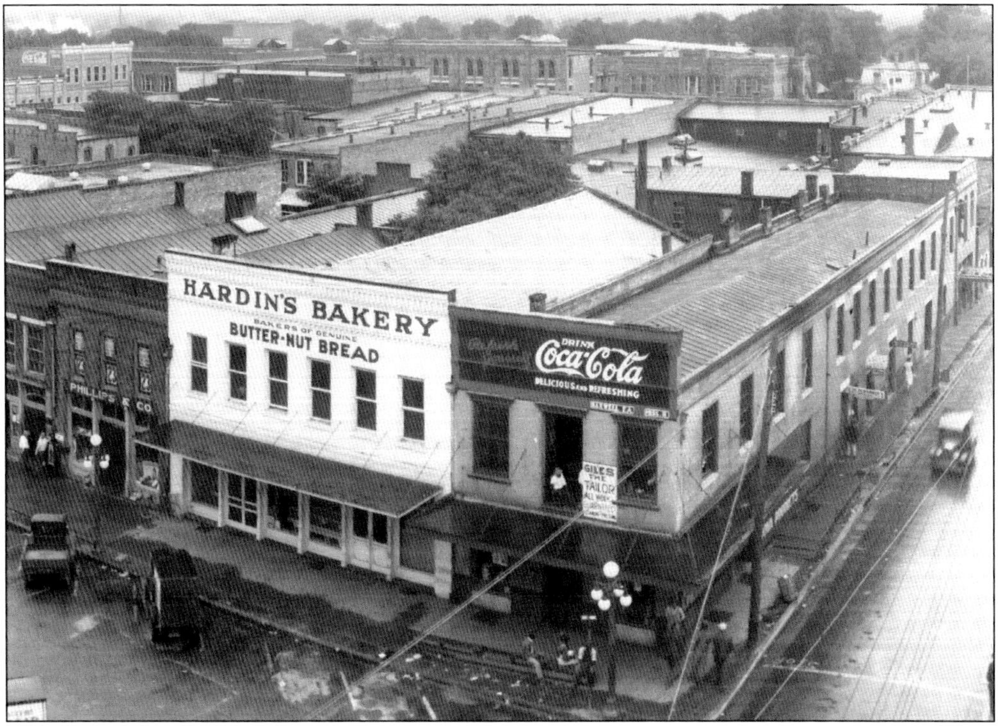

The road to the right of Hardin's Bakery, Fourth Street South, is known as Catfish Alley, an epicenter of African American commerce, culture, food, and music. The street contained numerous African American businesses such as barbershops, grocers, furniture stores, restaurants, physician offices, and much more. The alley most likely received its name from the smell of catfish cooked and sold along the street. In 2007, Catfish Alley received a Mississippi Blues Trail historic marker. (Courtesy of the Southern Historical Collection, Wilson Library, the University of North Carolina at Chapel Hill.)

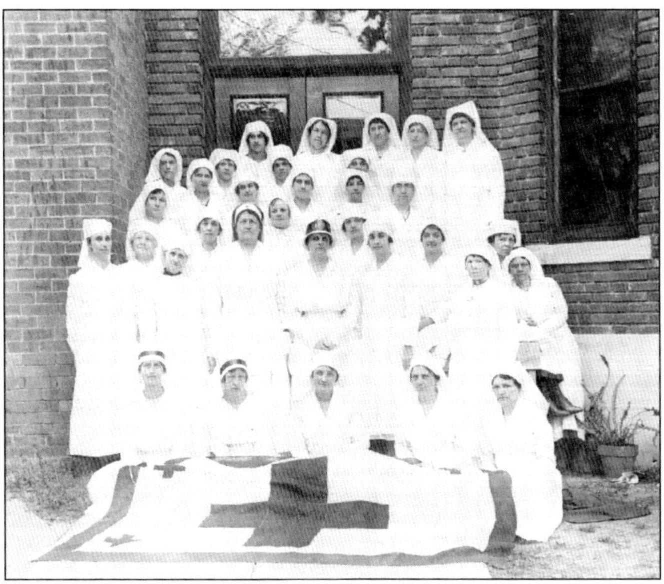

This photograph shows members of the local chapter of the Red Cross during World War I standing in front of the First Methodist Church. At the beginning of World War I, the American Red Cross only had 107 chapters. By the end of the war in 1918, there were over 3,800 chapters nationwide. The Columbus chapter was organized in June 1917.

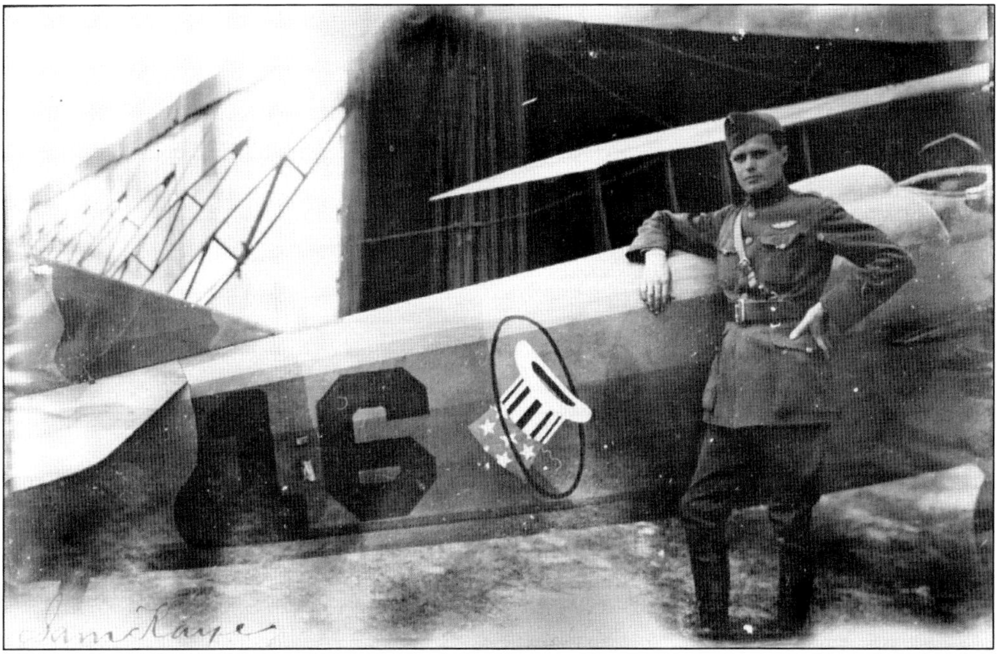

First Lt. Samuel Kaye Jr. poses beside his plane during World War I. Kaye fought in France with the 94th Aero Squadron, 1st Pursuit Group of the United States Army Air Service in the American Expeditionary Forces Division. The squadron's nickname was "Hat in the Ring" as indicated by the painting on the side of Kaye's plane. He is credited with four aerial victories and was awarded the Distinguished Service Cross, a Bronze Oak Leaf Cluster, and the French Croix de Guerre for his service and gallantry in action. In 2007, the Columbus Air Force Base theater was renamed the Kaye Auditorium in his honor.

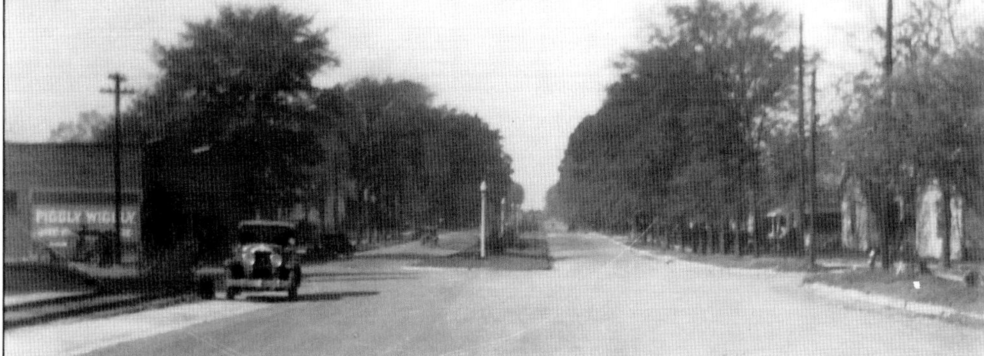

This image shows the intersection of Main Street and Thirteenth Street facing west in the 1930s. The steps of the Columbus and Greenville Railroad depot are on the left across from the Piggly Wiggly grocery store.

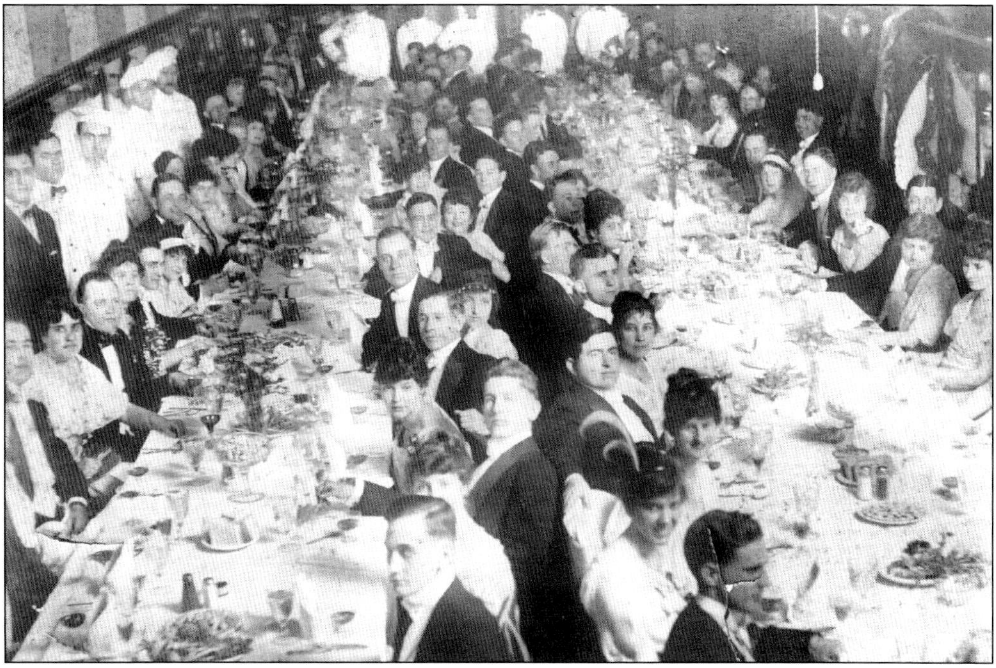

This photograph shows a domino dance and dinner given by the Choctaw Club on February 16, 1915. Over 120 people attended the Mardi Gras inspired carnival ball, which was held at the Gilmer Hotel. The hotel's New Bell Café served dinner, while the Princess Theatre orchestra, led by Professor A.M. Jacob, provided the music. The Choctaw Club was a social club organized on March 5, 1911, and E.W. Humphries served as the first president.

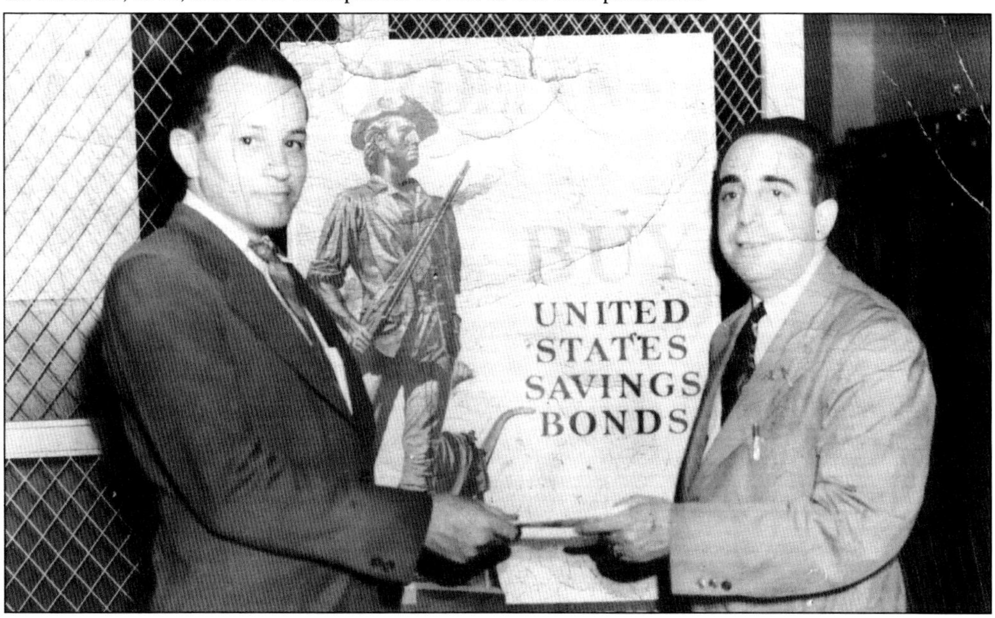

During World War II, Columbus residents helped support the war by purchasing war bonds that were issued by the government in order to raise money for the war effort. This photograph shows Leo Spatz and Herbert Perry buying the first war bonds sold in Columbus in 1941. (Courtesy of the Southern Historical Collection, Wilson Library, the University of North Carolina at Chapel Hill.)

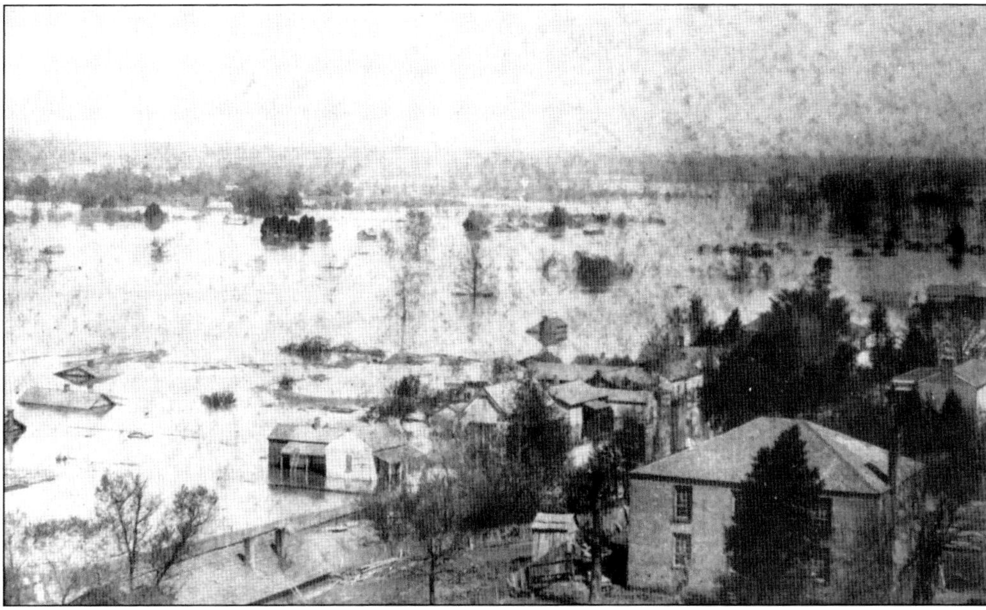

On April 8, 1892, the Tombigbee River crested to a record 42.6 feet. This image of the flood was captured from the roof of the Gilmer Hotel looking north out over the present-day site of the Hitching Lot Farmer's Market. About 50 people lost their lives, and there was heavy loss of property, such as cattle, mules, and homes, floating downriver. In one night alone, the river rose 14 feet. It is considered the benchmark of Tombigbee River floods.

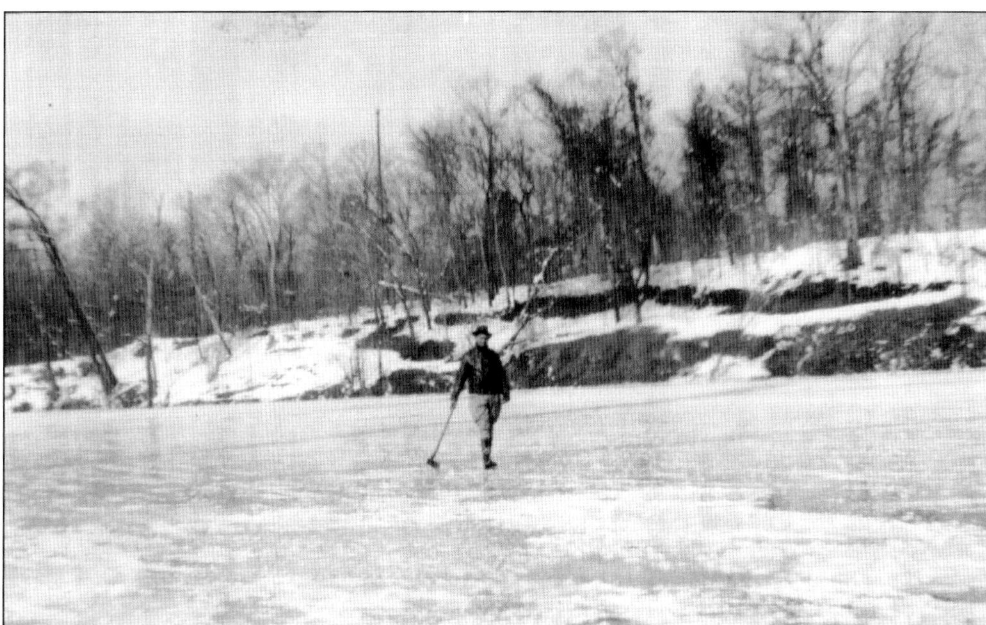

The Tombigbee River froze in the winter of 1940 as temperatures dipped to eight degrees below zero. Tradition states that it was frozen so solid that a team of oxen was driven across it.

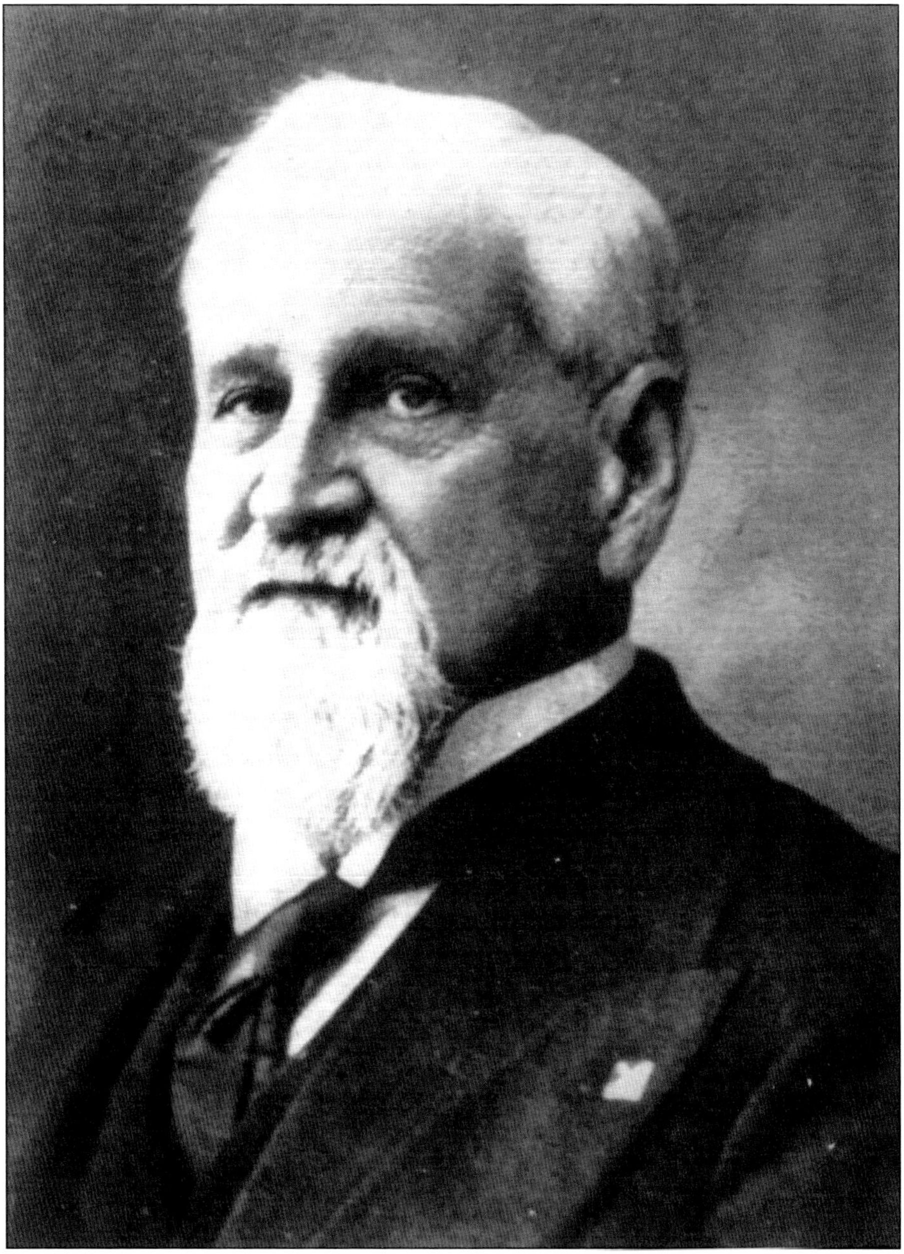

Stephen Dill Lee was born September 22, 1833, and died May 28, 1908. He was the youngest lieutenant general in the Confederate army and served as aide-de-camp to Gen. P.G.T. Beauregard in Charleston Harbor. It was Lee who, under Beauregard's command, ordered the Confederates to begin firing on Fort Sumter, initiating the Civil War. Later, Lee commanded General Pemberton's artillery at Vicksburg. He married Regina Harrison in 1865 and represented Lowndes County in the Mississippi Senate in 1878. From 1880 to 1899, he served as first president of the Mississippi Agricultural and Mechanical College (now Mississippi State University). He was president of the State Historical Society in 1898 and the first president of the trustees of the Mississippi Department of Archives and History. In 1899, Lee organized the United Confederate Veterans and, in 1904, was elected their commander-in-chief.

A division of the Navy during World War II, WAVES stood for "Women Accepted for Volunteer Emergency Services." A year after it was created, Marcella Billups, seen here in her officer uniform, joined the organization on February 9, 1943. She served three years and, while on duty, was stationed in New Orleans, Louisiana, and Jacksonville, Florida.

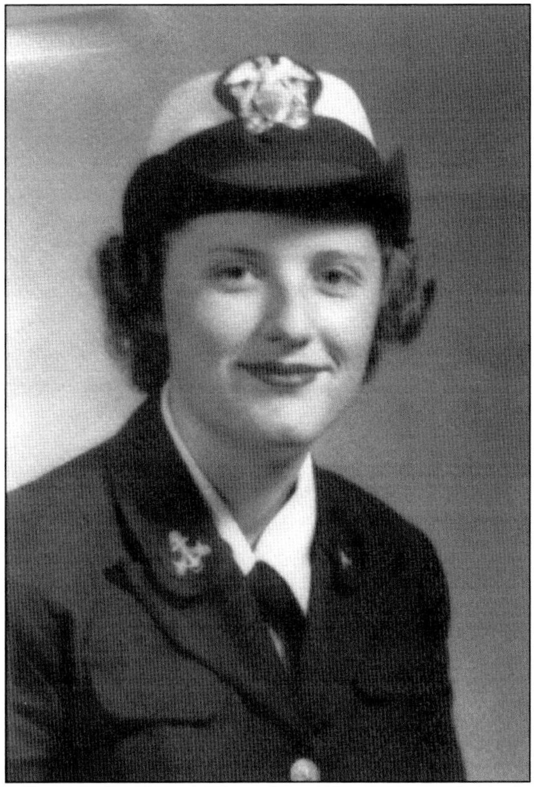

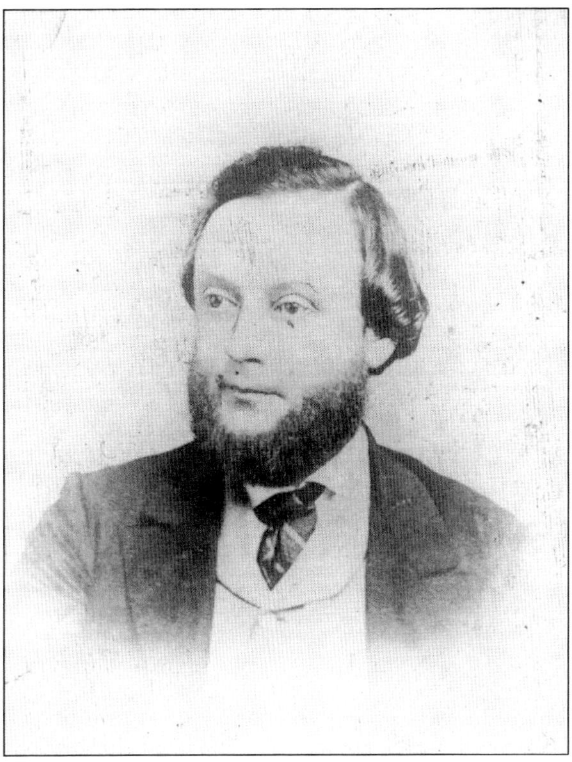

Almanacs are used to find information on weather forecasts, planting dates, astronomical data, and much more. It was within such almanacs that Oscar Thaddius Keeler (1824–1870), editor and printer of *Keeler's Almanac*, was able to preserve some of Columbus's earliest history. Keeler first published his almanac in Columbus in 1847. By 1859, he was printing 10,000 copies. His publication also included advertisements for local businesses and institutions.

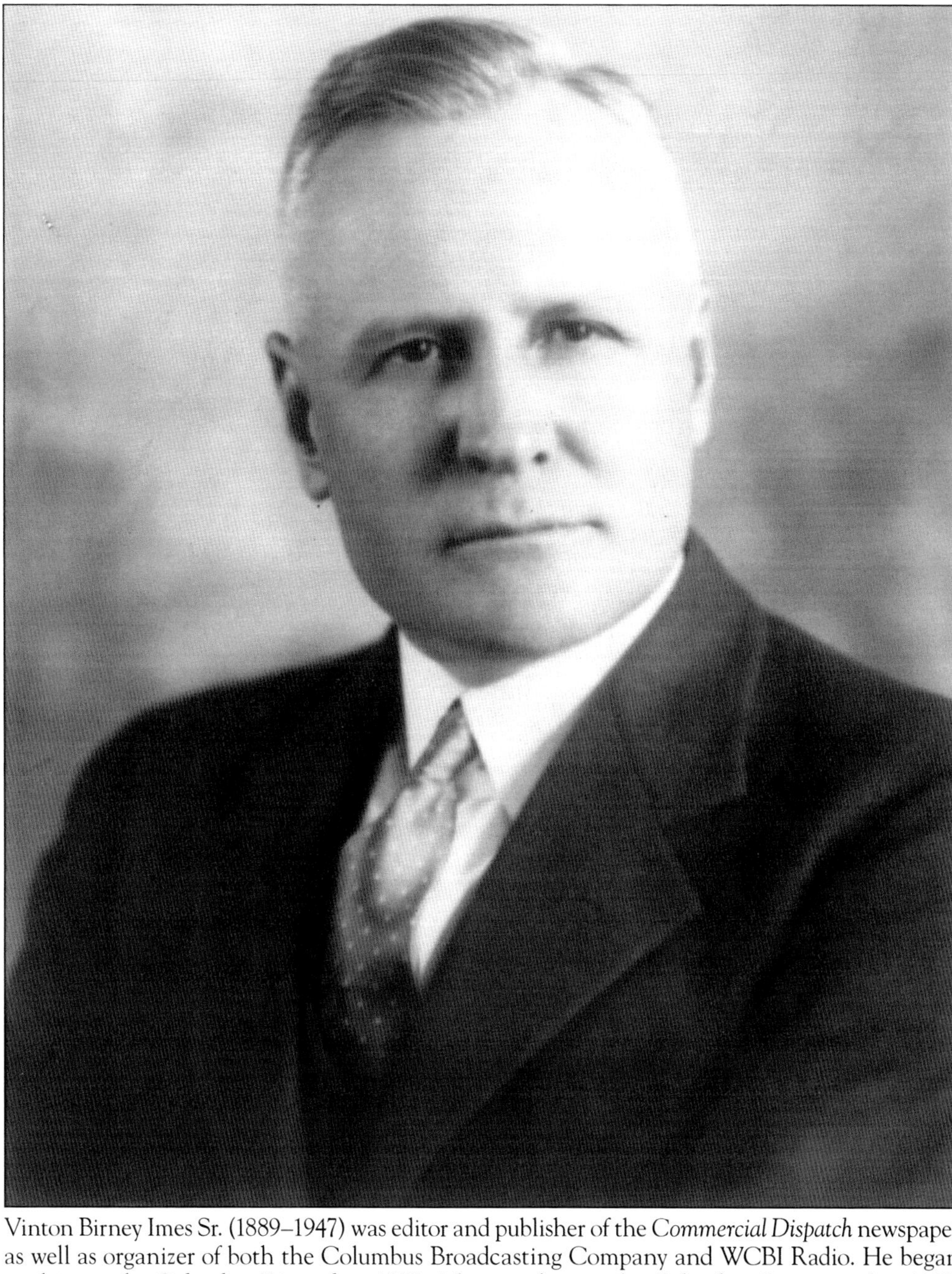

Vinton Birney Imes Sr. (1889–1947) was editor and publisher of the *Commercial Dispatch* newspaper as well as organizer of both the Columbus Broadcasting Company and WCBI Radio. He began working at the *Columbus Dispatch* in 1910. After purchasing the *Columbus Commercial* in 1922, he combined the two papers into the present-day *Commercial Dispatch*. Imes served as executive secretary of the State Board of Trustees of Universities and Colleges, president of the Mississippi Press Association, and founder and president of the Columbus Rotary Club. Imes was named a member of the US delegation to the Conference of Ministers of Foreign Affairs in Havana, Cuba, as special assistant to Secretary of State Cordell Hull in 1940. Imes was also director of the Columbus Chamber of Commerce and worked toward the establishment of the air base in Columbus in the 1940s.

African Americans took advantage of the growing photography business in Columbus. Seen here is Henry Davis Alston posing at W.C. Echard's Photography Studio sometime in the late 1800s. Today, one of Echard's former buildings is occupied by The Globe clothing store.

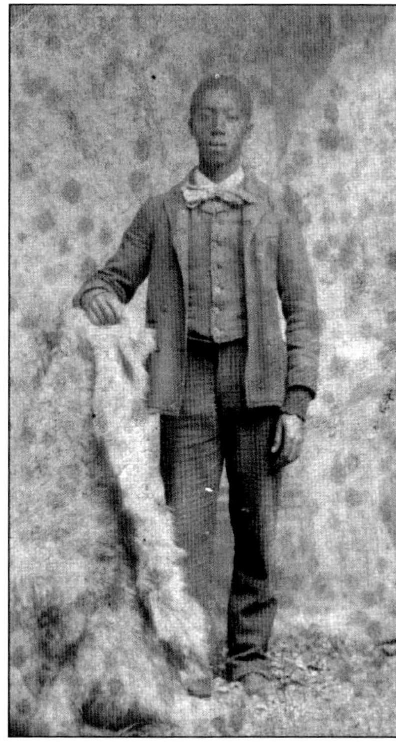

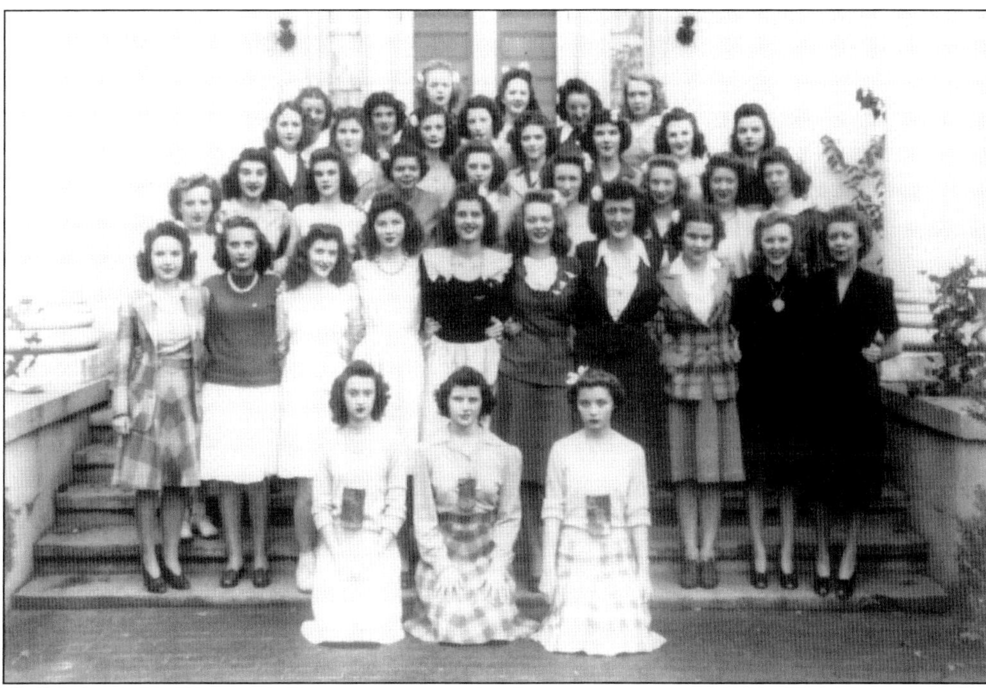

Delta Beta Sigma, seen here in front of Polly Puckett's house in 1943, is a national high school sorority founded in 1903. The local chapter of the club held bridge parties, dances, and organized fundraisers for various causes. (Courtesy of the Southern Historical Collection, Wilson Library, the University of North Carolina at Chapel Hill.)

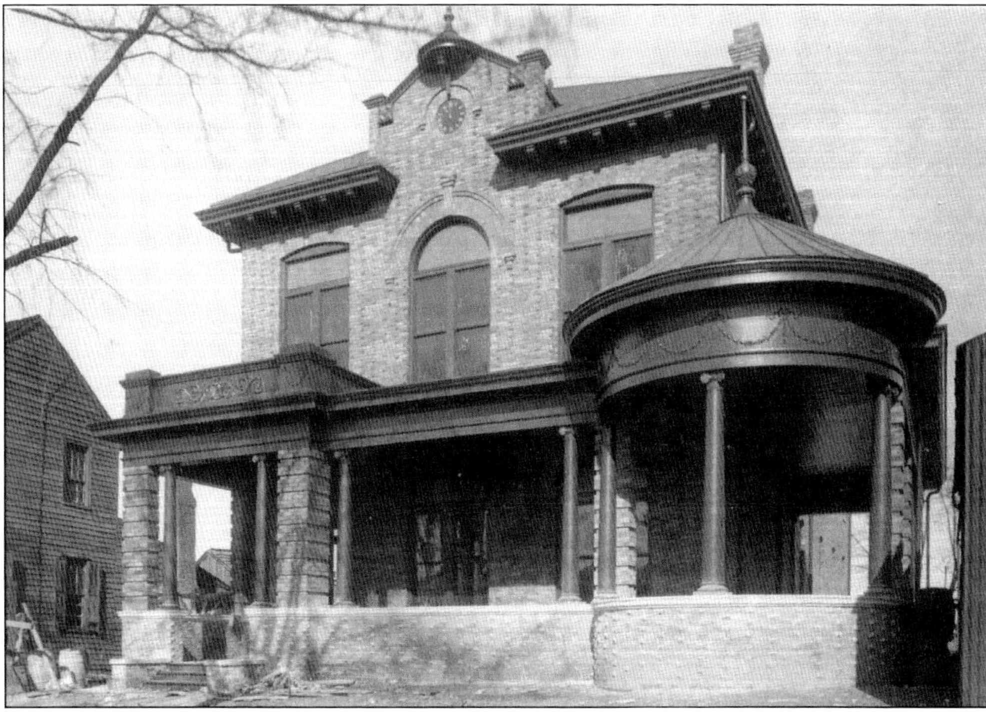

Local Lodge No. 555 of the Benevolent and Protective Order of Elks Club or "The Elks" was organized in Columbus in March 1900 with Thomas J. Cady as the first exalted ruler. The Elks are a national fraternal, charitable, and service order dating back to 1868. By 1901, Lodge No. 555 built the structure (above), located at 309 Main Street. The building contained a lodge room, ornate hallway, and a parlor (below). By 1979, the Elks Club began construction on a new house on Baldwin Road.

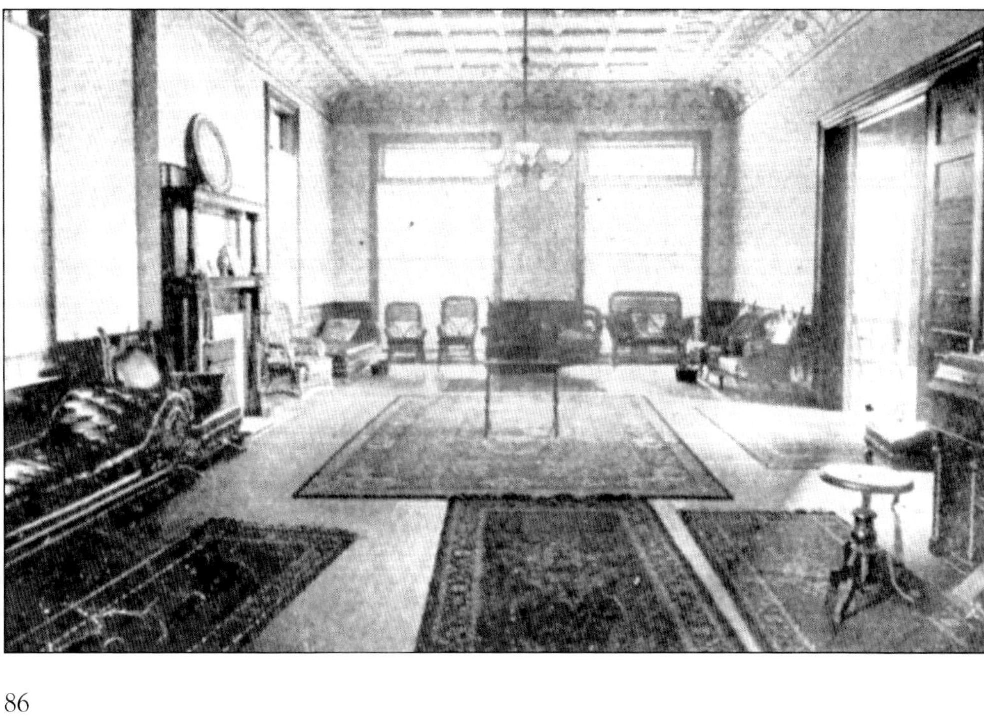

Edith Colvin Bradley (right) was born on April 15, 1900 and worked as a quilt-maker. She married Ed Bradley and lived at 1104 Ash Street. Edith died on October 23, 1997, at the age of 97.

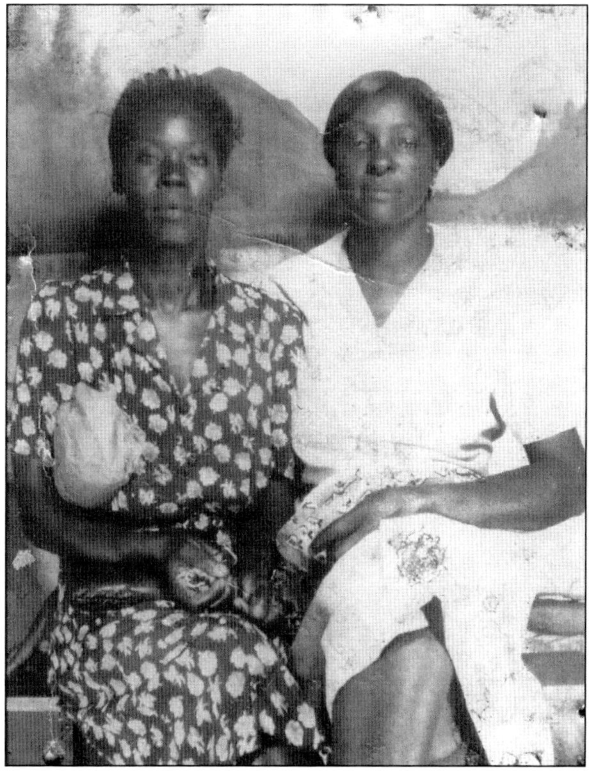

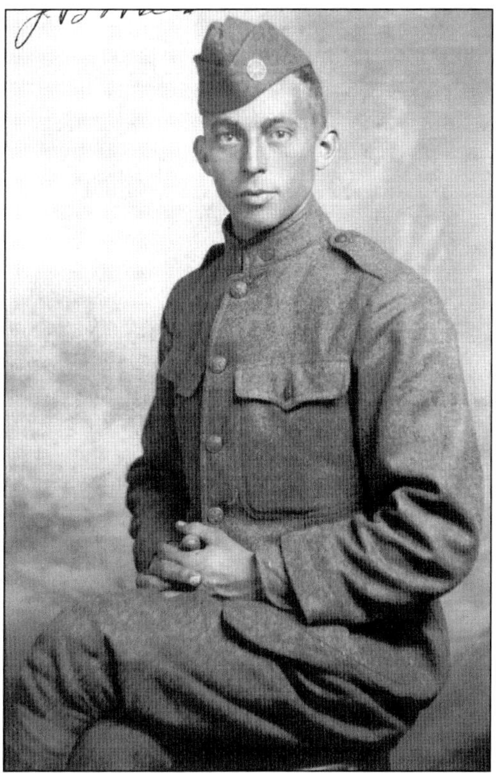

When America joined in the Great War, or World War I, men from Columbus and surrounding areas registered for service. One such man was John Berry Wells, shown here in his uniform.

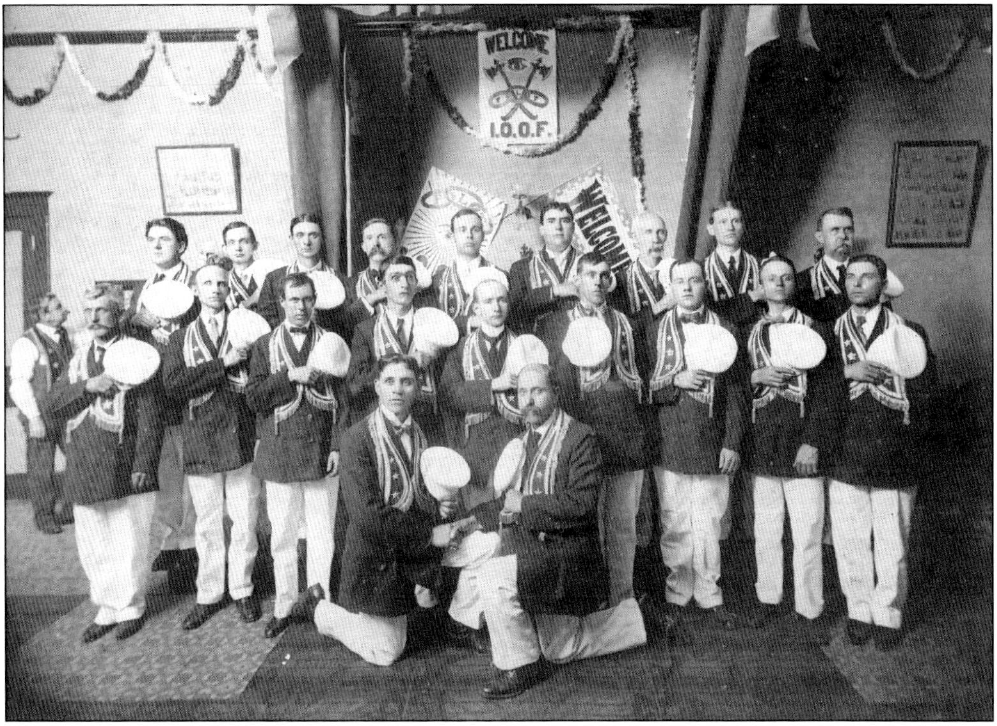

One of many fraternal organizations in Columbus is the Independent Order of Odd Fellows (IOOF) Union Lodge No. 35. It was created in 1868 by the combining of the Covenant Lodge (1845) and McKendree Lodge (1847). The hall, a three-story structure located on Main Street known as the Odd Fellows Building, was built in 1858 and then rebuilt and enlarged in 1906. In the 1850s, the organization operated a collegiate high school and, during the Civil War, allowed its hall to be used as a hospital for wounded soldiers. The IOOF also owned Friendship Cemetery from 1849 to 1957.

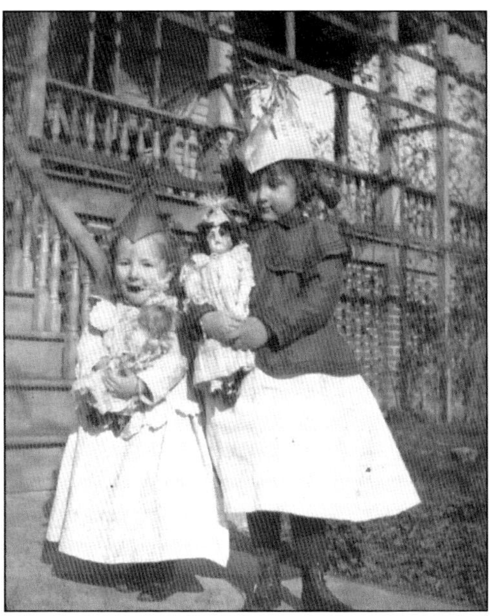

Margeretha (left) and Catherine E. Donnell play with their dolls in front of their home at 515 Military Road around 1910. Catherine went on to work as a bookkeeper for Columbus Marble Works.

Photographer Henry Emil Hoffmeister, born in Germany in 1855, moved to Columbus in 1900 after having studios in both West Point and Macon, Mississippi. Here, he captured many images of local people, events, and businesses. In 1901, he started teaching photography classes at the Industrial Institute and College, where he later served as head of the Department of Photography until 1909. His studio, located at 424 ½ Main Street, is the current location of The Globe clothing store. In 1921, he sold his studio to another well-known local photographer, O.N. Pruitt.

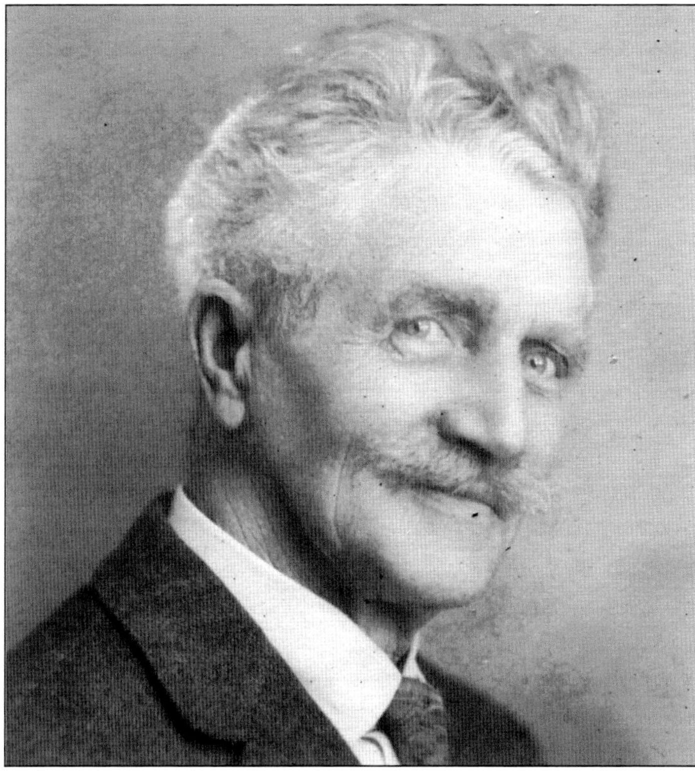

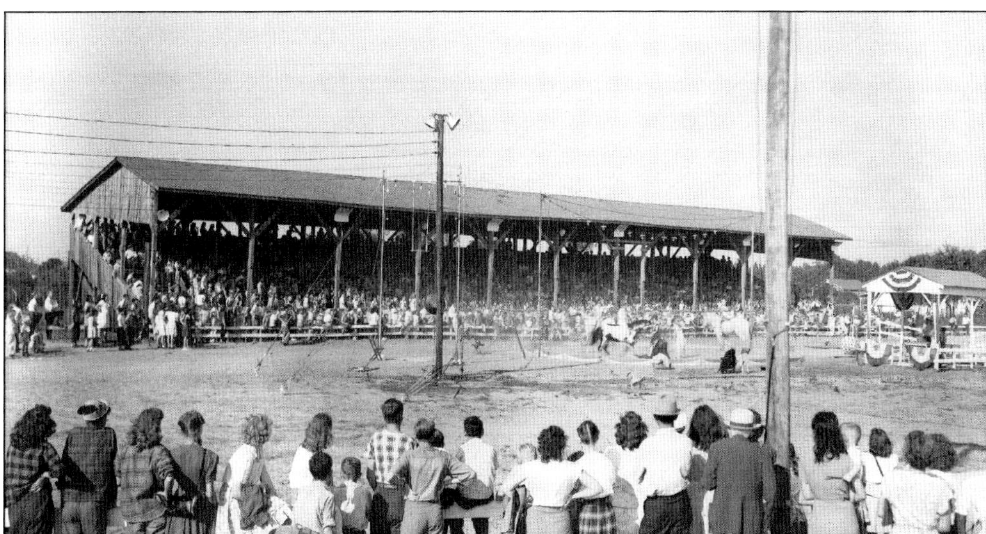

Over 7,000 people attended the Lowndes County Fair and Livestock Association Fair at the Columbus Fairgrounds in 1947. Held September 26–27, the fair included agricultural and livestock exhibits as well as a circus performance.

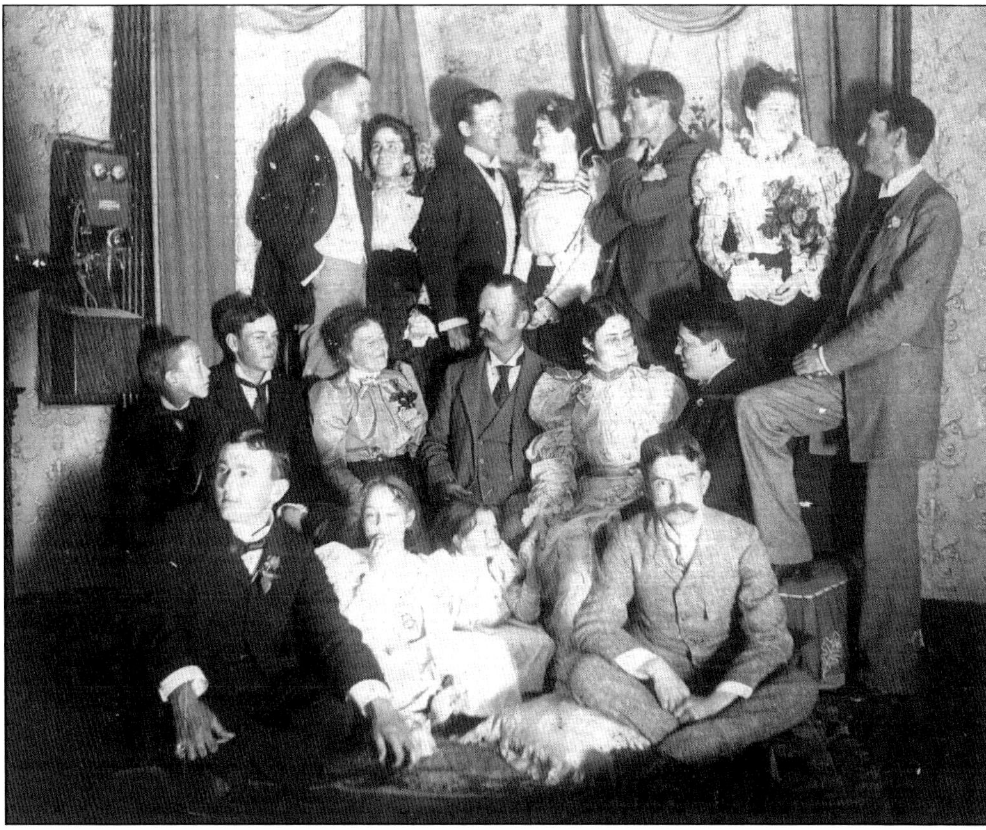

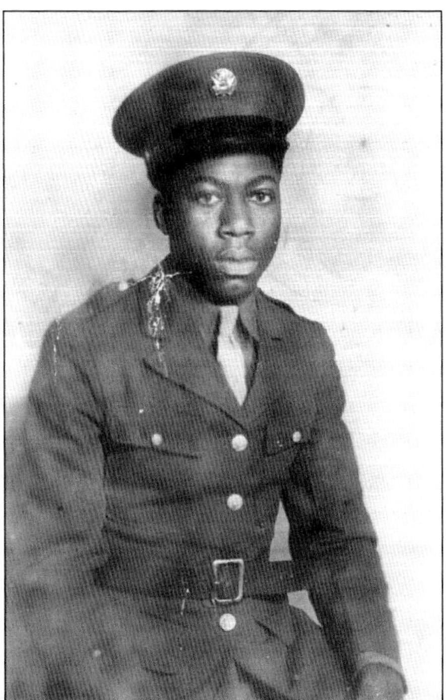

Ever since the advent of photography, the people of Columbus have enjoyed capturing images of friends and family. Seen here are members of the Billups family and their friends at the home Snowdoun around 1900.

Many men from Lowndes County joined the military during World War II. James Quilla Salter or "Captain Salter" was one of those who enlisted. Born on January 15, 1921, to Will and Cindy Salter, he joined the army as a private on October 2, 1942, at Camp Shelby, Mississippi. Upon returning from the war, Salter worked for Columbus Brick Company and married Annie Lee Colvin. Together, they raised 11 children. Salter died on June 9, 1999.

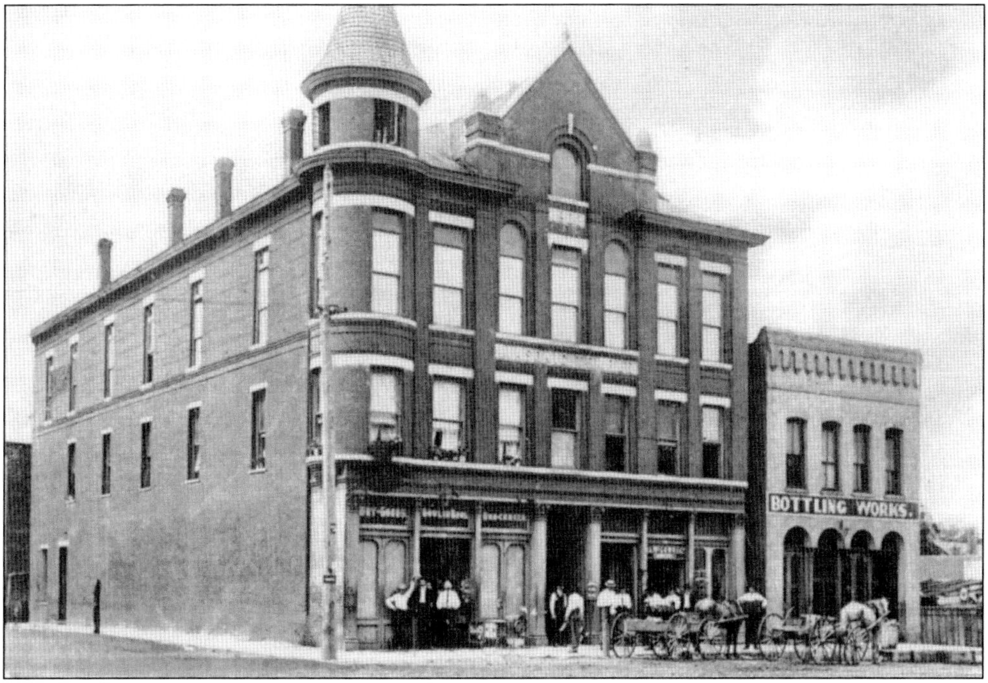

The Masonic Temple was built by the Columbus Lodge No. 5 of the Free and Accepted Masons in 1902. The first floor housed various businesses while the second and third floors were ceremonial chambers. The third floor was called the "Blue Hall" and consisted of 2,000 square feet of space and 15-foot ceilings. The Masons continued to meet at the Main Street structure for over 80 years until the roof was damaged in a fire in 1982.

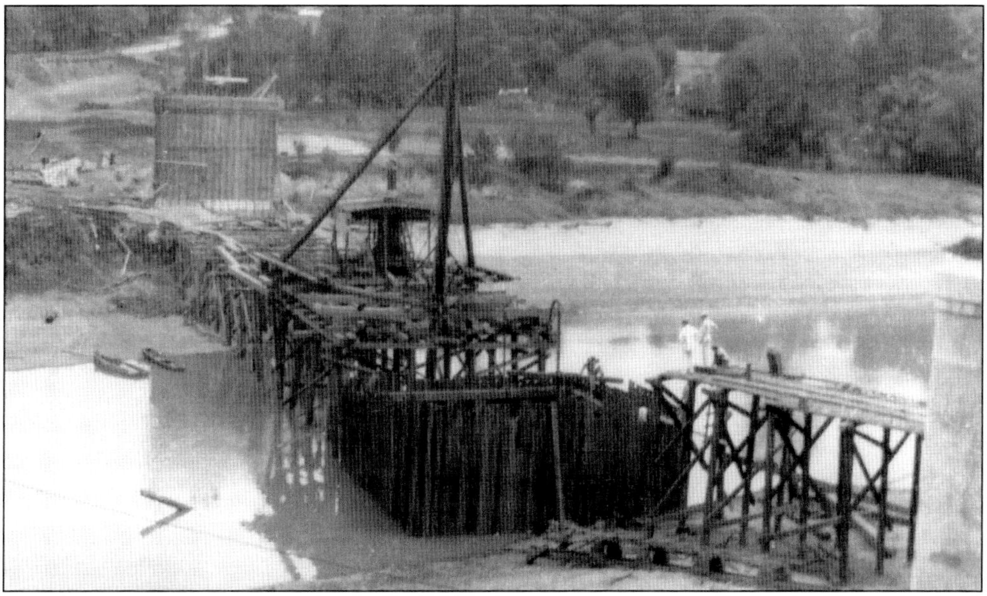

This image shows the construction of the Tombigbee River Bridge (facing east) in 1925. The bridge, completed in 1927, is a steel-and-concrete swing bridge. This allows the bridge to pivot horizontally, thus permitting large river traffic to pass. This bridge was preceeded by a wooden one built in 1840 and then by a wrought iron drawbridge in 1877.

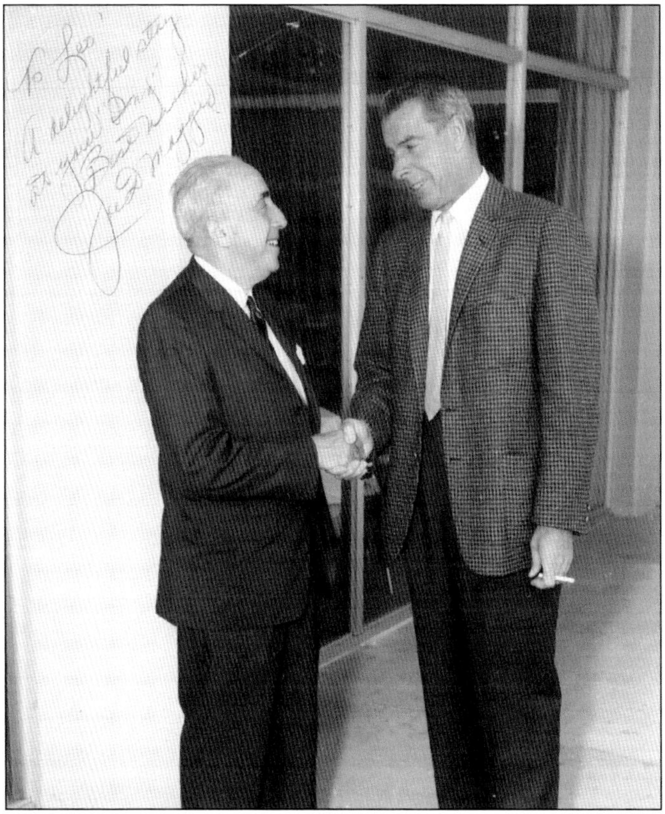

In the summer of 1962, baseball Hall of Famer and New York Yankee Joe DiMaggio visited Columbus. DiMaggio was in town to hold a baseball clinic for Little Leagues at the Columbus Air Force Base. He is pictured here with local restaurant and hotel owner Leo Spatz. Spatz was known as "Mr. Hospitality."

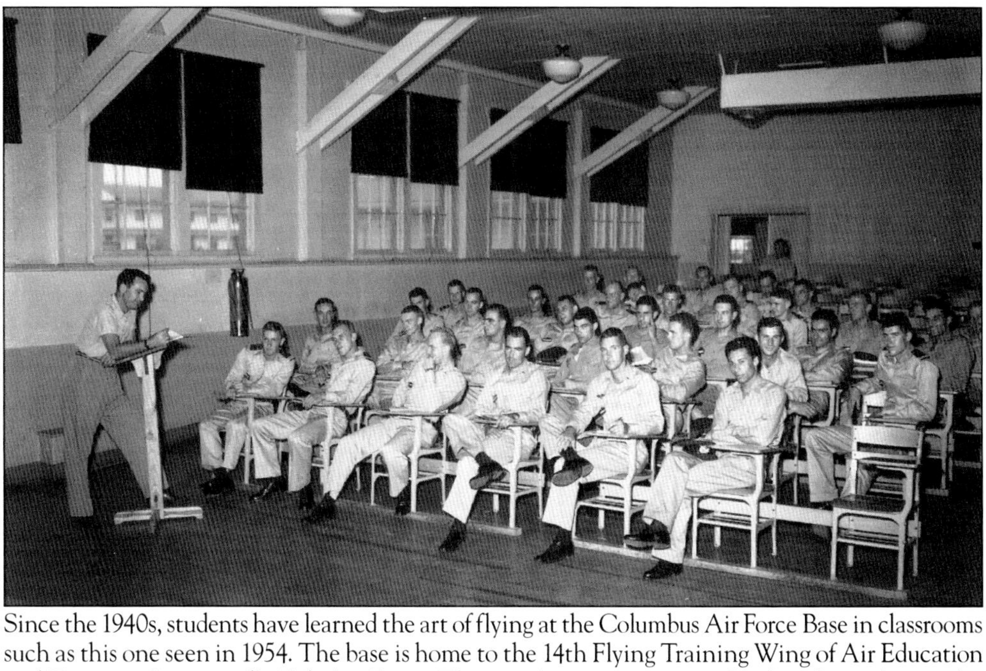

Since the 1940s, students have learned the art of flying at the Columbus Air Force Base in classrooms such as this one seen in 1954. The base is home to the 14th Flying Training Wing of Air Education and Training Command's 19th Air Force. The wing's mission is specialized undergraduate pilot training, and it flies an average of 350 sorties each day from three parallel runways.

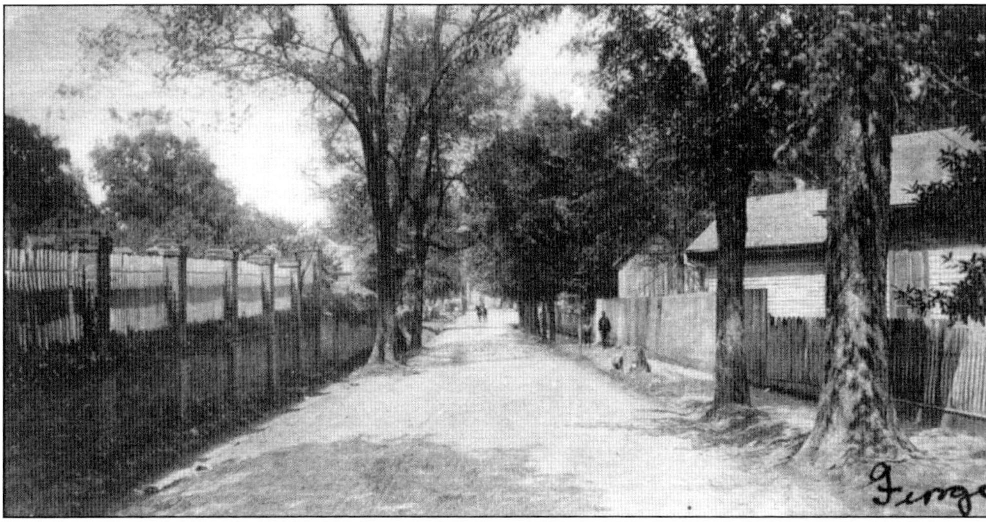

Military Road passes straight through Columbus on its way from Nashville, Tennessee, to New Orleans, Louisiana. On the recommendation of Gen. Andrew Jackson, the US War Department built the road, which took from 1817 to 1820 to complete. It was constructed to allow for easier transportation of the military in times of war. Prior to the construction of Military Road, the only route from Nashville to New Orleans was by way of the Natchez Trace, an added distance of over 200 miles. It was primarily used as a commercial and telegraph route, although parts of the road eventually fell into disuse. This is a postcard of the road as seen in 1907.

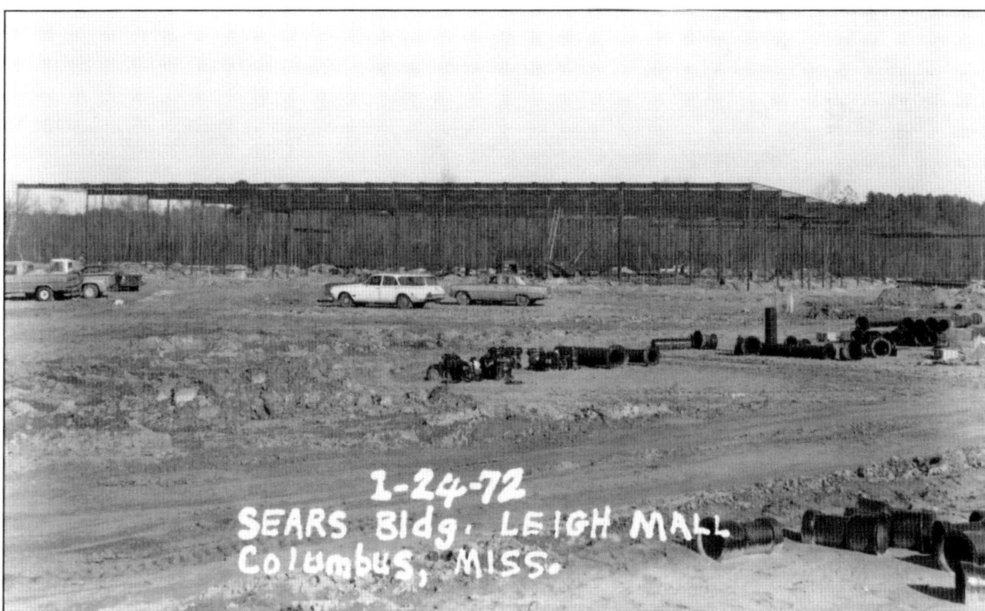

This image shows the construction of the Sears, Roebuck, and Co. department store on January 24, 1972. It was the first part of Leigh Mall to be built.

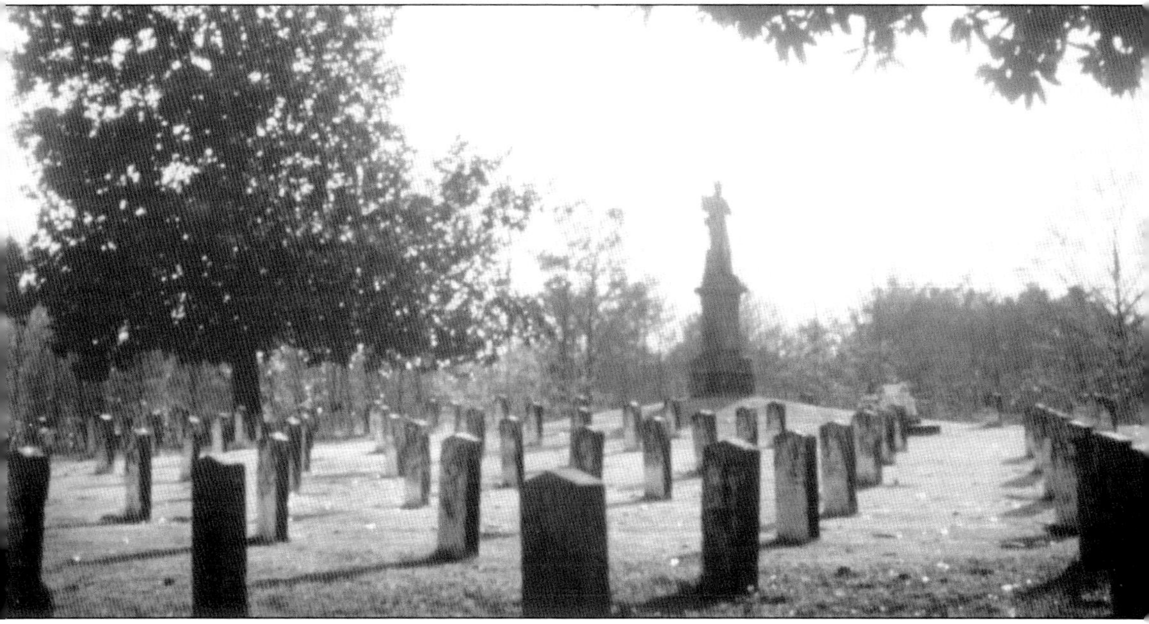

The Independent Order of Odd Fellows owned Friendship Cemetery, founded in 1849 on a five-acre parcel of land. The first person buried there was Mary Elizabeth Bell Sinclair, who died in childbirth in July 1849. It is the site where the first Memorial Day was held on April 26, 1866. In March 1957, the cemetery was deeded to the City of Columbus. The cemetery includes two Mississippi governors, one Revolutionary War soldier, four US congressmen, the only volunteer Confederate nurse recognized by the federal government, and many more influential individuals. There are over 2,190 Confederate soldiers buried there. It is the location of "The Angel of Grief," popularly known as "The Weeping Angel," tombstone belonging to Rev. Thomas Teasdale. In 1980, Friendship Cemetery was listed in the National Register of Historic Places.

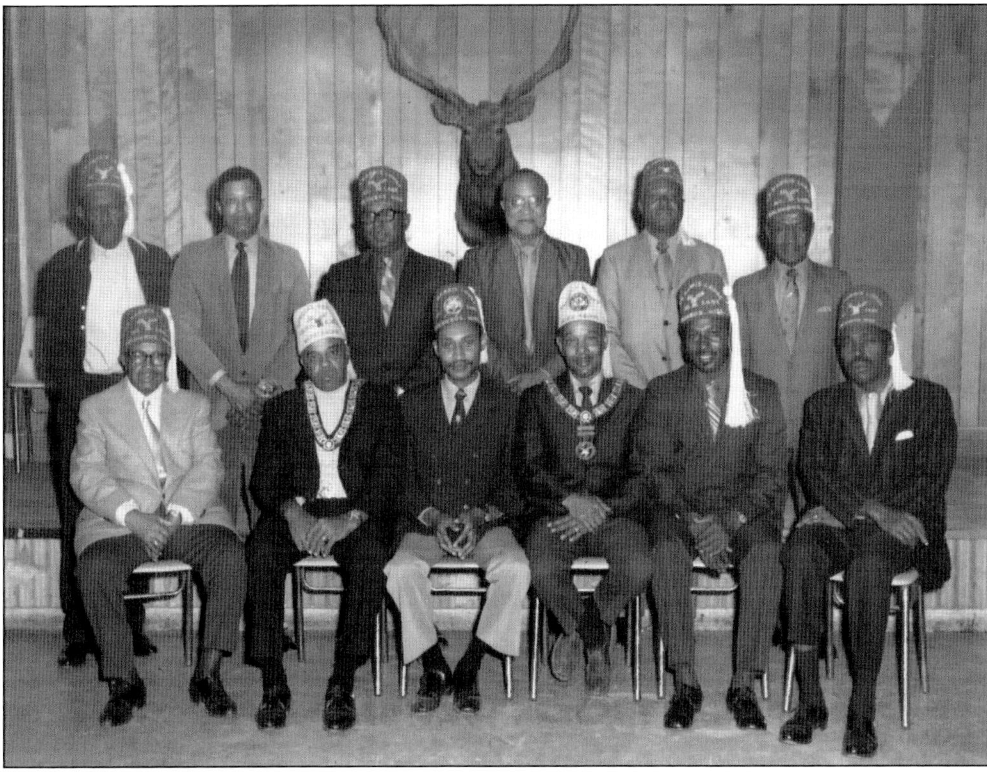

One of the African American fraternal organizations in Columbus is the Improved Benevolent and Protective Order of Elks of the World T.P. Harris Lodge No. 1495 or "IBPOEW." Seen here in the 1970s, A.L. Ryan served as exalted ruler. The organization continues to meet at its lodge located on Sixteenth Street North. The national fraternity, founded by B.F. Howard and Arthur J. Riggs in 1898, is the largest African American fraternal organization in the world.

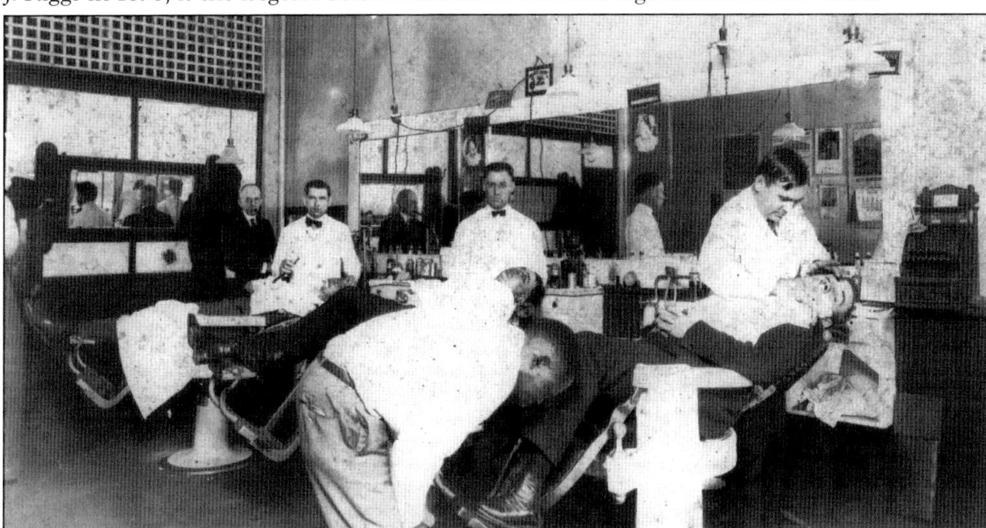

The Gilmer Hotel barbershop, seen here around the 1920s, was operated by Titus Gilmer until the early 1900s. The shop was a popular gathering place for many Columbus citizens. Standing in the center is barber John D. Wright.

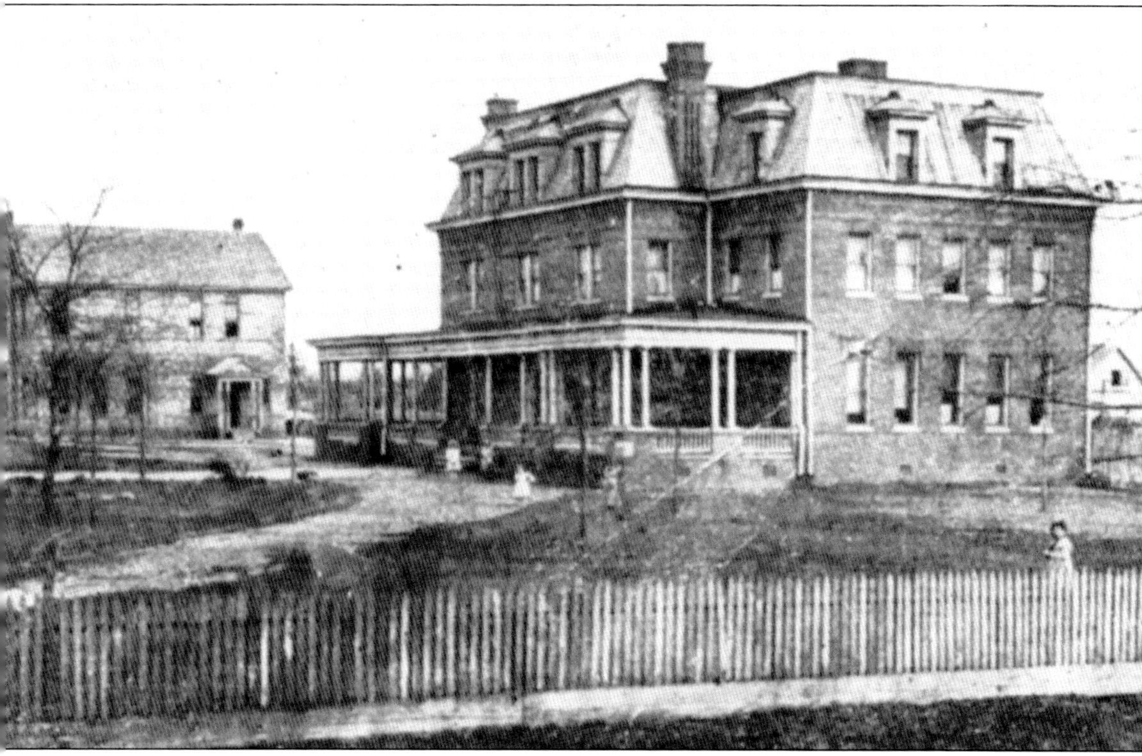

The Palmer Orphanage, now the Palmer Home for Children, was made possible through the work of Rev. W.S. Jacobs, a Presbyterian minister. It is named for Dr. Benjamin Morgan Palmer, a leading Presbyterian preacher of the 19th century. The first building was erected in 1898 on 20 acres of land located at 912 Eleventh Avenue South. The Palmer Orphanage accepted children between the ages of six to twelve regardless of their religious faith or place of residence. The children were given an education and religious training, as well as manual and technical training. Today, the Palmer Home for Children is an independent institution serving nearly 100 boys and girls.

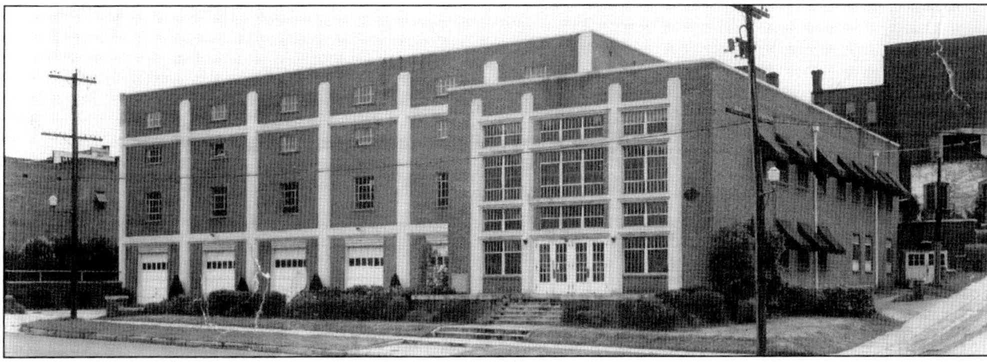

The City Auditorium (above), located on the corner of Second Avenue and Fourth Street North, was dedicated on July 28, 1942. Erected by the city of Columbus in conjunction with the Works Progress Administration (WPA), the building cost approximately $125,000. The dedication was broadcast live over WCBI Radio. The program included a speech by Q. Edward Gatlin, Mississippi administrator for the WPA. Seen below is a dance held at the auditorium and sponsored by the United Service Organization (USO), a group that provided support and entertainment to military troops. The building was replaced by the current James M. Trotter Convention Center, named for long-time mayor James M. Trotter, in 1987. (Courtesy of the Southern Historical Collection, Wilson Library, the University of North Carolina at Chapel Hill.)

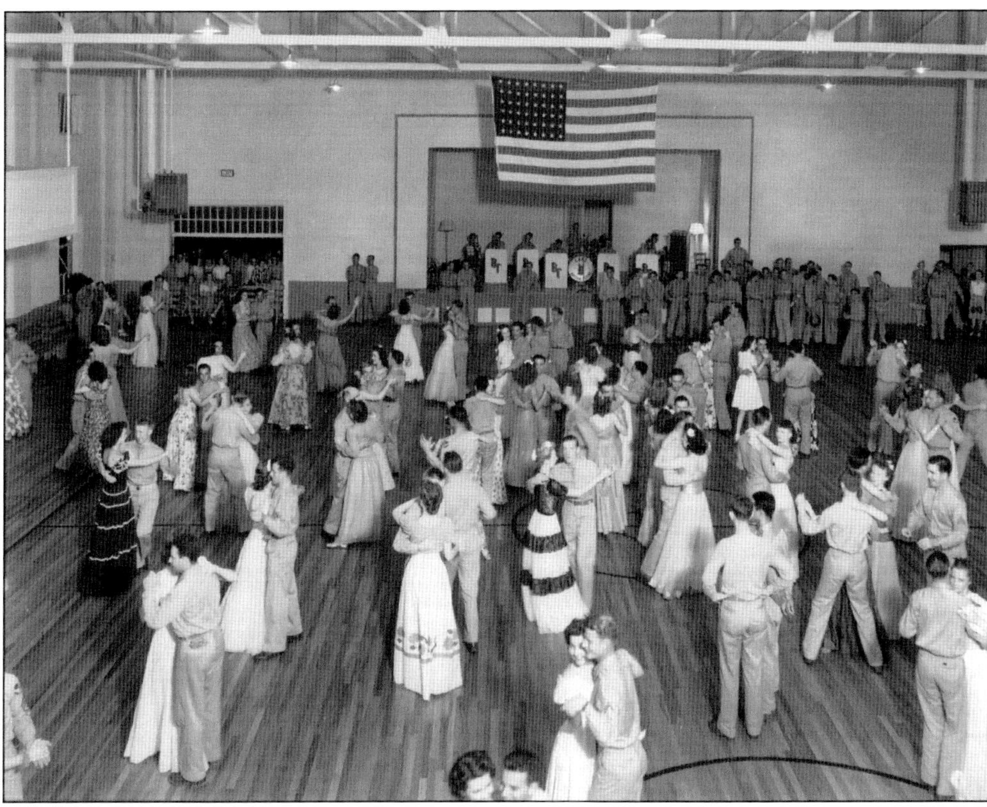

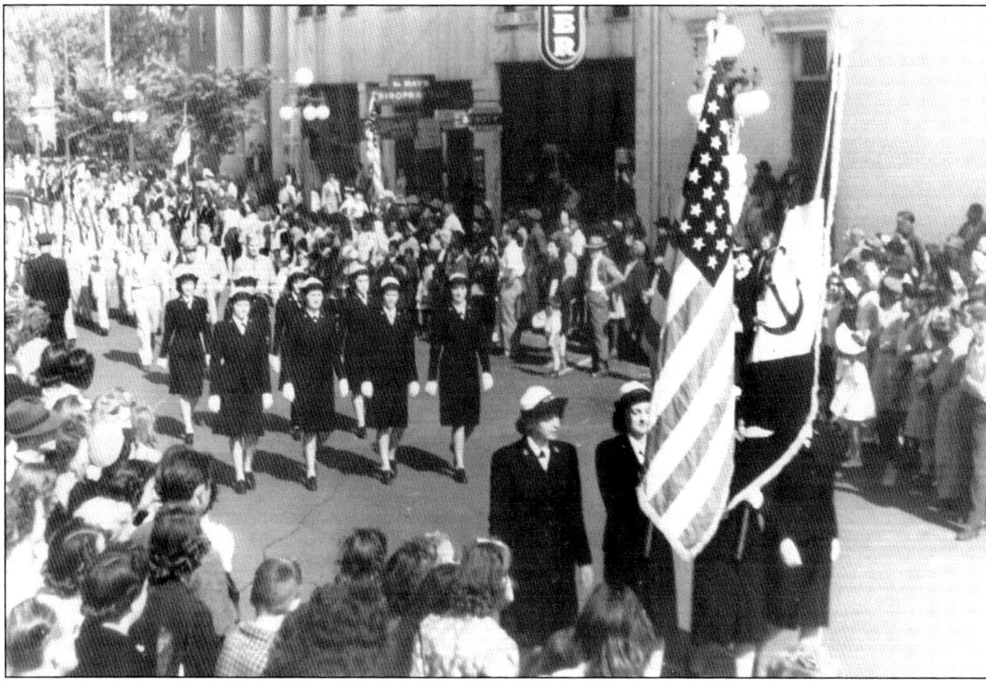

This image captures a World War II parade marching east on Main Street. Buildings in the background include, from left to right, the US Post Office, Ralph W. Hays Chiropractor, Vanity Beauty Shoppe, Higgins Jewelry Company (now part of the *Commercial Dispatch* building), and Ruth's Department Store.

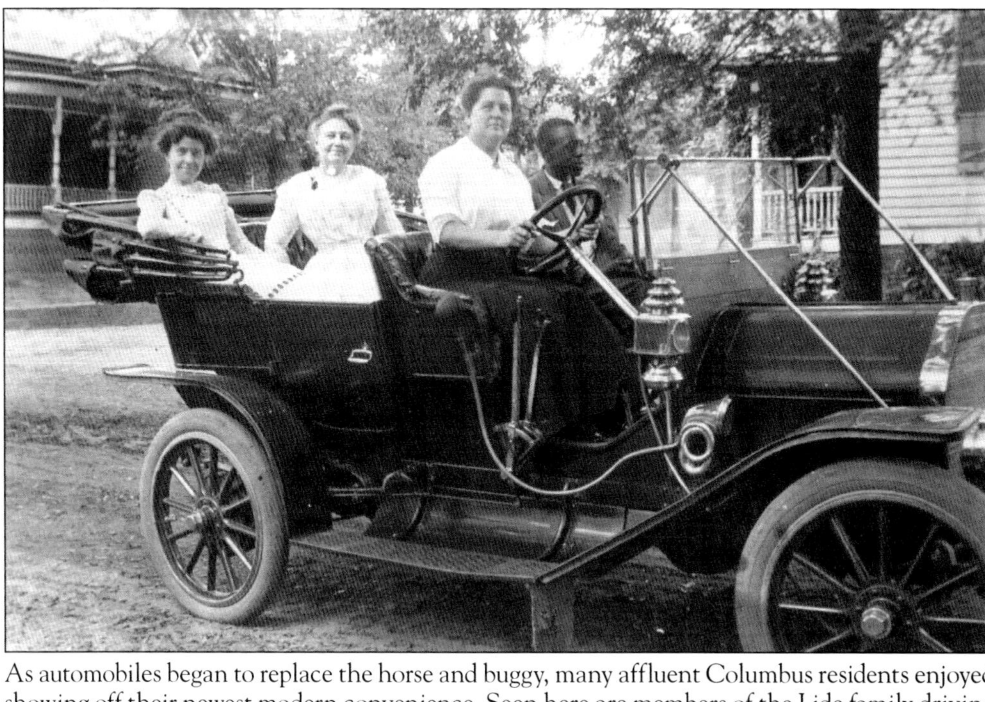

As automobiles began to replace the horse and buggy, many affluent Columbus residents enjoyed showing off their newest modern convenience. Seen here are members of the Lide family driving in Columbus sometime around 1910.

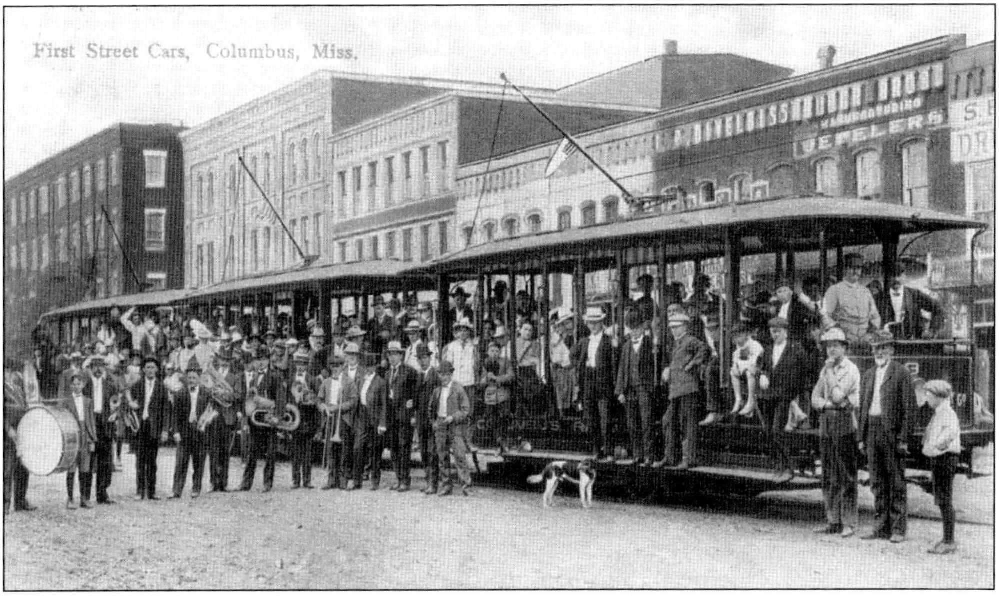

Streetcars came to Columbus in 1905 under the ownership of the Street Railway Company. The streetcars ran at a speed of 6–12 miles per hour and cost roughly 5¢ for a single ride. The streetcars were replaced in popularity by automobiles, and the company, which by then was the Columbus Railway Light and Power Company, dissolved in 1928. Below is the construction of the railway lines in July 1905.

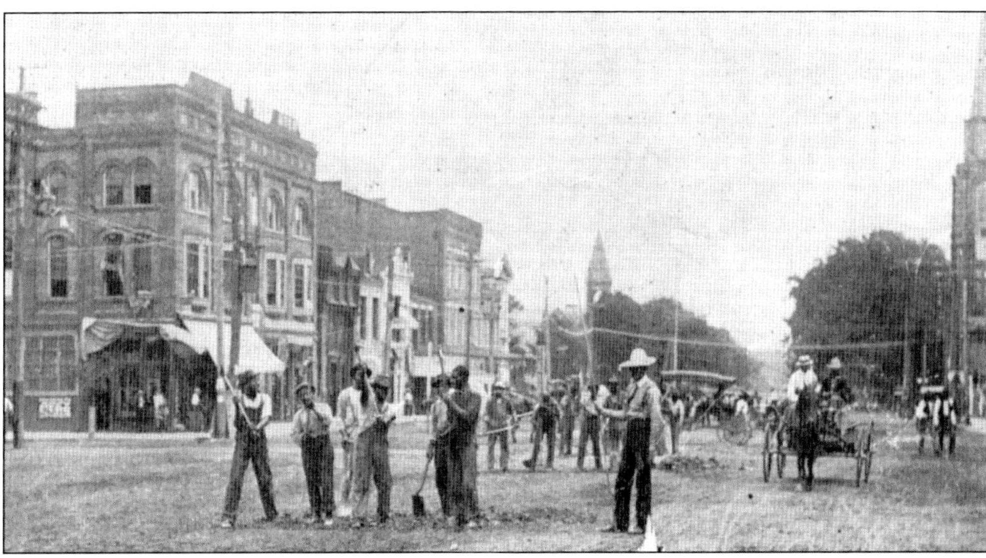

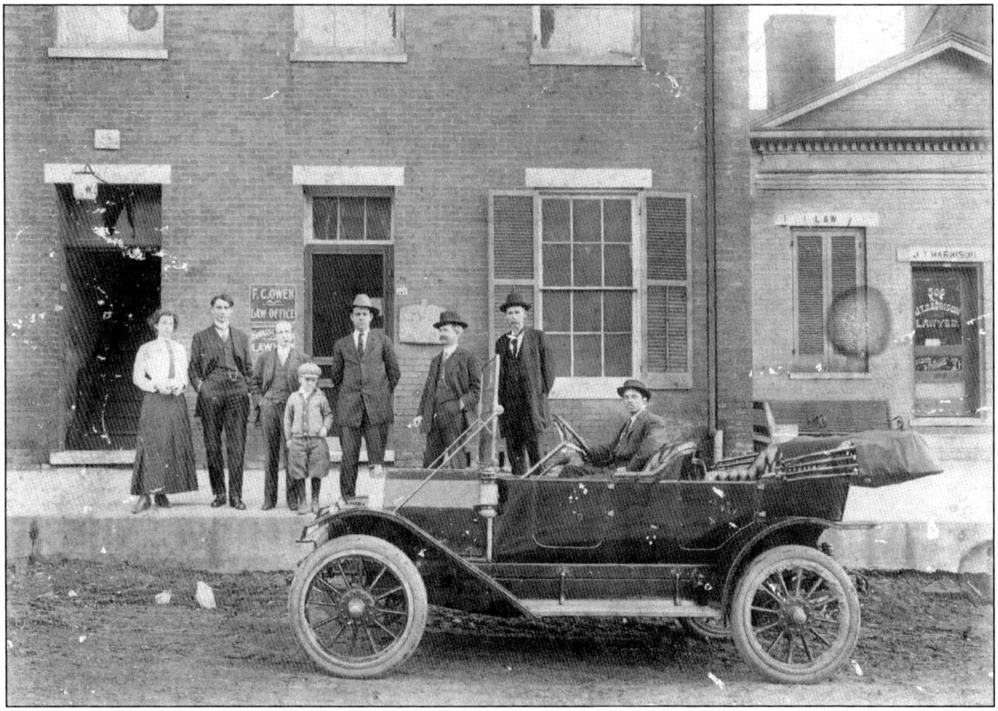

"Lawyer's Row" included the buildings along Second Avenue North between Fifth and Sixth Streets. It was referred to as Lawyer's Row because of the number of lawyers who occupied the buildings across the street from the Lowndes County Courthouse. The small building on the right was occupied by Judge James T. Harrison. Seen here around 1908 are Charles L. Garnett, standing second from the left, and, to his right, Frank C. Owen. Judge Jennings I. Sturdivant is second from the right, and the young boy in the center is Evans Sturdivant.

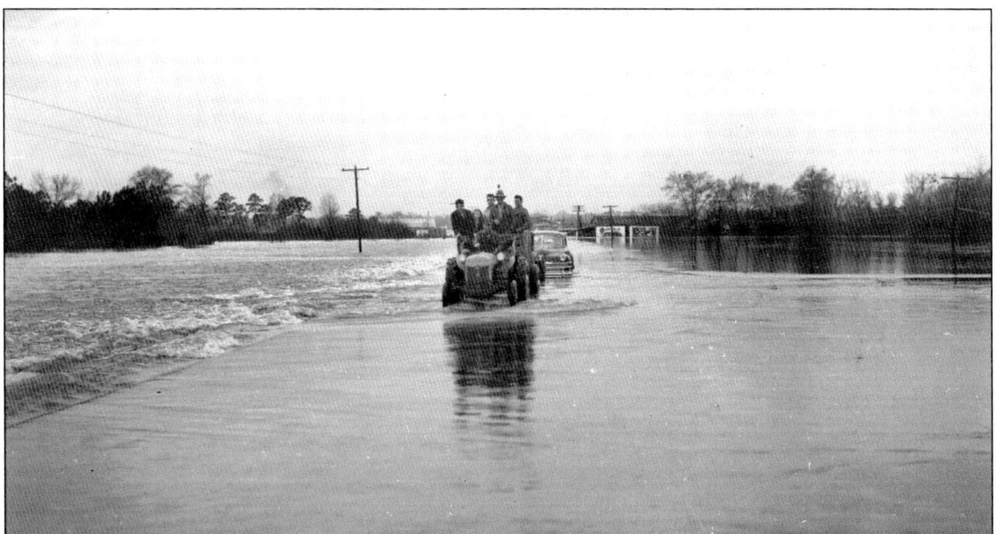

The Luxapallila River overflowed its banks in March 1951 and crested at 31.6 feet. In addition to flooding, temperatures dipped to 36 degrees. This image captures a tractor and car braving a trip through the shallow spill running across Highway 82.

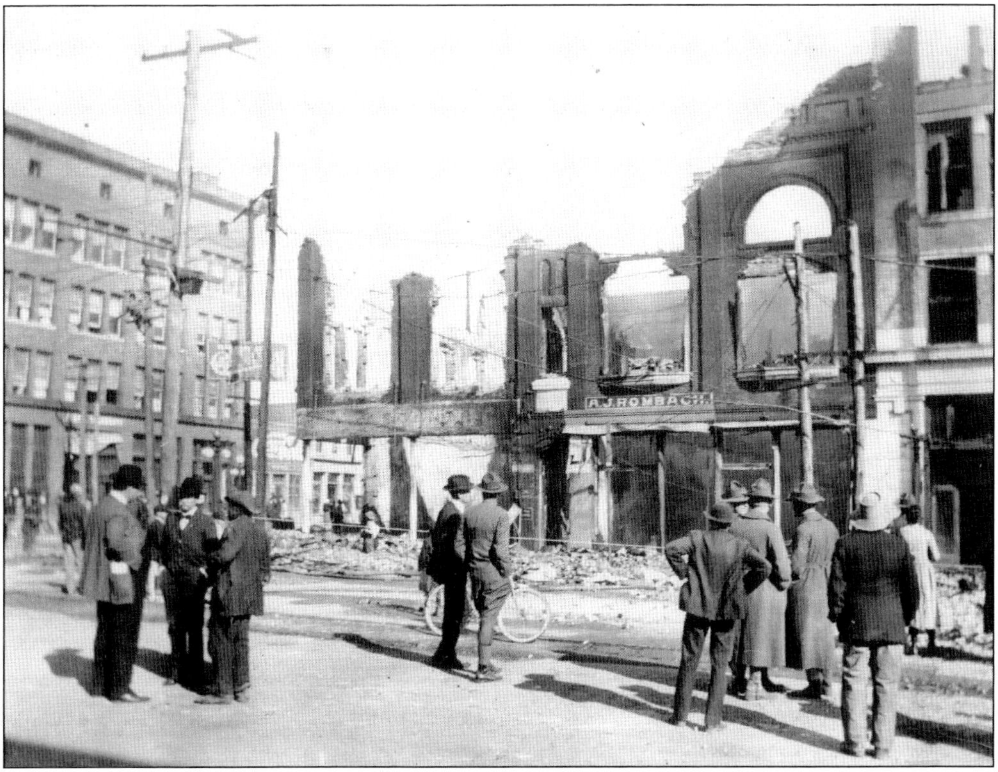

Columbus has been the victim of many fires over the course of its history. One such fire occurred on March 18, 1919. It began in the Burleson Barbershop, located on the southeast corner of Main and Market Streets, at 3:30 p.m. in the afternoon. Home to many businesses, including the Columbus Clothing Company, the three-story structure was completely destroyed. The six-story Columbus National Bank next door also caught fire and sustained damage (right). The bank, however, was rebuilt but only up to the first four stories.

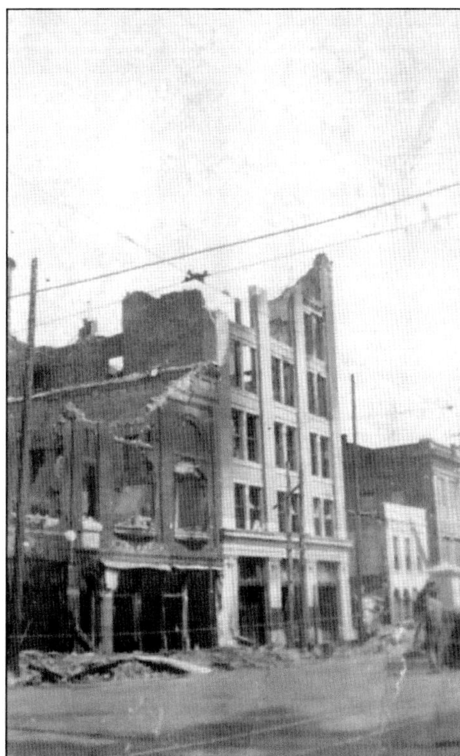

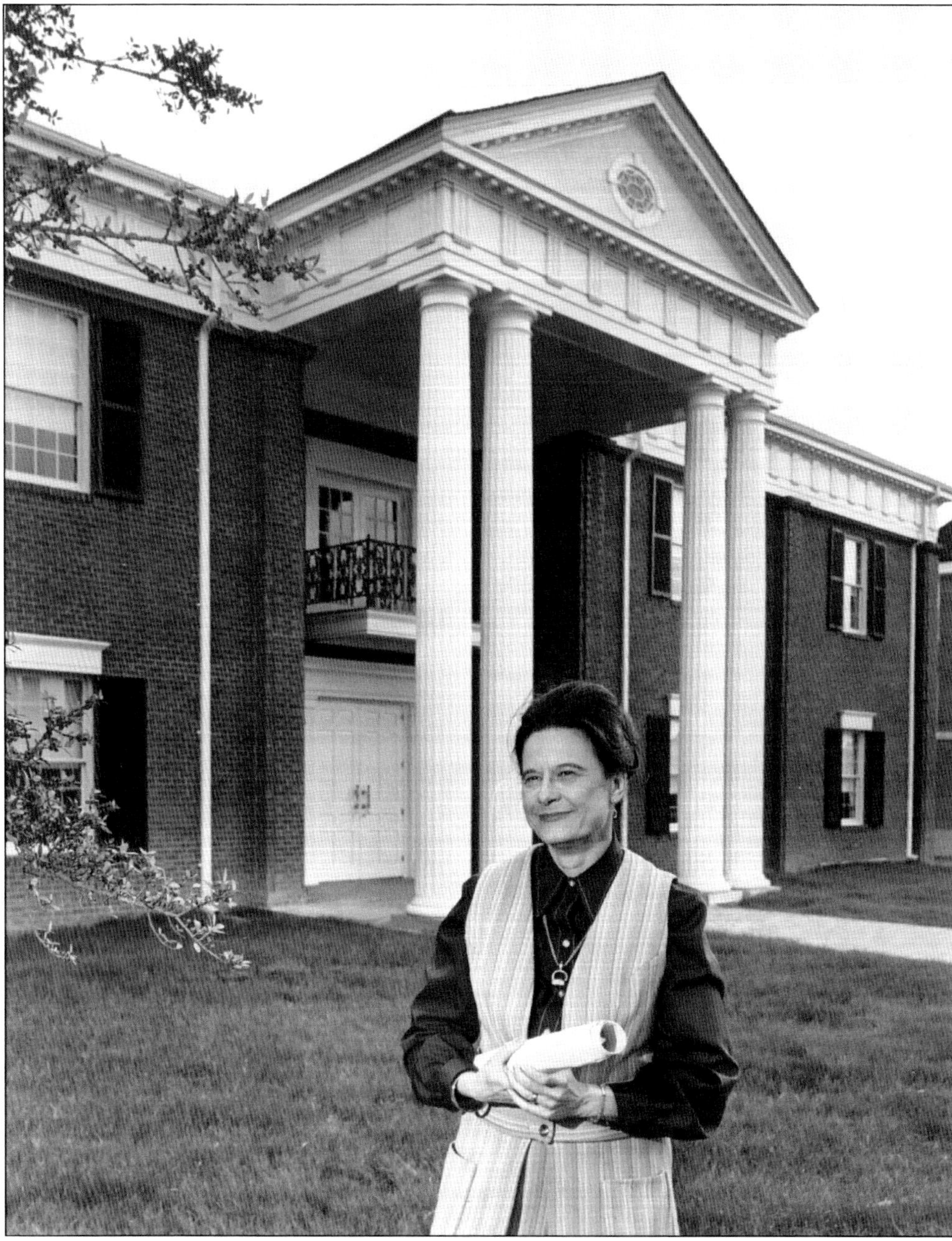

The history of a public library in Columbus stretches back to the 1800s. During this time, a library operated out of the Simon Loeb and Brother mercantile store and even city hall. The current organization dates to 1934, when the Works Progress Administration opened a public library with Grace Lawrence George as the first librarian. Over time, the library moved to various locations, including the former Stephen D. Lee High School Band Room. In 1958, branches in Artesia and Caledonia opened and Crawford joined the system in 1981. In 1960, Chebie A. Gaines Bateman (shown here) became Columbus librarian and then director in 1961, a position she maintained until 2004. It was because of Bateman's determination that the current building housing the public library in Columbus was completed in 1973. This building bears Bateman's name in her honor.

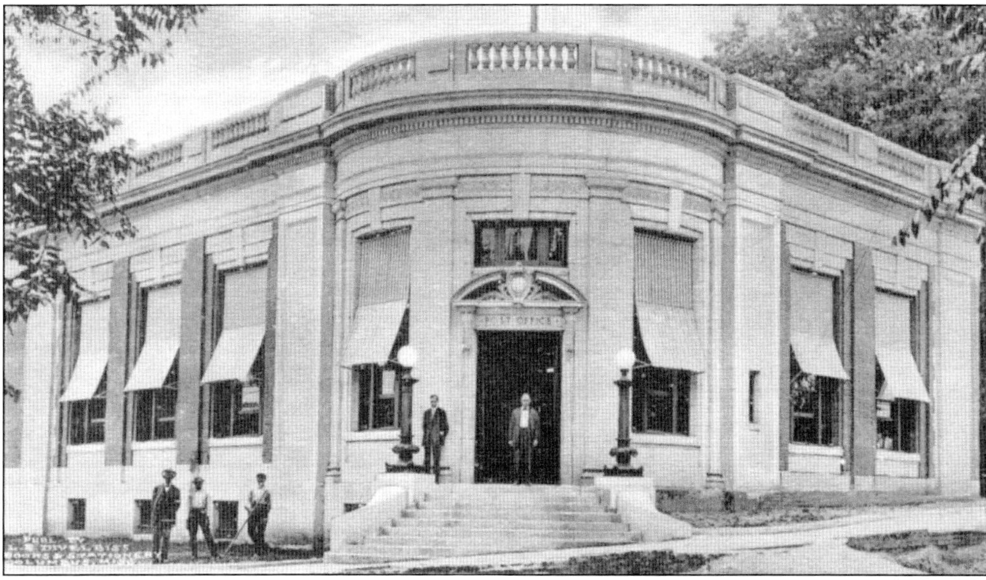

Prior to 1903, the Columbus Post Office operated out of the Gilmer Hotel. From 1903 to 1910, it was located in city hall. Then, the post office built its offices at 220 Second Avenue South (now the Columbus Light and Water Department). The cornerstone for the current downtown post office was laid in July 1938. The building was constructed on the former site of Cady Livery Stable on the corner of Main and Sixth Street South. This building also contains a mural painted by artist Beulah Bettersworth in 1939 on behalf of the Federal Works Agency.

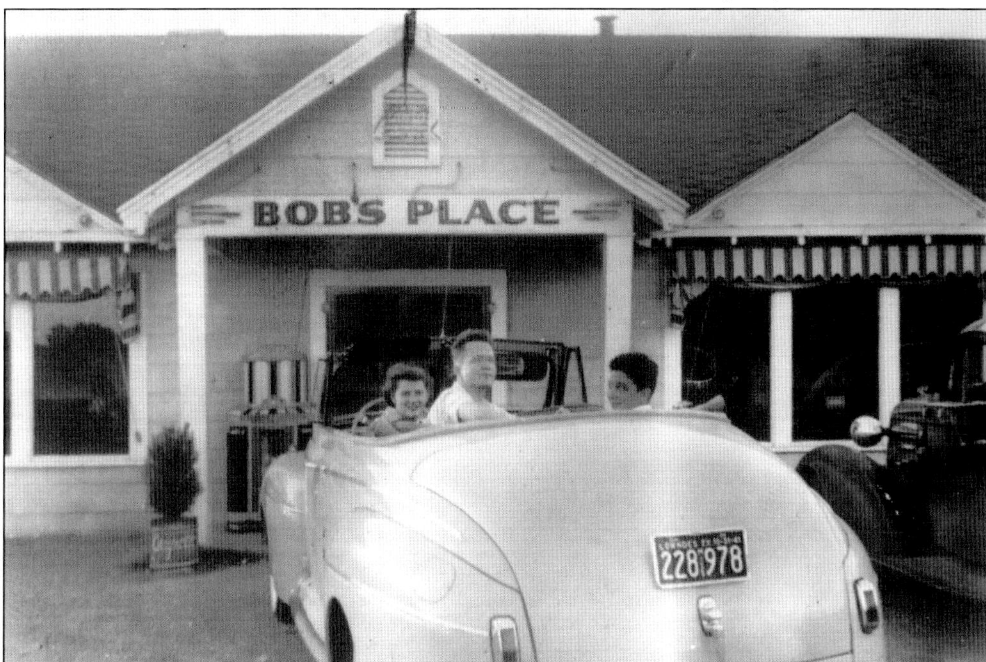

One popular hangout in Columbus was Bob's Place. Owned and operated by Robert William and Eva Ruth Thweatt, the restaurant was located on Highway 82 West. Seen here around 1940 are, from left to right, Marcella Billups, Gene Beard, and Jim William Cox.

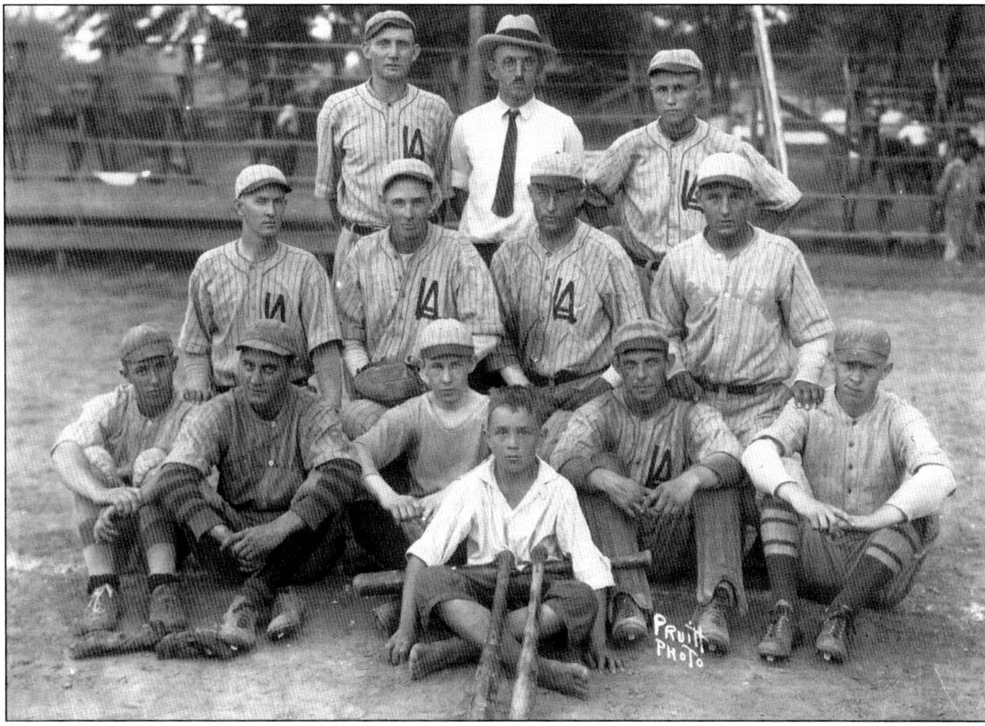

Columbus has a long history with the game of baseball. Seen here is the American Legion baseball team in the 1920s. Seated in front is bat boy Gala Curtiss. Members of the team are, from left to right, (first row) Archie Breast, Fred Propst, Ted Patton, Johnny Lipsey, and Leroy Wood; (second row) Leslie Wood, Bill Cooper, Henry Pope, and John Roberts; (third row) Red Campbell, Coach Bader, and Zam Pegues. (Courtesy of the Southern Historical Collection, Wilson Library, the University of North Carolina at Chapel Hill.)

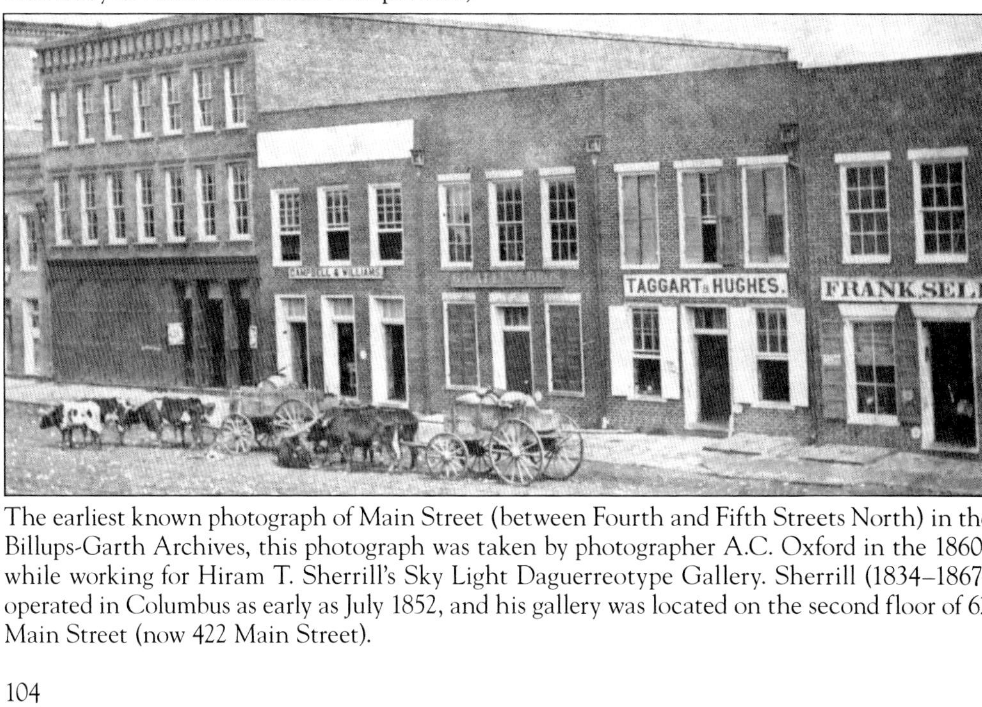

The earliest known photograph of Main Street (between Fourth and Fifth Streets North) in the Billups-Garth Archives, this photograph was taken by photographer A.C. Oxford in the 1860s while working for Hiram T. Sherrill's Sky Light Daguerreotype Gallery. Sherrill (1834–1867) operated in Columbus as early as July 1852, and his gallery was located on the second floor of 62 Main Street (now 422 Main Street).

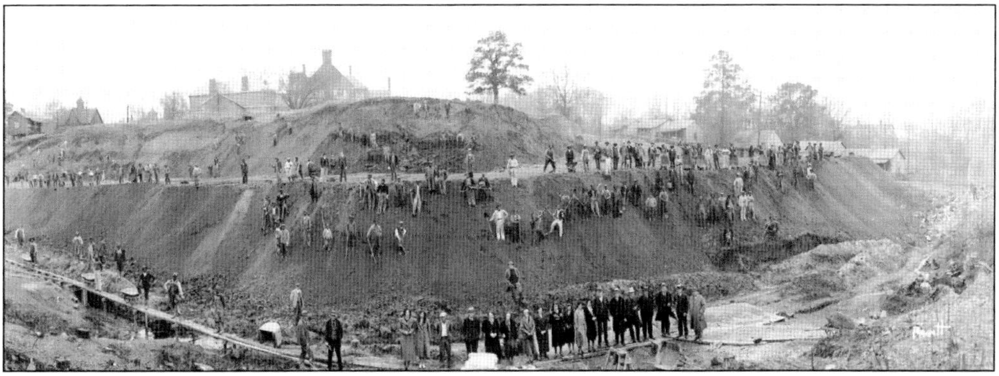

The Magnolia Bowl, located behind Franklin Academy, was constructed in 1933. When built, a valley was filled in with 25 feet of dirt and 40 old automobiles in order to create the field and stands. The playing field at Magnolia Bowl was renamed Willie B. Saunders Field on October 1, 1976. Saunders was coach at Stephen D. Lee High School and arranged for the creation of the bowl. The Magnolia Bowl witnessed its last official high school football game when the Columbus Falcons played on October 30, 1998. (Courtesy of the Southern Historical Collection, Wilson Library, the University of North Carolina at Chapel Hill.)

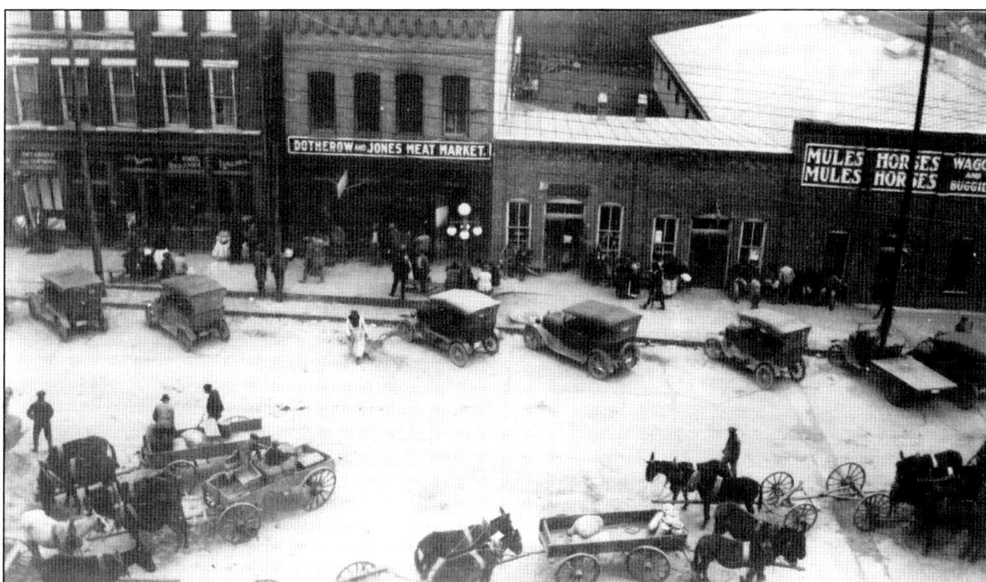

Many amateur photographers enjoyed capturing the city bustling around them, as in this image of Main Street South taken in March 1914 from the roof of the former Gilmer Hotel. Only the two structures on the left, the Masonic Building and the former Dotherow and Jones Meat Market, still exist.

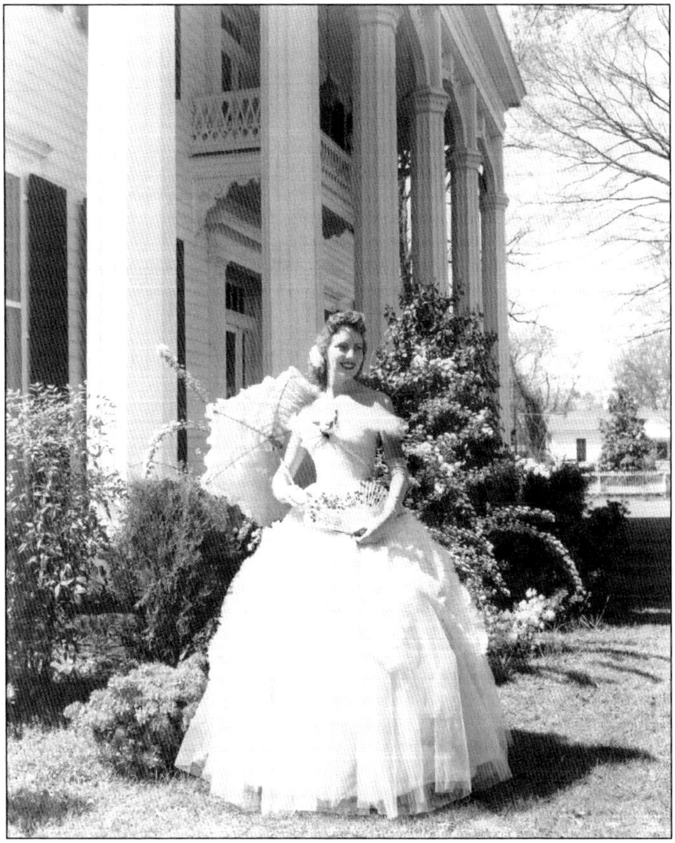

Columbus opened its doors for the first Pilgrimage in April 1940. A Pilgrimage includes a tour of the area's historic homes and gardens with guides dressed in period costume. A few of the first homes on the Pilgrimage included the Cedars, Shadowlawn, Whitehall, Camelia Place, and Whitearches. Seen here is Sandra Clayton Schweiger giving a tour of Errolton, built in 1848. The Pilgrimage continues to draw thousands of visitors to this day. (Courtesy of the Southern Historical Collection, Wilson Library, the University of North Carolina at Chapel Hill.)

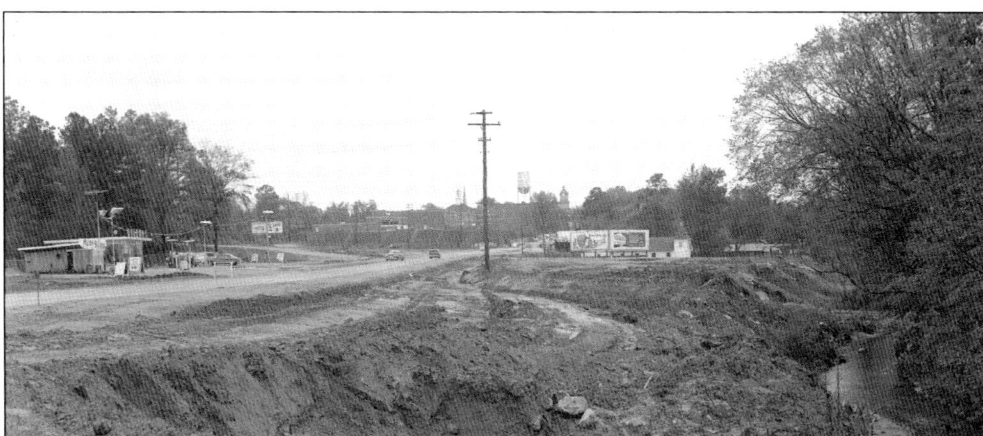

Taken on April 10, 1959, this image was taken on Highway 45 facing south towards downtown Columbus. It shows the Magnolia Bowl football stadium and the old water tower in the distance. It also shows Billups Service Station No. 3 (left) owned by Jason S. and John W. Billups. The area is now occupied by many businesses including Columbus Inns and Suites and The Little Dooey restaurant.

Seven

ENTERTAINMENT

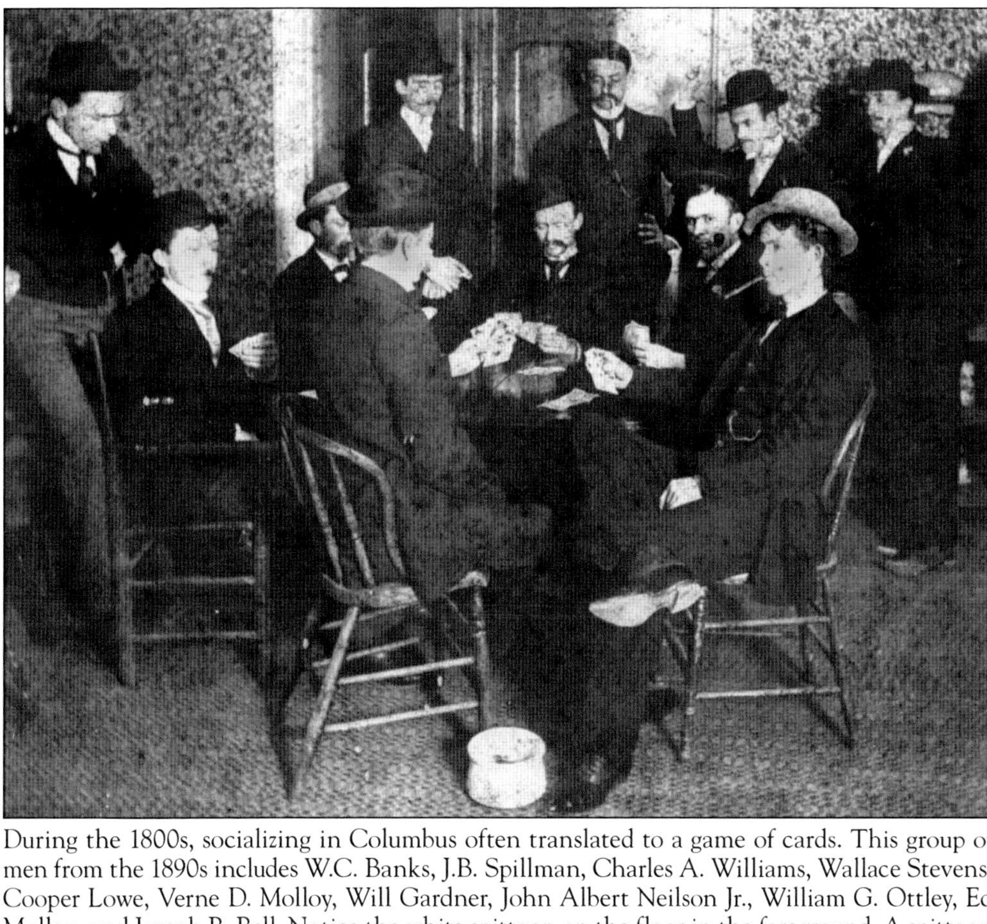

During the 1800s, socializing in Columbus often translated to a game of cards. This group of men from the 1890s includes W.C. Banks, J.B. Spillman, Charles A. Williams, Wallace Stevens, Cooper Lowe, Verne D. Molloy, Will Gardner, John Albert Neilson Jr., William G. Ottley, Ed Mullen, and Joseph B. Bell. Notice the white spittoon on the floor in the foreground. A spittoon is used for disposing of one's chewing or dipping tobacco by spitting into the receptacle.

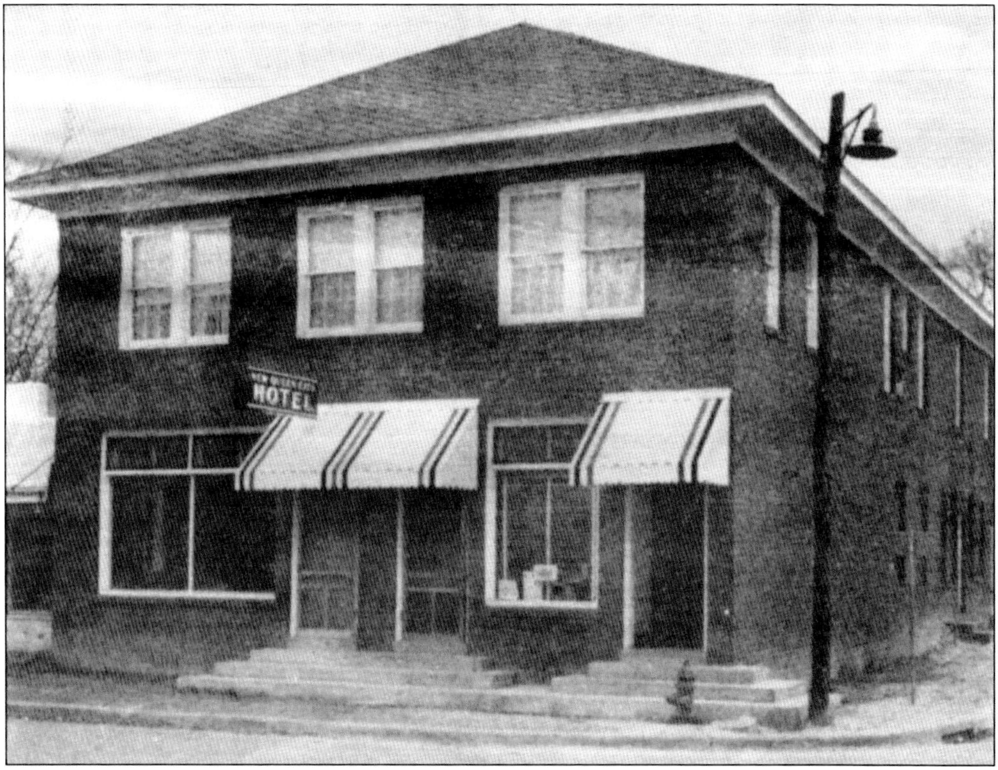

The Queen City Hotel, formerly located on the corner of Seventh Avenue and Fifteenth Street North, stood at the center of African American life and entertainment in Columbus. Built by Robert Walker in 1914, the hotel was renovated by Ed and Bessie Bush and reopened in 1948. Major-league baseball players Jackie Robinson and Don Newcombe stayed at the hotel. Musicians, such as Count Basie, Louis Armstrong, B.B. King, and Little Richard, also stayed at the hotel when they performed nearby at either the Savoy Room or the Blue Room.

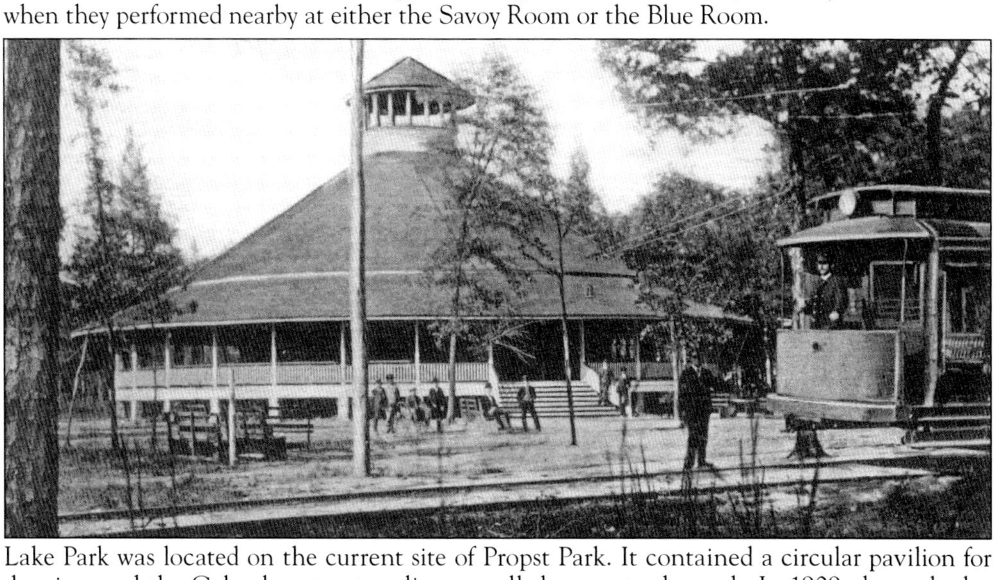

Lake Park was located on the current site of Propst Park. It contained a circular pavilion for dancing, and the Columbus streetcar line ran all the way to the park. In 1909, the park also featured an Airdome with "picture shows" from Vaudette's Theatre.

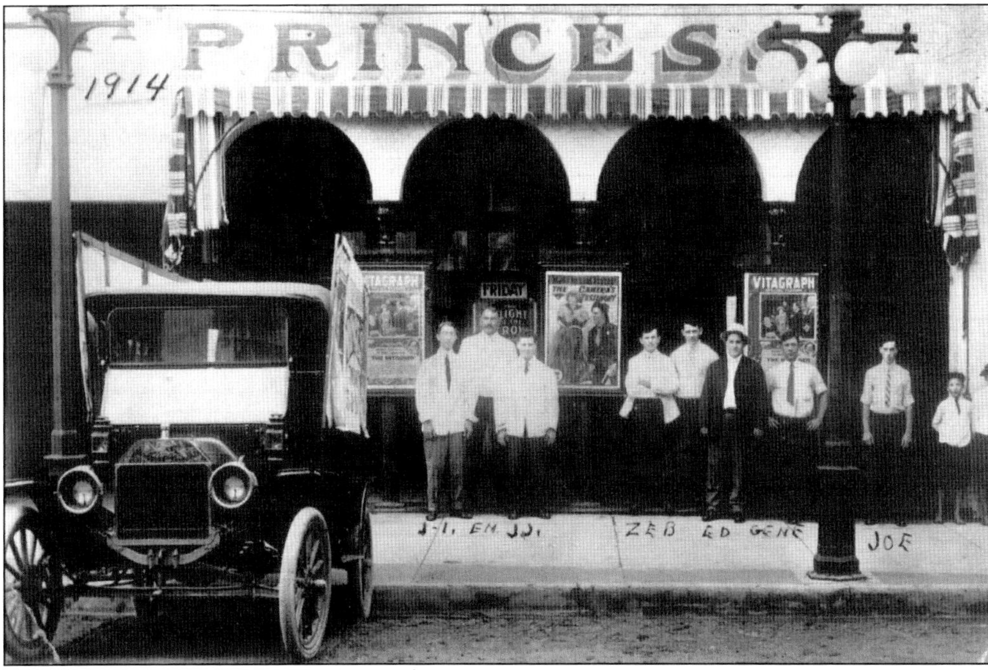

Ed Kuykendall first operated the Princess Airdome before opening his first indoor theater, seen here, located on Fifth Street North directly behind the present-day Rosenzweig Arts Center. By June 1925, he opened the Princess Theatre at its current location on Fifth Street South. Kuykendall was president of both the Mississippi Theater Owners Association and the Motion Picture Theater Owners of America. Standing fourth from the left is Zeb Therne, sixth is Ed Kuykendall, seventh is Eugene Bearden, and eighth is Joe Wood.

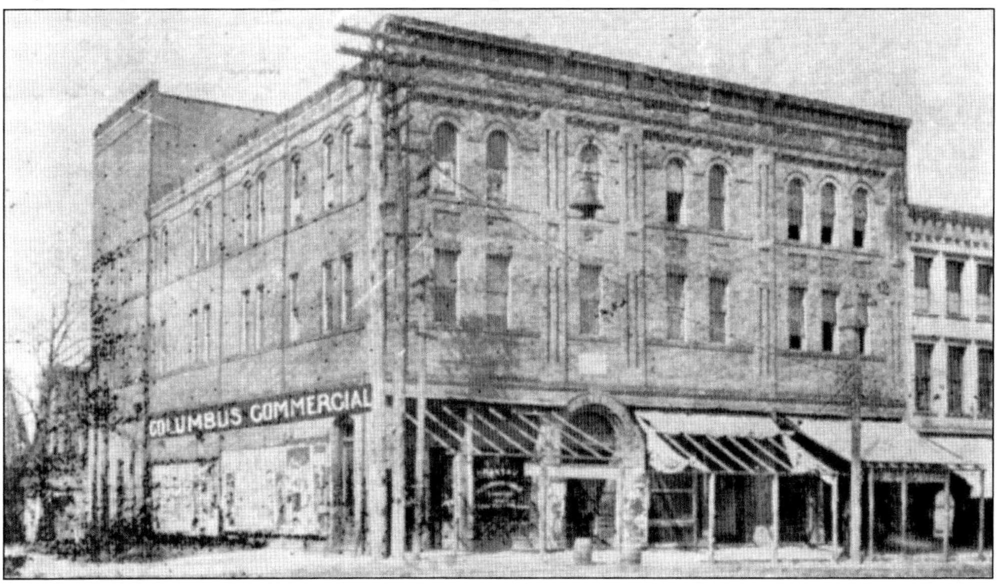

W.N. Puckett built the Columbus Opera House in 1897. It featured plays, operas, vaudeville shows, minstrels, movies, and talkies. By 1902, the house was leased and managed by Thomas J. Locke Jr. The building was later converted into a movie theater, called the Varsity Theatre, which burned on April 9, 1978.

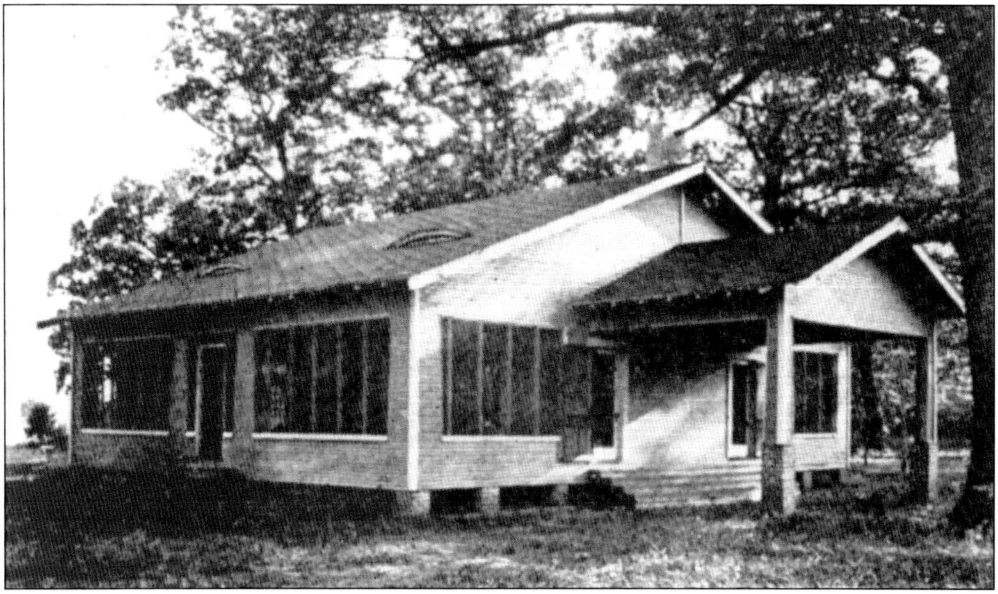

The Magowah Gun and Country Club, south of Columbus, is a favorite spot for many locals to enjoy skeet shooting and barbecue. Originally planned as a birthday picnic around 1906, twenty acres of Collier Hardy's land were donated for the project. It included a barbecue pit, a lake for fishing and swimming, a tournament tract, and later a clubhouse. The name was chosen from the creek that ran through part of the Hardy plantation.

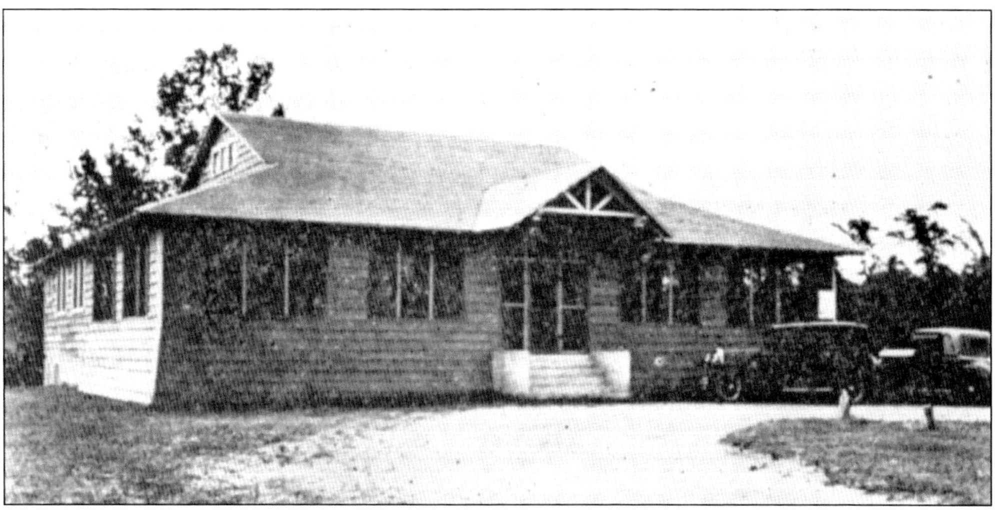

The Columbus Country Club dates back to 1924 and was established to promote the cultivation of social interactions, games, and physical exercises among its members. The club consisted of 100 acres on Military Road and included a golf course, swimming pool, clubhouse, and tennis court. The clubhouse, or assembly hall (above), was used for events such as dances and receptions.

Eight

Homes

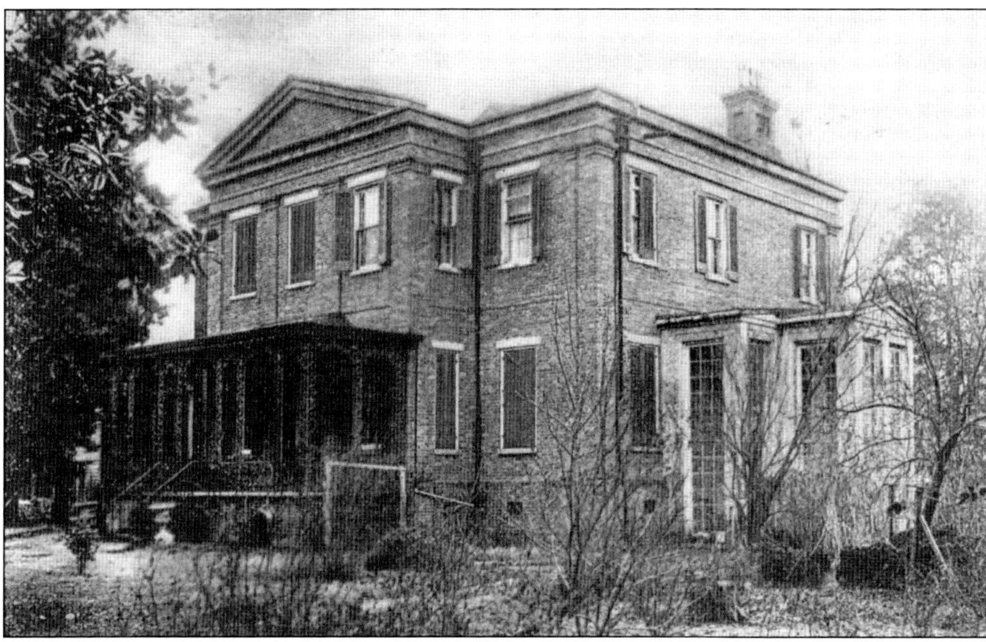

The Stephen D. Lee Home was built in 1847 by Maj. Thomas Garton Blewett and originally consisted of the entire city block. After Maj. Blewett's death on May 2, 1871, the property passed to his daughter, Regina Harrison. Harrison's daughter, also named Regina, married Stephen D. Lee, founding president of the Agricultural and Mechanical College (Mississippi State University). In 1909, President Taft visited the home during his trip to Columbus. Beginning in 1918, the Stephen D. Lee High School, built next door, used the house for home economics and a cafeteria. Located at 316 Seventh Street North, the home is now open for tours of both the house and the Florence McLeod Hazard Museum on the second floor. The Stephen D. Lee Home is listed in the National Register of Historic Places and is a Mississippi Landmark.

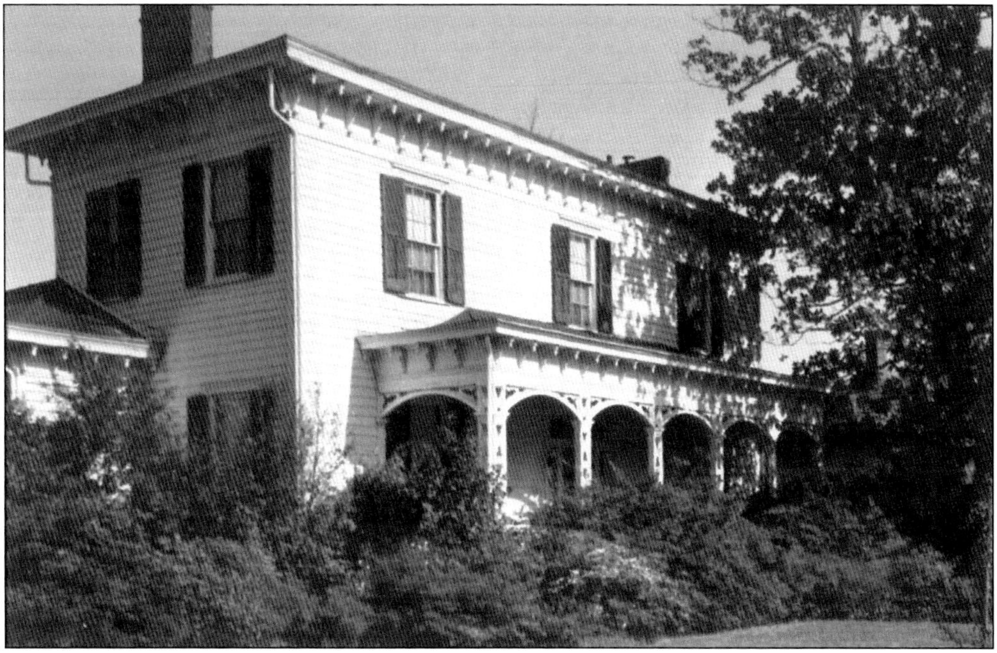

The Amzi Love House was built by Maj. Amzi Love for his bride, Edith Wallace, in 1848. It combines Greek and Italianate architectural designs and is located at 305 Seventh Street South. The home has remained in the family for seven generations and open to visitors of the Columbus Pilgrimage for over 70 years. The home is open for tours and is listed in the National Register of Historic Places.

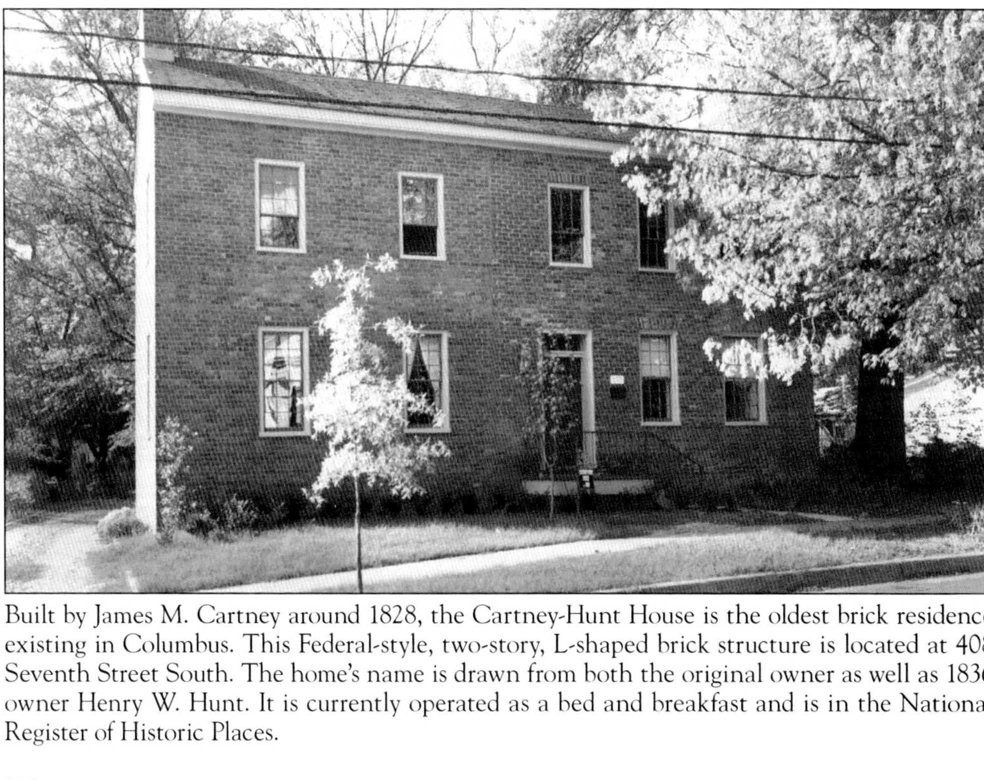

Built by James M. Cartney around 1828, the Cartney-Hunt House is the oldest brick residence existing in Columbus. This Federal-style, two-story, L-shaped brick structure is located at 408 Seventh Street South. The home's name is drawn from both the original owner as well as 1836 owner Henry W. Hunt. It is currently operated as a bed and breakfast and is in the National Register of Historic Places.

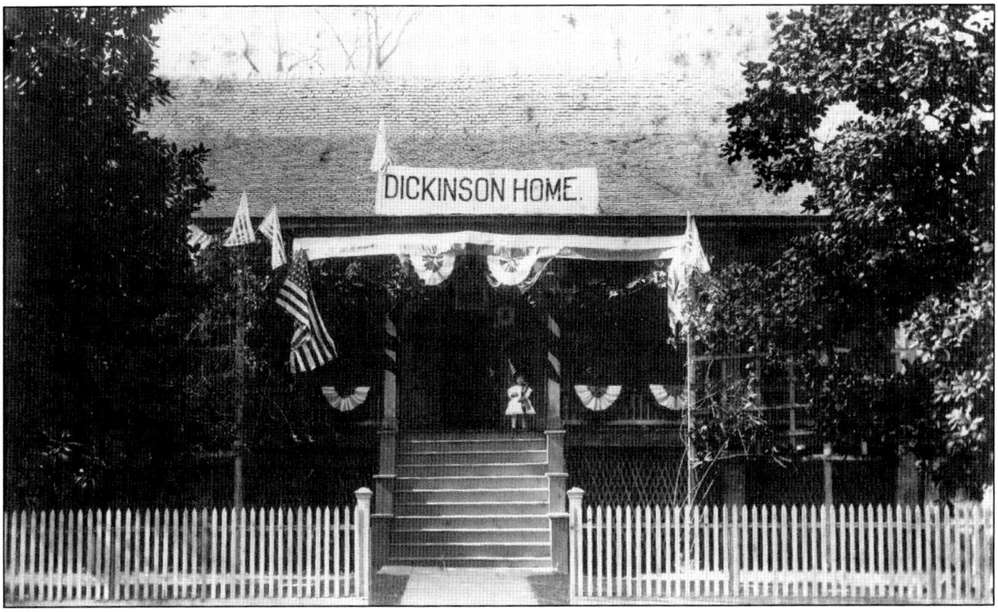

The Craven-Dickinson-Estes house, built around 1840, is shown here decorated for the arrival of Pres. Howard Taft on November 2, 1909. The house was the birthplace of Jacob McGavock Dickinson, secretary of war during President Taft's administration (1909–1912). Located at 221 Seventh Street North, the house was torn down in the mid-1960s to build a physician's complex.

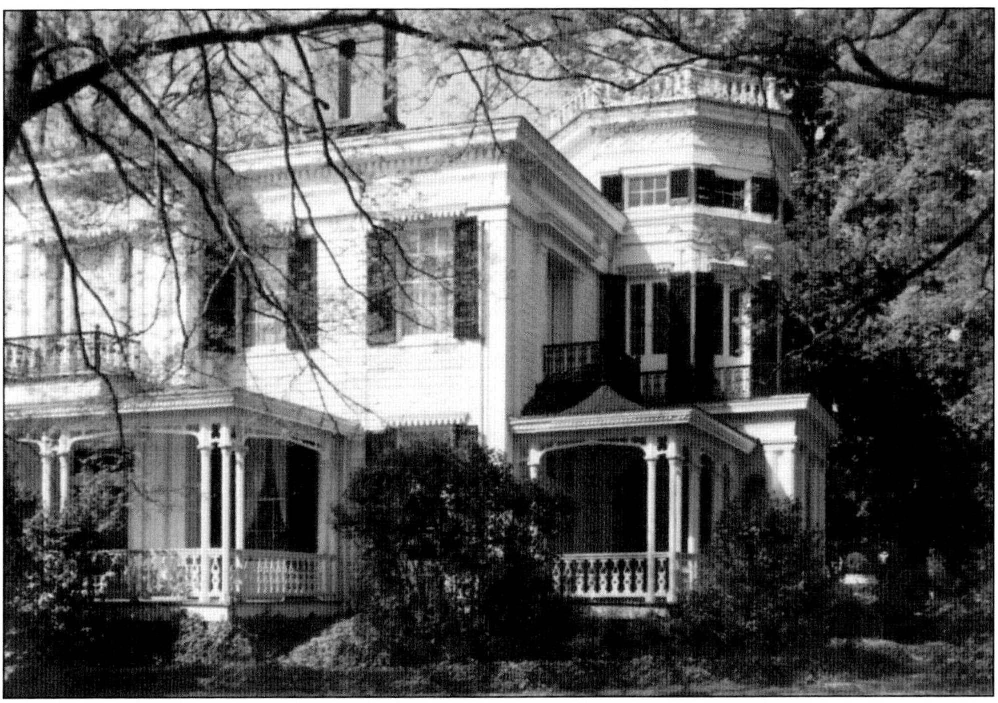

White Arches was built around 1857 by planter and politician Gen. Jeptha Vining Harris. The home combines Gothic, Greek Revival, and Italianate architectural elements and has a central octagonal tower with an observatory on the top floor. Located at 122 Seventh Avenue South, it is in the National Register of Historic Places.

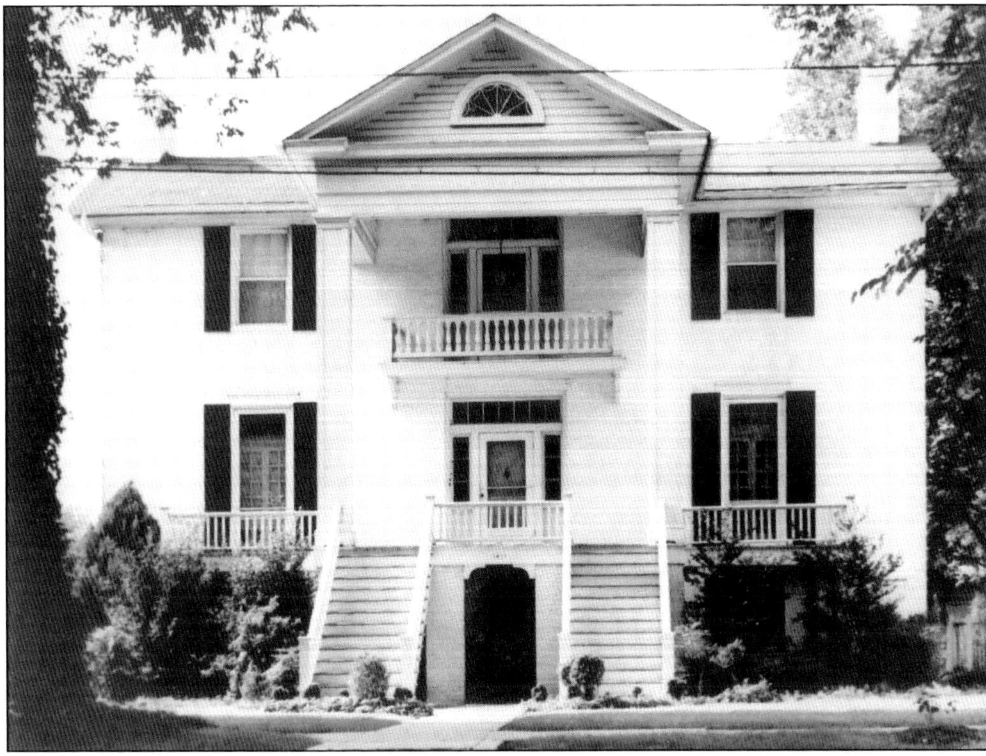

The Kenneth-Gatchell House was built around 1829 by Gen. J.D. Montgomery on acreage reaching all the way to Alabama. The three-story structure contains a double exterior staircase. During the Civil War, it was used as a prison. The home, located at 1411 College Street, was named after 1945 owners Kenneth P. and Alice Gatchell. It is listed in the National Register of Historic Places.

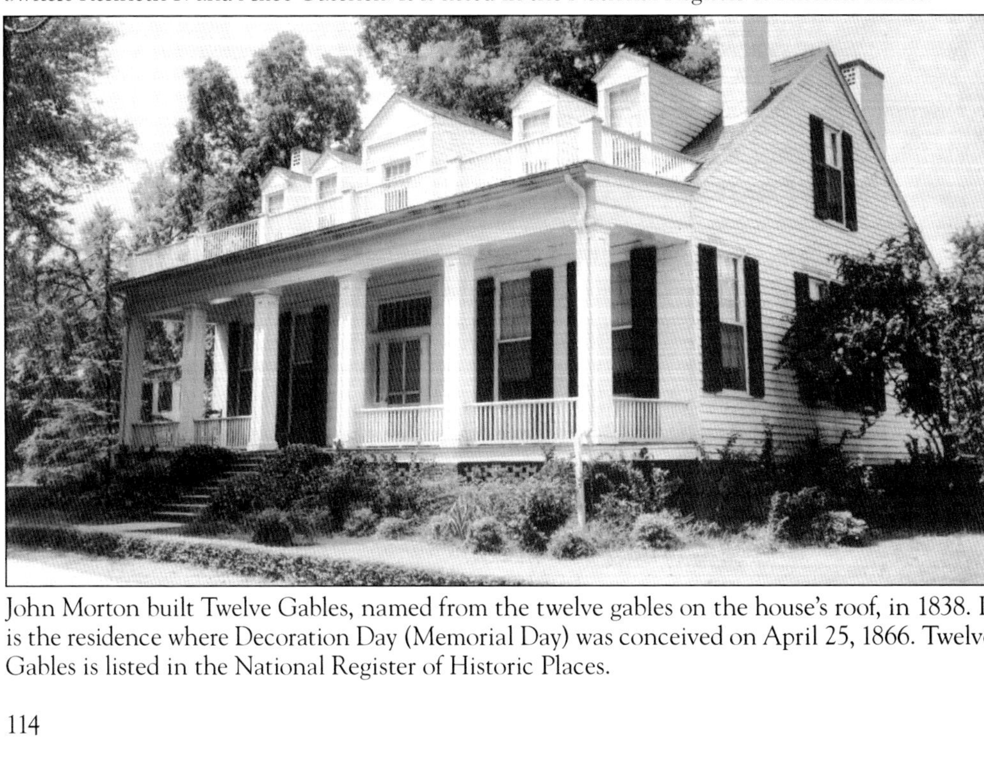

John Morton built Twelve Gables, named from the twelve gables on the house's roof, in 1838. It is the residence where Decoration Day (Memorial Day) was conceived on April 25, 1866. Twelve Gables is listed in the National Register of Historic Places.

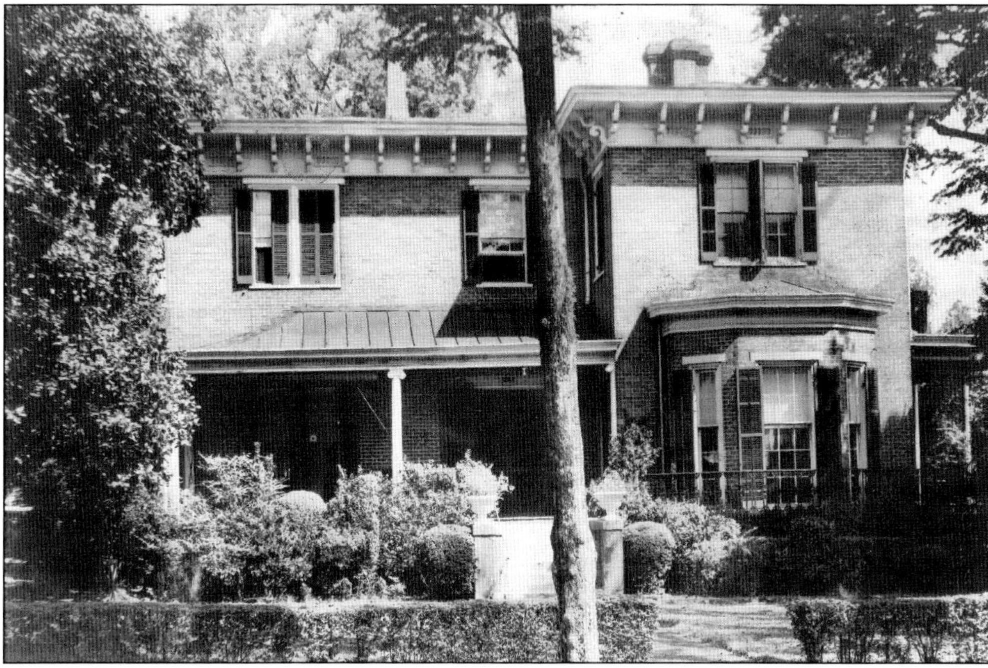

Built by Gov. James Whitfield in the 1860s, Hamilton Hall was a wedding gift for his son Henry and his bride, Laura Young. The architecture is of Italian design, and it contained its own water system, speaking tubes, and bell system. It was named Hamilton Hall after owners H. Coleman and Anna W. Hamilton and is listed in the National Register of Historic Places.

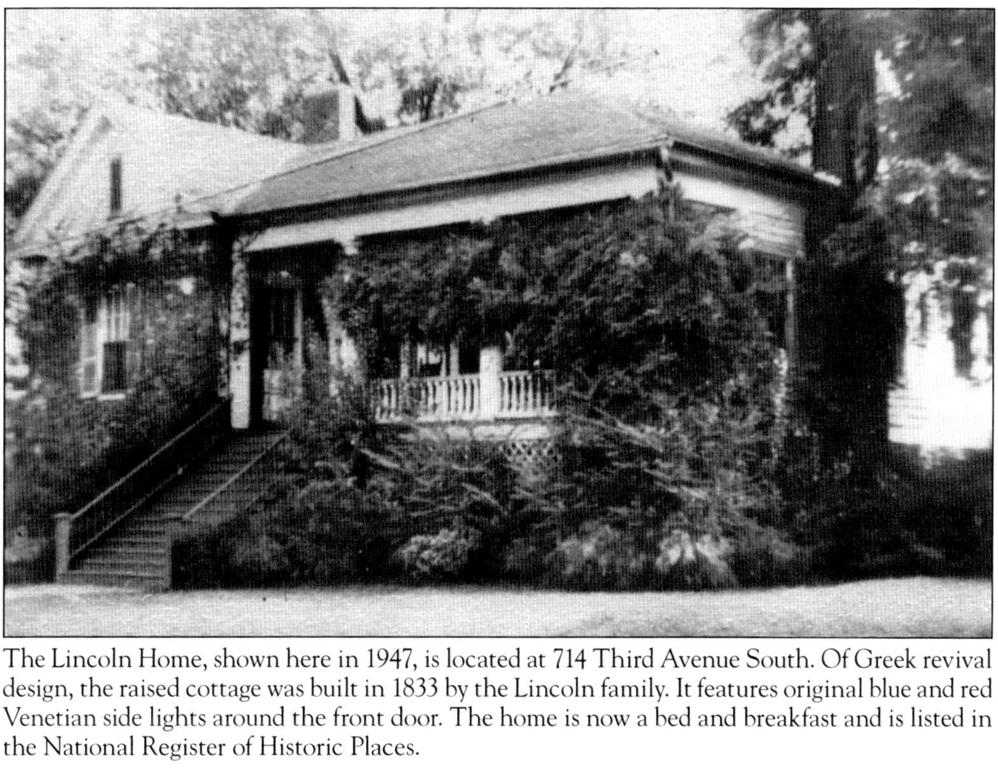

The Lincoln Home, shown here in 1947, is located at 714 Third Avenue South. Of Greek revival design, the raised cottage was built in 1833 by the Lincoln family. It features original blue and red Venetian side lights around the front door. The home is now a bed and breakfast and is listed in the National Register of Historic Places.

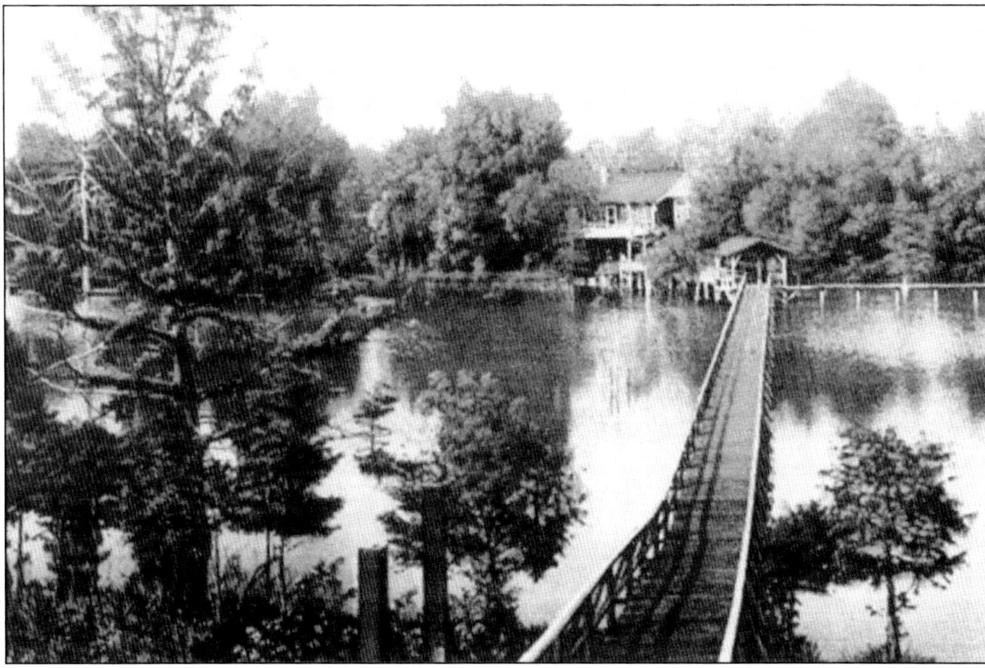

Thomas J. Locke Jr. owned and operated T.J. Locke & Son, a wholesale grocery business. In 1921, he purchased lake property that included a clubhouse, boathouse, pier, and pavilion. He later built cages to house a growing zoo that included bears, lions, deer, camels, a panther, and more. "Locke's Zoological Gardens" was open to the public on Sundays during the warm months of the year.

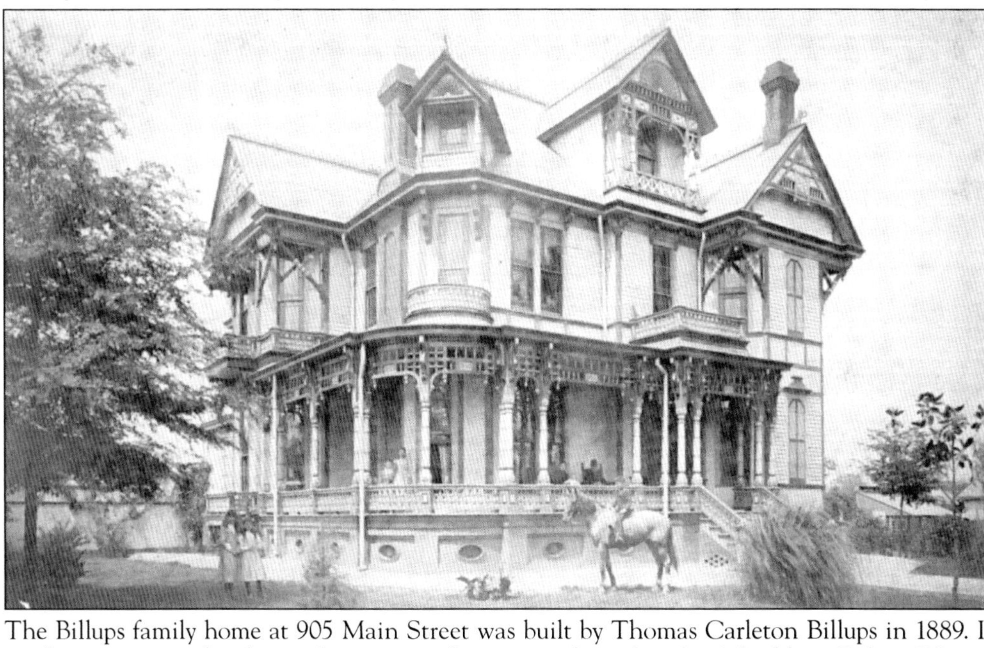

The Billups family home at 905 Main Street was built by Thomas Carleton Billups in 1889. It was home to many family members prior to being torn down for a bank building. Robert Edward Johnston, long-time secretary of the Columbus Chamber of Commerce, married Billups's daughter, Elizabeth "Bessie" Billups, in 1899 and resided in the house. The last family members to live there were Dr. John Richards and Marcella Billups Richards.

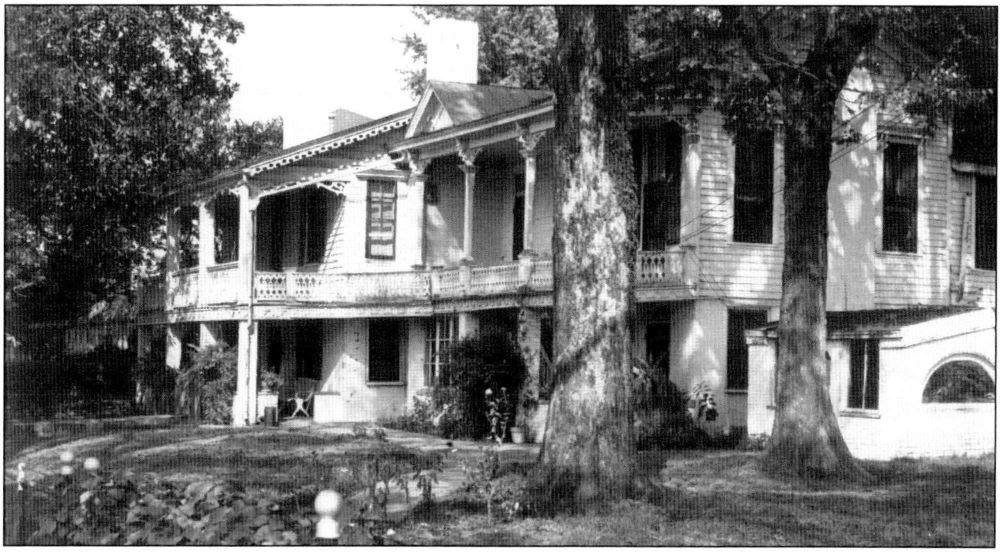

Isaac and Thomas Williams built The Haven in 1843. The home is unique because the Williams brothers were free African Americans prior to the Civil War. Located at 315 Second Avenue North, the raised cottage was enlarged in the 1870s by William Steen. It was named by owners Frank and Esther Troskey and is listed in the National Register of Historic Places.

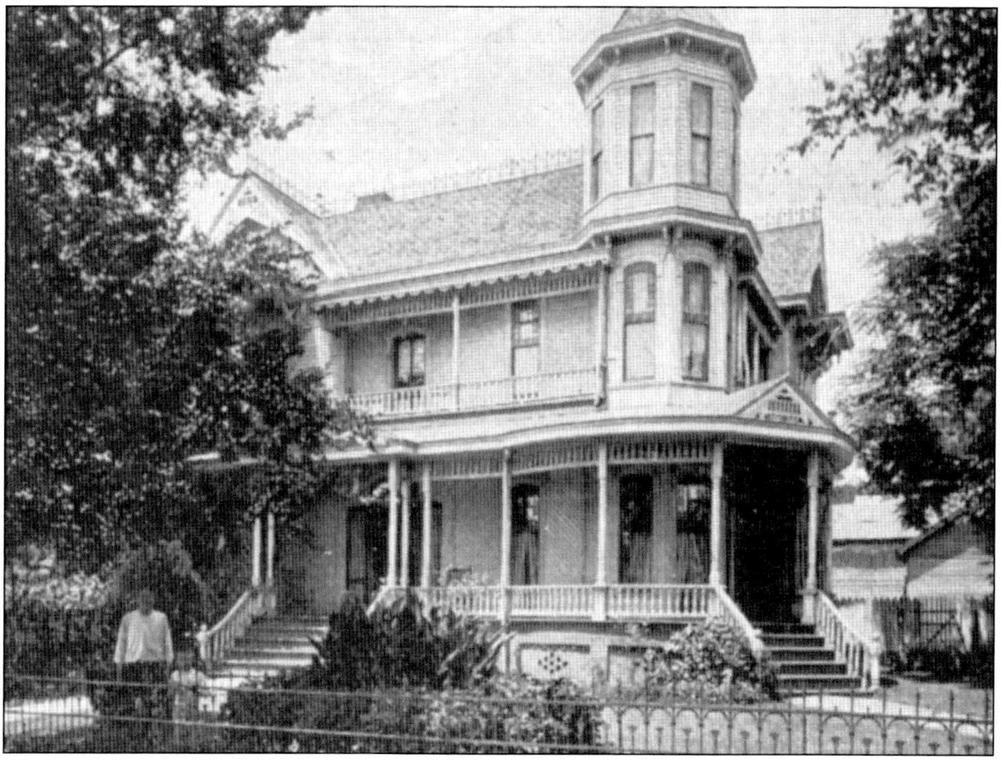

The Victorian house known as the Painted Lady, seen here in 1905, was built by Thomas O. Burris in 1892. Burris, who died in 1922, worked as a dry goods merchant, president of a cotton mill, and a banker. In 2003, the home was renovated and is now operated as a bed and breakfast. The Painted Lady is listed in the National Register of Historic Places.

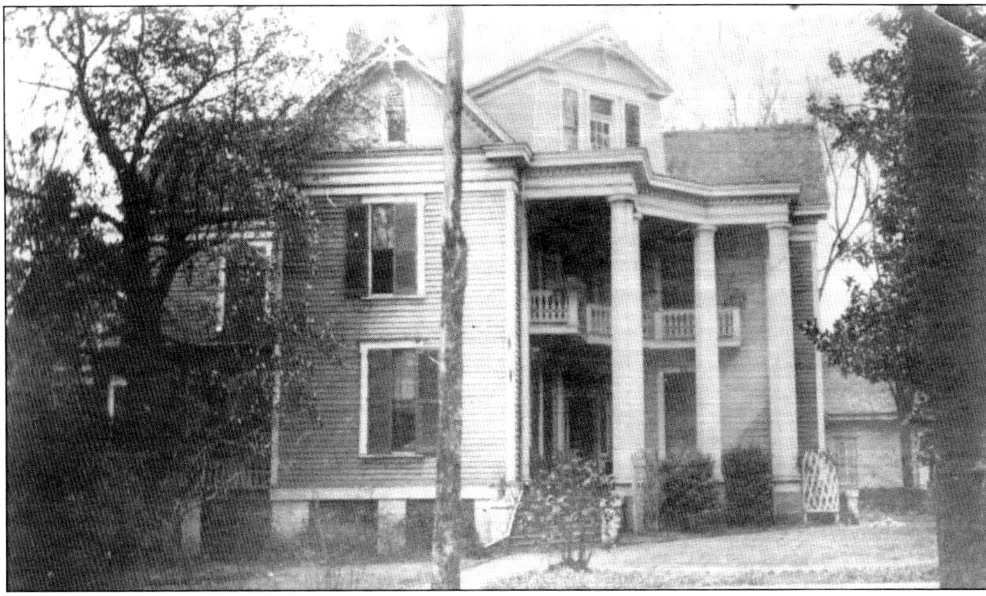

Built in 1854 for Gov. James Whitfield, Snowdoun was purchased by Maj. John M. Billups in 1864. The home, located on the corner of Third Avenue North and Ninth Street, contains a distinct octagonal front porch. While a candidate for US Senate, Jefferson Davis (the president of the Confederate States of America) spoke to a crowd of Columbians from a balcony window. The home is in the National Register of Historic Places.

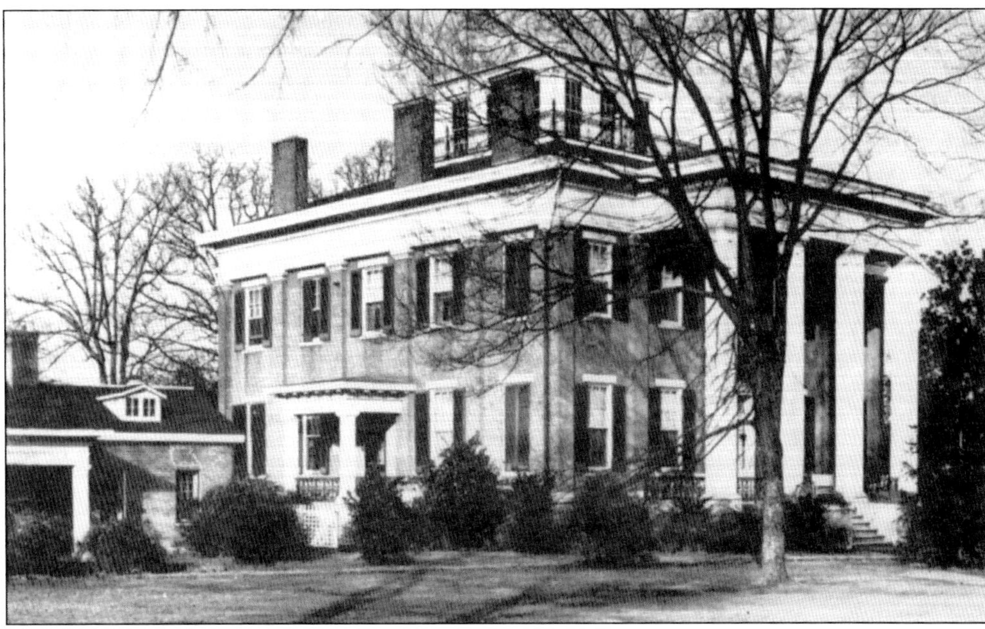

Built by architect James S. Lull in 1852 and encompassing an entire city block, Riverview was used as a townhouse by Col. Charles McLaran. McLaran was one of the founders of the First National Bank of Columbus. The house, located at 514 Second Street South, is three stories, with the fourth floor containing a 19-foot-square cupola. The home is in the National Register of Historic Places.

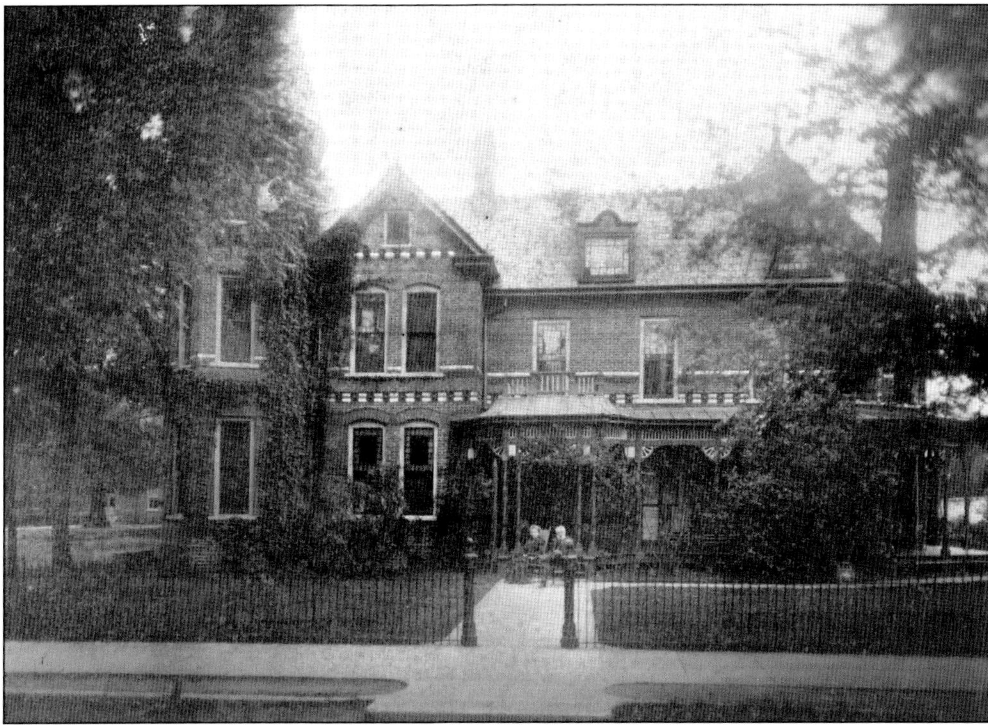

The Garth house was located at 603 Third Avenue North. A portion of the home, built by John Moore, was made of logs and dated back to 1839. Moore's grandson Lt. Gov. William H. Sims, remodeled the entire house. In 1899, Col. J.W. Garth purchased the home. He and his wife, Virginia Manning Garth, are seen sitting in front of the house. In 1963, it was sold to the city and razed to build a playground for Franklin Academy.

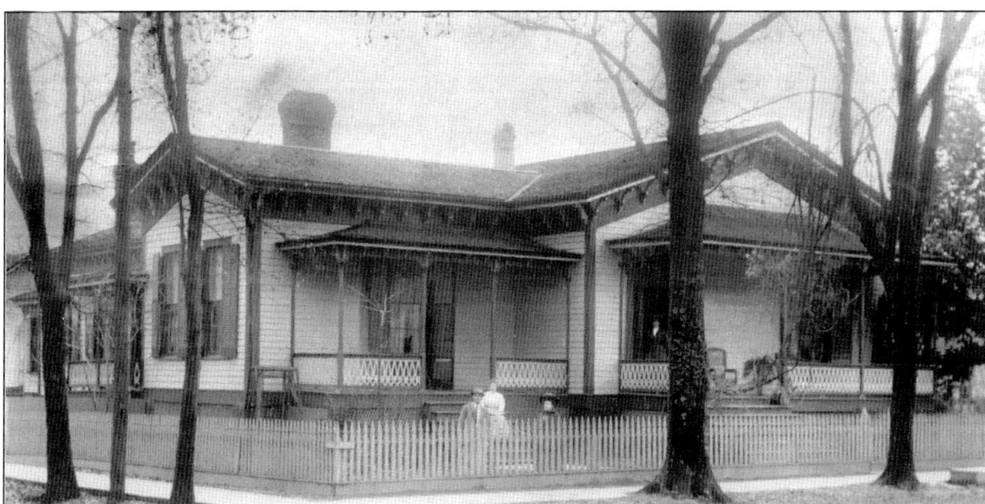

Columbus has many styles of antebellum architecture, including the cottage. One such house was built in 1860 with a "twin-look," which consisted of two front careened porches and two sets of concrete steps. Located at 224 Fourth Avenue South, it was built by Tilghman M. Tucker, one-time governor of Mississippi. Later, it was sold to local historian Edward R. Hopkins in 1888.

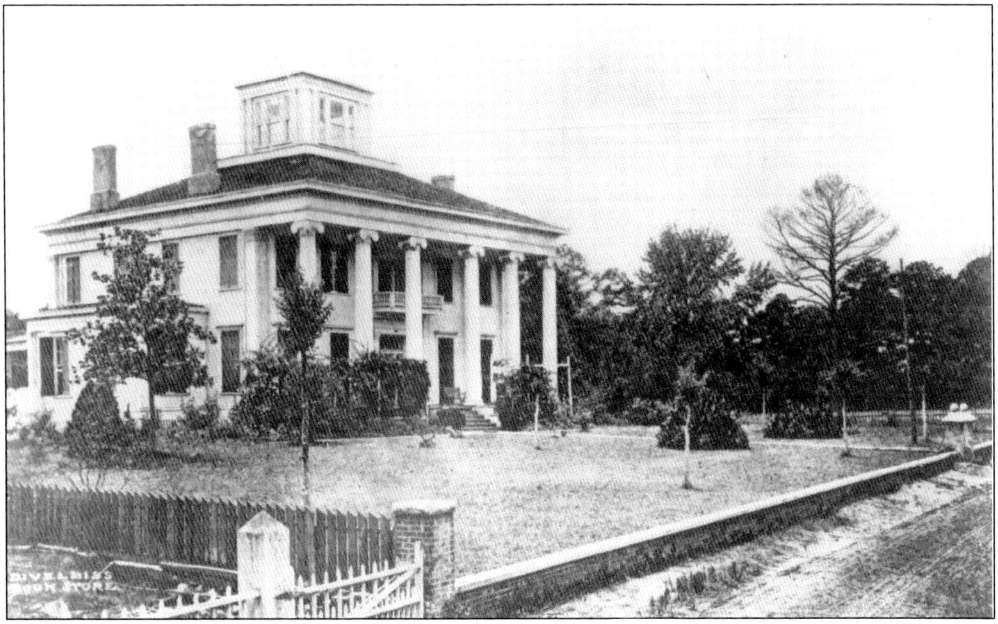

Charles F. Sherrod began construction of the home Highlands (above) in 1862. The architect was James S. Lull, builder of the Lowndes County Courthouse. Later it was sold to W.S. Lindamood. In 1909, a fire broke out, and the house was destroyed. The home was rebuilt, however, using brick, in 1910 (below) and is currently operated as a bed and breakfast located at 810 Highland Circle.

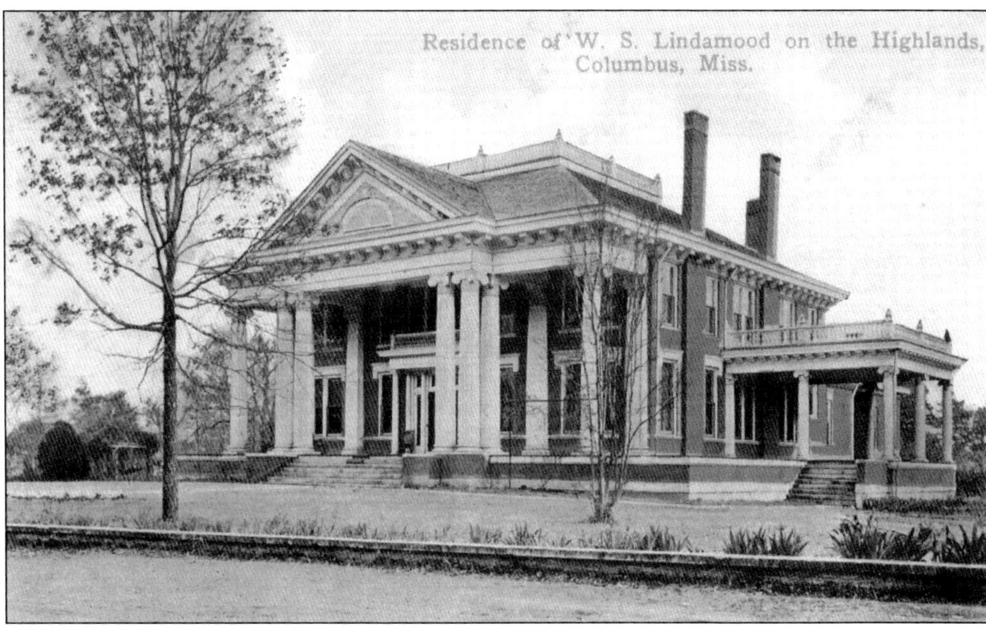

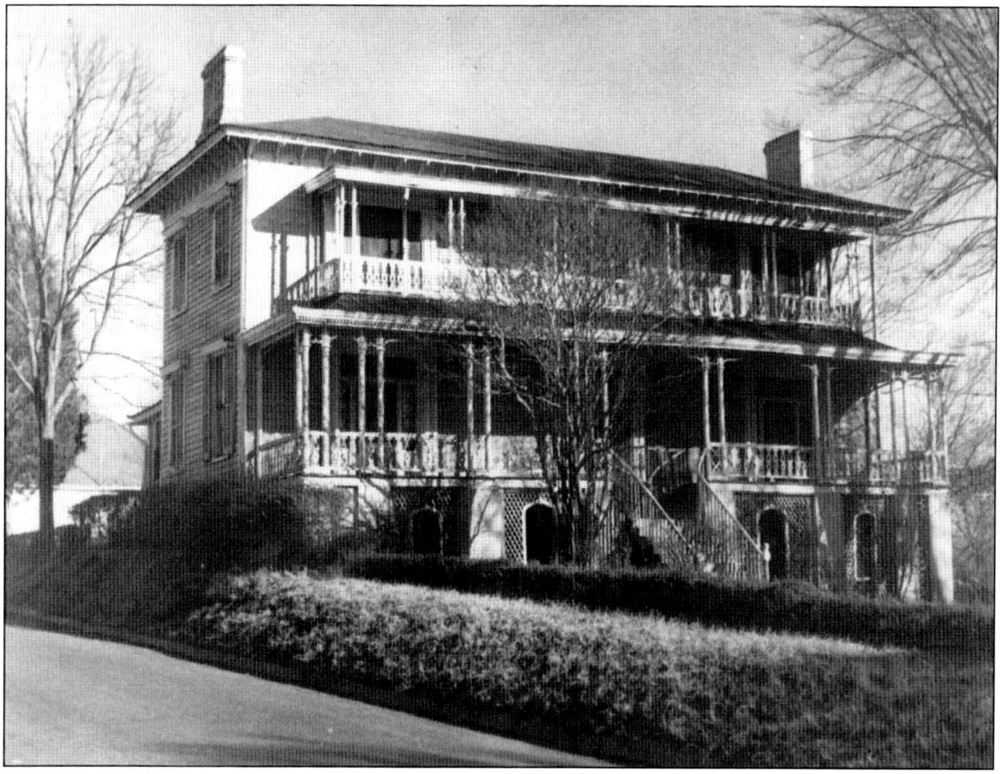

Sometimes called the Steamboat House because of its unusual shape, Dawnview was built in 1856 by architect W.H. O'Neal. Charles E. Dancy, mayor of Columbus, also resided in the home for a number of years. Ernest N. and Laura Lipscomb Beard then purchased it. Laura was both a teacher and principal at Franklin Academy. The site is now occupied by an apartment complex.

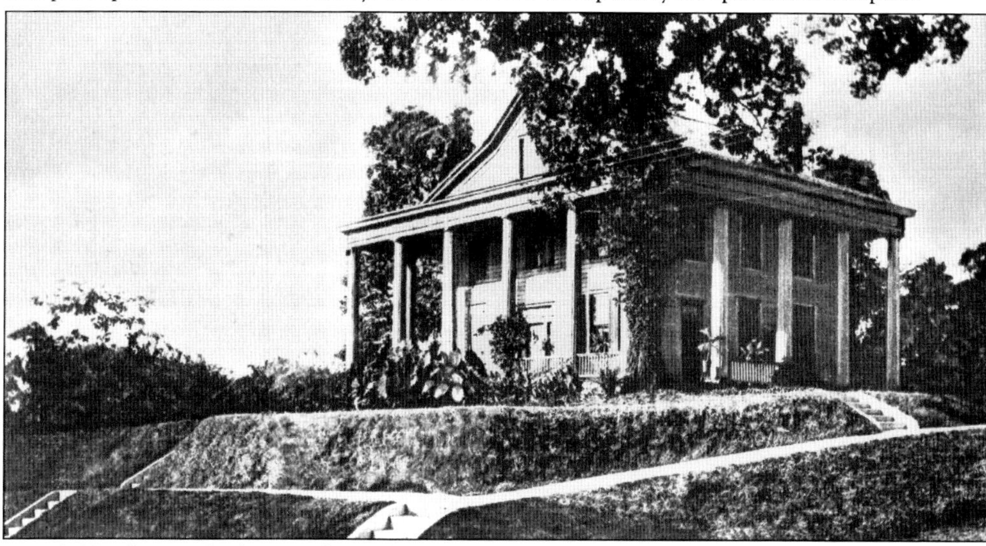

Temple Heights was built around 1837 by Gen. Richard T. Brownrigg, a pioneer settler of Columbus. Later, it was home to Jane Fontaine, one of the women who inaugurated the first Decoration Day in 1866. Located at 820 Sixth Avenue North, the home is in the National Register of Historic Places and is a Mississippi Landmark.

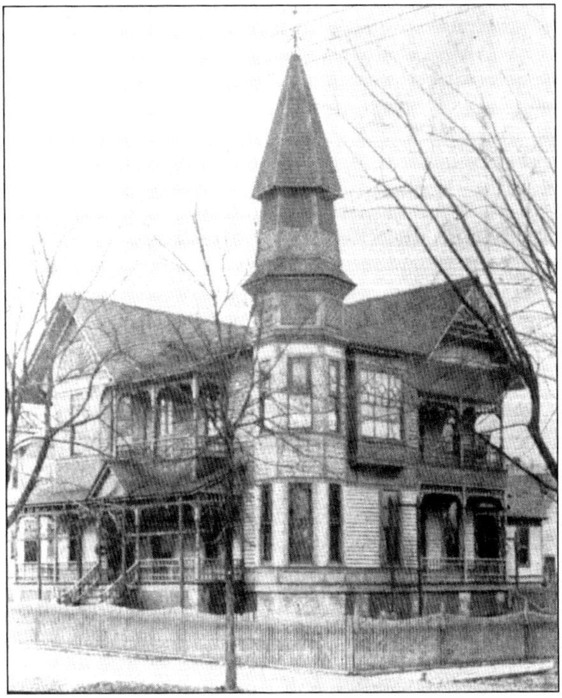

Edward C. Chapman (1865–1919) was a cashier at the National Bank of Commerce, member of the city council, deacon at First Baptist Church, and a member of a fraternal organization. His house, seen here in 1903, was located at 821 Main Street but was later replaced by a bank.

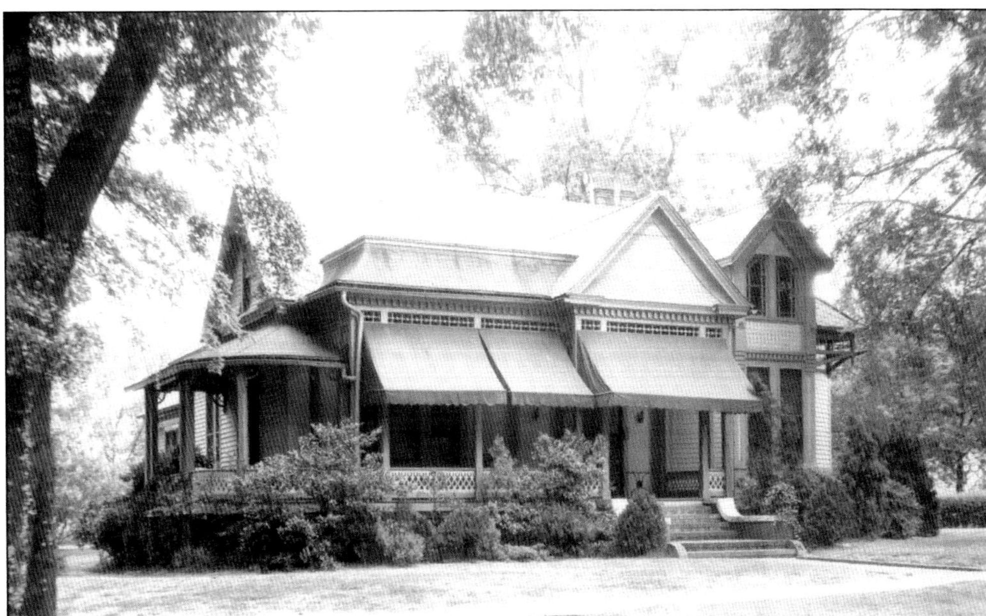

Once the home of Henry P. and Bess Sherrod, of McGowan-Sherrod Hardware Company, this house sat across the street from Annunciation Catholic Church at 724 Second Avenue South (now College Street). The location is now a parking lot.

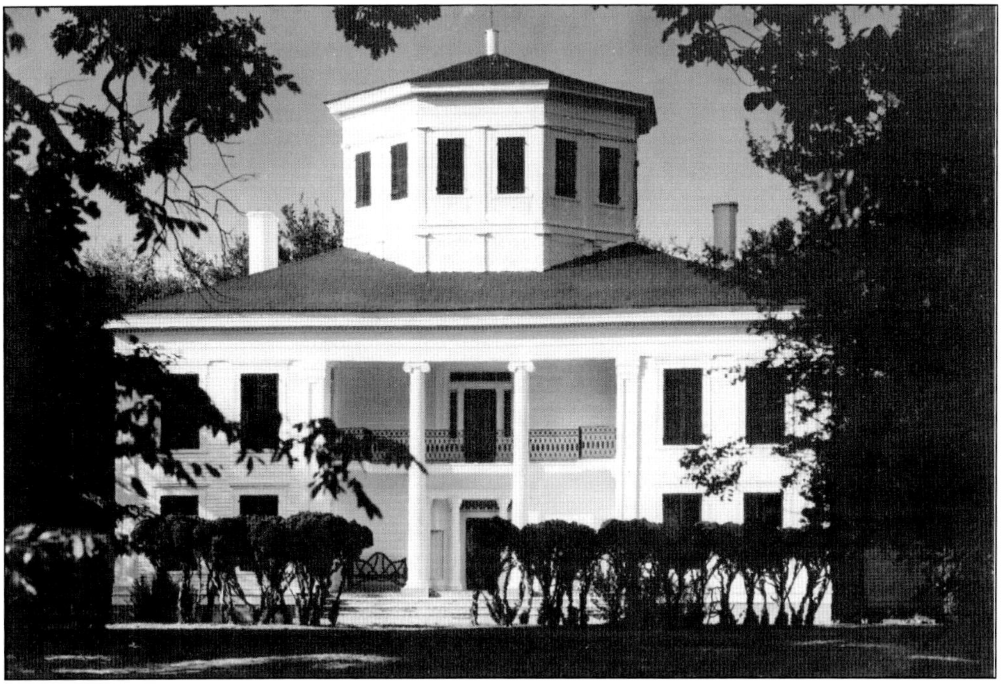

Farms, known as plantations, once surrounded the city of Columbus. George Hampton Young completed one such plantation, known as Waverly, in 1852. Then considered Lowndes County, it is now located within Clay County. The house contains an octagonal rotunda centered in the roof, known as a cupola. At one time, the plantation produced its own energy, meat, and textiles. It was also the site where the National Fox Hunters Association was organized. The second photograph shows one of the winding staircases inside the home in 1929. The mansion eventually fell into disrepair but was restored by the Snow family starting in 1962. The home was placed in the National Register of Historic Places in 1973 and is open for tours.

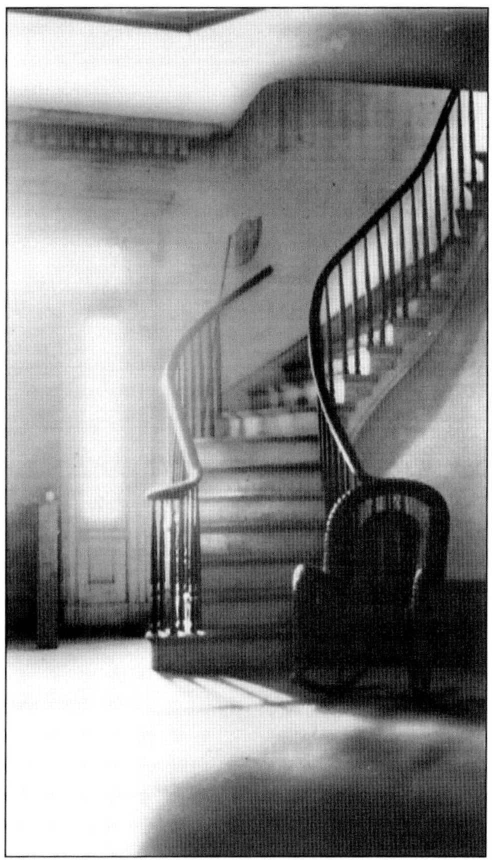

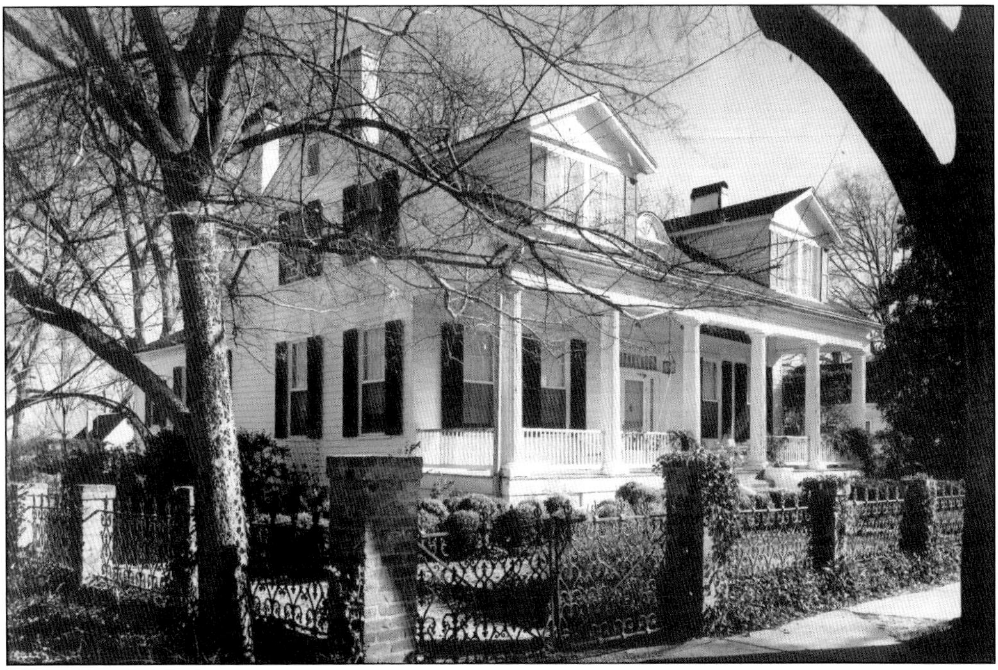

Lehmquen is a cottage of Greek Revival style surrounded by a distinctive iron fence. Located at 613 South Second Street, the home was built by Judge George R. Clayton in 1838. Lehmquen is listed in the National Register of Historic Places.

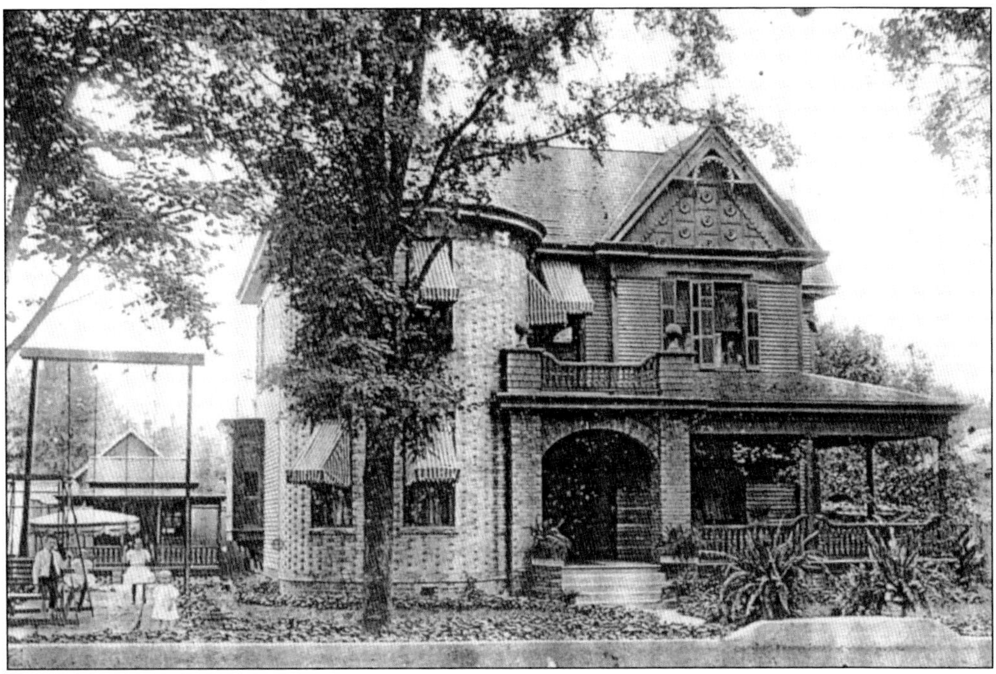

The Alexander Home, located on College Street, was built around 1899 by Peter and Caroline Alexander. The home features Flemish bond header style brick, seven fireplaces, and a hand-carved box staircase. The house was later divided into apartments until it was renovated and restored in 1996. The Alexander Home is listed in the National Register of Historic Places.

Nine

National Figures from Columbus

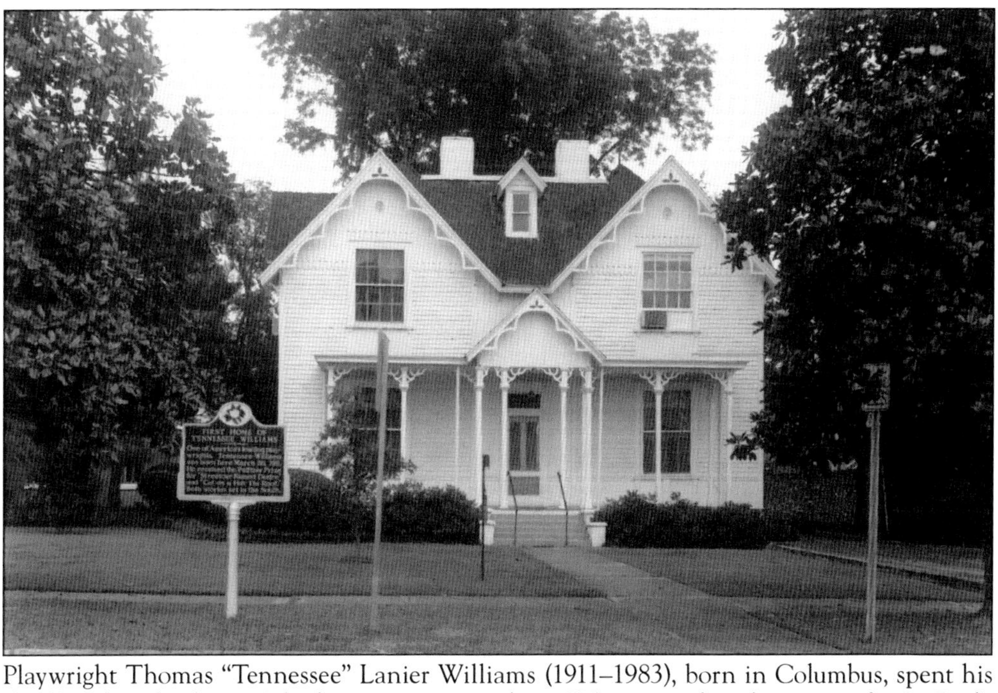

Playwright Thomas "Tennessee" Lanier Williams (1911–1983), born in Columbus, spent his childhood in this home. The house, constructed in 1875, was used as the rectory for St. Paul's Episcopal Church, where Williams's grandfather Rev. Walter Dakin served as minister from 1905 to 1913. It originally sat to the right of the church, as seen here. Williams went on to write plays such as *A Streetcar Named Desire*, *Cat on a Hot Tin Roof*, and *The Glass Menagerie*. The house was moved to Main Street from College Street in 1995 and is now used as an official Mississippi Welcome Center.

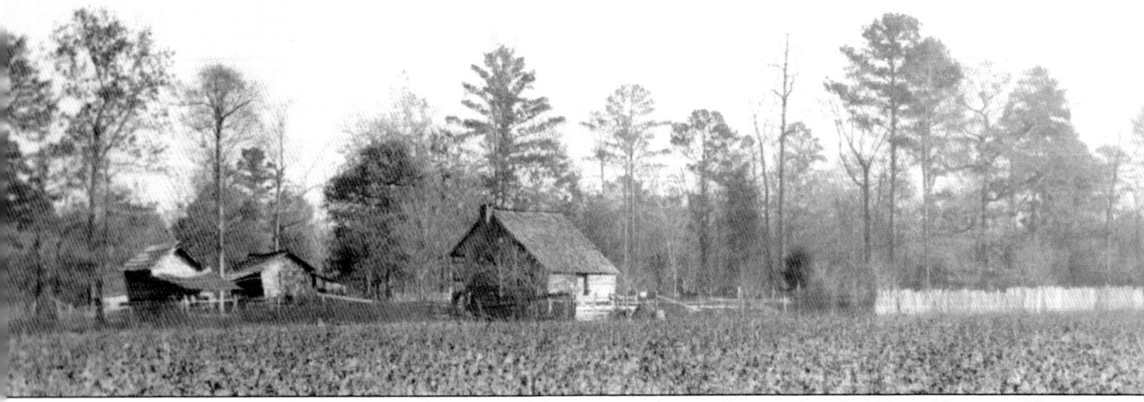

Here is the Strawbridge family house and farm, once located near the childhood home of boxer, actor, and minister Henry Armstrong (born Henry Jackson Jr.). The house, off of Wilkins-Wise and Waverly Roads, was similar to what Armstrong's would have looked like. Born in Columbus on December 12, 1912, Armstrong is considered one of the greatest fighters of all time. Armstrong is the only fighter to simultaneously hold three world titles in three different weight divisions—featherweight, lightweight, and welterweight. Armstrong had 152 victories in 181 fights throughout his career. Armstrong is a member of the International Boxing Hall of Fame. In 2010, he was inducted into the Mississippi Sports Hall of Fame. Armstrong died in October 1988 in California.

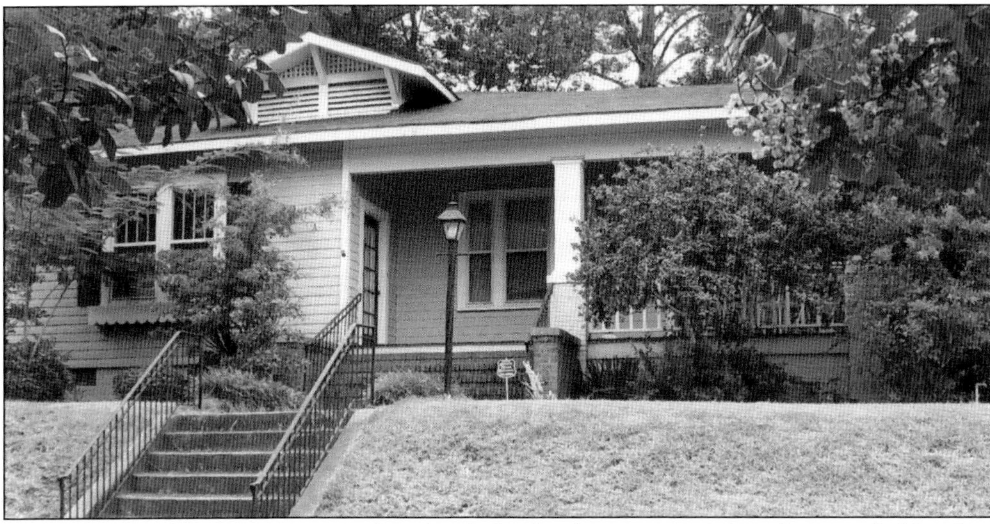

Joshua Meador, born in 1911, moved to this Columbus home in 1918. Meador attended Stephen D. Lee High School before going to work for Walt Disney Studio as an animator, special effects artist, and animation director on such movies as *20,000 Leagues under the Sea* (1954), which won an Academy Award; *Fantasia* (1940); *Cinderella* (1950); and *Sleeping Beauty* (1959). Meador created special effects for MGM's classic science-fiction film *Forbidden Planet* in 1956. He died in 1965.

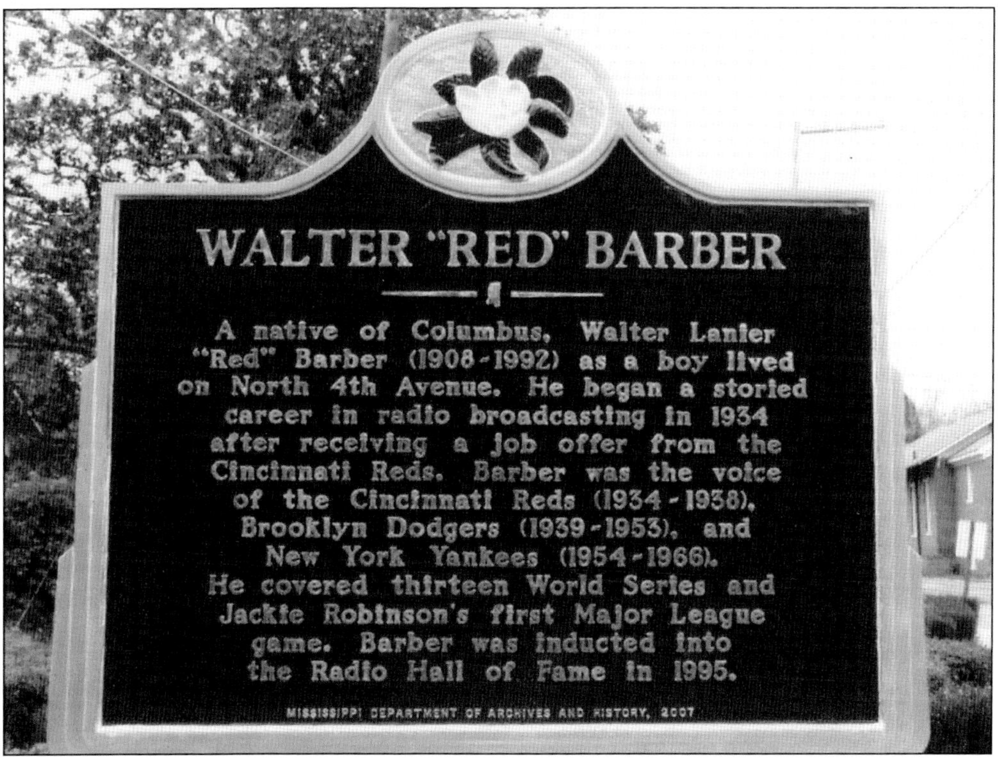

Walter Lanier "Red" Barber (1908–1992), born in Columbus, grew up at 922 Fourth Avenue North. Barber was a radio sportscaster with the Cincinnati Reds (1934–1938), Brooklyn Dodgers (1939–1953), and New York Yankees (1954–1966). Barber went on to cover 13 World Series as well as Jackie Robinson's first major-league game. In 1995, he was inducted into the Radio Hall of Fame.

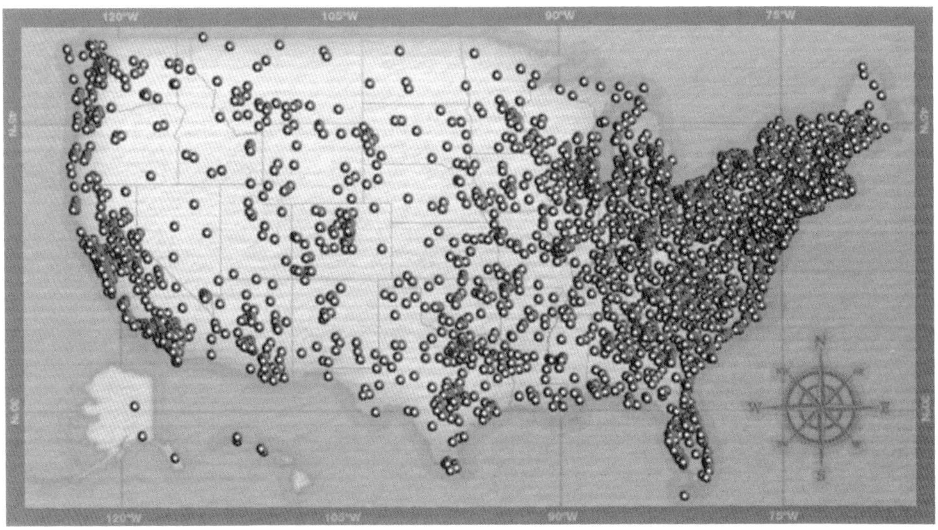